GLOBALIZATION, THE THIRD WORLD STATE AND POVERTY-ALLEVIATION IN THE TWENTY-FIRST CENTURY

Globalization, the Third World State and Poverty-Alleviation in the Twenty-First Century

Edited by
B. IKUBOLAJEH LOGAN
The University of Georgia, USA

ASHGATE

#5061648

© B. Ikubolajeh Logan 2002

Published by
Ashgate Publishing Ltd
Gower House
Croft Road
Aldershot
Hants GU11 3HR
England

Ashgate Publishing Company
131 Main Street
Burlington, VT 05401-5600 USA

Ashgate website: http://www.ashgate.com

British Library Cataloguing in Publication Data
Globalization, the Third World state and
    poverty-alleviation in the twenty-first century
    1.Globalization 2.Poverty - Developing countries
    3.Developing countries - Economic conditions 4.Developing
    countries - Politics and government
    I.Logan, Bernard Ikubolajeh
    338.9'0091724

Library of Congress Control Number: 2002102831

ISBN 0 7546 0923 5

Printed and bound in Great Britain by Antony Rowe Ltd., Chippenham, Wilts.

Typeset by Martingraphix, Cape Town, South Africa.

Contents

List of Tables

List of Contributors

B. Ikubolajeh Logan, Associate Professor, University of Georgia

Lakshamn Yapa, Professor, Pennsylvania State University

Severine Rugumamu, University of Dar es Salaam

Padriig Carmody, Assistant Professor, University of Vermont

Kidane Mengisteab, Professor, Pennsylvania State University

Julius Nyango'ro, Professor, University of North Carolina at Chapel Hill

Susan Walcott, Associate Professor, Georgia State University

Johnathan Walker, Visiting Assistant Professor, University of Illinois, Chicago

Carlos Rozo, Professor, Produccion Economica, Mexico

Richard Peet, Professor, Clark University

Timothy M. Shaw, Professor, Dalhousie University

Kent Glenzer, Emory University

William Moseley, Assistant Professor, Northern Illinois University

Alejandro Ochoa Arias, Universidad de Los Andes, Merida, Venezuela

Chapter 1

Introduction: Globalization and Third World Development in the Twenty-First Century

B. Ikubolajeh Logan

Introduction

Globalization is a process that continues to elude clear definition and, for this reason, possesses different meanings for different groups having a variety of agendas. Its lack of clarity imbues the process with a certain strident contentiousness when it is directed at Third World development, because it takes on shades of earlier discourses (for example, north-south, dependency, world structures, post-colonial). Much of the critical energy expended on the current debate on globalization centers on the nature of the process, whether it is merely another stage in the inexorable march of capitalism, or whether it is a distinct and nouvelle experience which locates capitalist expansion within a broader political, environmental, social and cultural super-structure more so than earlier global excursions of capital.

Strong globalizationists, those who argue that the current globalization is a distinctly new phenomenon, make the point that previous periods of capitalist expansion into the Third World lacked the speed, technological sophistication, economic integration and ideological universalism which are the hallmarks of globalization in the twenty-first century (c.f. Ohmae, 1990; 1995; Bryan and Farrell, 1996; Mathews, 1997). Strong globalizationists also adhere to the efficacy of the market over the state and take the neoliberal position that globalization has universally benign economic effects.

Soft or weak globalizationists, on the other hand, describe current global processes simply as another stage in capitalist expansion (see, for example, Sassen, 1998; Kennedy, 1993; Sjolander, 1996). They insist that technology merely makes the process more efficient, not different from earlier phases, in fundamental characteristic and objectives. Weak globalizationists contend further that the current globalization is merely a hiccup in Western hegemony or, at best, a remodification of the structures that underpin that hegemony. The phenomenon is not new, it has merely been recast in the scintillating hues of high tech. The internet may have replaced ocean vessels, but the basic operations of accumulating resources at the core remain essential to the process. While the global political economy of the immediate post-second World War era may have required the formalization of strategies at Bretton Woods, the new order is more flexible. It continues to use the agency of the Bretton Woods institutions, but is particularized by the speed of communication and information technology whose versatility allows global forces easy access to Third World economies (c.f. Hirst and Thompson, 1996; Kapstein, 1991/92).

The scholarly exercise of differentiating between weak versus strong globalization may not be so relevant for the Third World where the major concern is with the effects of the process on the poor. Whether weak or strong, as in earlier historical episodes, the encounter between Western capital and the Third World has not been a meeting of minds. To the contrary, the process has always been a specific drama orchestrated by strong hegemonic forces to solidify the interests of global capital. Towards this end, new rules of admission and engagement are constantly being formulated with the express purpose of excising ineffective/inefficient regions and peoples. In the process, Third World economies become fragmented, selected sectors and classes become co-opted into the global system and the majority of the region's peoples become increasingly marginalized.

The chapters in this book revolve around a number of themes, three of which are particularly relevant for understanding the effects of globalization on Third World poverty during the first few decades of the twenty-first century; state-market relationships; civil society and the emergence of new regional configurations (new regionalisms); and environment, resource exploitation and economic polarization. The chapters attempt to comment on the mechanisms through which globalization is unfolding in the Third World, with the objective of assessing the degree to which these same mechanisms provide opportunities for economic development and political stability in the region. In the next section, I preface the discussion of the three themes above with a few comments on globalization.

Considering Globalization

Perhaps, at the heart of the present conundrum over what globalization might imply for Third World development is the fact that the term attempts to appropriate for itself a precedence in meaning on the basis of a number of supposedly unique signatures. Among them is the current neoliberal position that the dissolution of the state-market wedlock is an unproblematic requirement for the political and economic survival of the Third World (c.f. Brodhead, 1996; Bryant and Farrell, 1996). Unfortunately, this position does not make clear how widespread privatization of education, health, electricity, water supply and other basic services will improve standards of living in the Third World. Similarly, current attempts to meld democratic reform with economic reform have ambiguous implications. What mechanisms exist for Third World countries to achieve 'a free market in a free democracy'? What are the commonalities and mutualities between these 'freedoms' and how is the freedom to 'consume' political participation and to 'consume' economic products likely to coexist in poor economies? What happens when/if the state abrogates all its responsibilities to its people in favor of establishing an enabling environment for the market? A number of the chapters in this book attempt to address these fundamental questions.

The current globalization is characterized also by its insistence on human rights as a necessary condition for political and economic change (this is certainly a new engagement since dehumanization of 'natives' characterized earlier global extensions of capital into the Third World). There is no doubt that many present

Third World regimes violate the human rights of their citizens in ways that are even more uncharitable than in the colonial period. Yet, it has become difficult to promote universal human rights because the same forces, which champion human rights, ignore such rights when their economic and political interests are at stake. For example, the West, in general 'boycotted' the 2001 Durban Conference on Racism, not because they do not believe racism to be a humanitarian issue, but precisely because the conference threatened to focus on issues that were against the political interest of Western allies. Actions of this nature by the West, indicate to the Third World that human rights, like democracy, is selectively expendable in the globalization agenda (support of tyrannical regimes like that of former Rawlings of Ghana and undemocratic regimes like that of Kuwait also make this point).

The role of human rights in socioeconomic change in the Third World requires some serious contemplation since advocacy for humanitarian benevolence comes amid advise for the state to abdicate its welfare obligations. The expectation that the private sector will fill any vacuum created by state withdrawal from these functions does not seem to have much merit. It is neither clear why the market will wish to provide some services (which?) out of goodwill, nor how the poor will afford privatized welfare without state assistance. One could argue that the same economic and political pragmatism that encourages Western governments to protect the interests of their large middle class should currently direct Third World governments to provide basic services, at almost any cost, for the poor.

Another interesting aspect of the current globalization is the role of the international financial institutions (IFIs), multinational organizations like the United Nations and a host of multilateral and bilateral organizations and international and local NGOs (Mathews, 1997). These are all key players in the formulation and implementation of national policy at various geographic and social scales. Their activities have often forced the Third World state to relinquish some of its sovereignty (this is especially significant with the structural adjustment agenda of the IFIs over the past two to three decades). In many instances, the objectives of these globalization agents are quite inimical to the welfare of local populations as evidenced by the number of public protests associated with structural adjustment programs in several countries around the Third World (Nigeria, Cote d'Ivoire, Zimbabwe, Indonesia, Malaysia, etc.).

The present wave of globalization is also characterized by a mixed array of issues – the environment, gender rights, debt relief, AIDS, the rights of children/child soldiers in civil conflicts, the role of minerals in financing civil unrest, the international transfer of arms and military expertise in the form of mercenaries, nuclear terrorism, immigration etc. Each of these is a priority for one international group or another. Yet, their various agendas do not always converge and actually contribute to the complexity of the globalization process and what it may portend for the Third World poor.

Despite claims to the contrary, all of these signatures do not quite differentiate globalization from, say colonialism. The particular strategies may be different because the specific targets are different, but the overall agendas and objectives have remained intimidatingly consistent. Additionally, the current globalization does shares several attributes with its antecedents, among them, institutionalized resource expropriation and the perpetuation of a dysfunctional socioeconomic order manifested in anomalies like dualism and informality.

Similarly, globalization in the twenty-first century shares a number of paradoxes (simultaneous polarizing processes) with its earlier counterparts.

1. Integration and marginalization, which is marked by the exclusion of large sections of the Third World from the cutting edge of research, technology, management and communications (see, for example, Connor, 1994). Even as some obviously significant world village dynamics are occurring, Third World economies are being systematically relegated to oceans of poverty which are attached to the capitalist mainstream largely through the activities of a few capital cities, export processing zones and miscellaneous mining and agricultural projects.
2. Globalization and regional specialization, is marked by the increasing relegation of Third World labor to unskilled activities (see, for example, Bergsten, 1996). Export processing zones, which use cheap, unskilled labor, are often localized, islands of economic isolation within their countries.
3. Globalization of culture and cultural isolation, is a paradoxical process by which sociocultural convergence (for example, through CNN, Microsoft, the London Times, electronic mail) seems to spawn a simultaneous process of cultural alienation (Barnett and Cavanaugh, 1994; Huntington, 1996). Global cultural homogenization has succeeded in integrating a small segment of Third world societies into the global family, while effectively disconnecting them socially and culturally from their counterparts in their own countries. As a consequence, Third World societies are being increasingly dichotomized in standards of living, quality of life and lifestyles.

A key attribute of the current globalization (elements of which it shares with earlier rounds) is manifested in what may be termed post Cold War one-worldism and political polarization. This process is reflected in the elevation of liberal democracy to a global dogma (Epsing-Andersen and van Kersbergen, 1992; Gill, 1996). Yet, this political philosophy has proved of limited utility in many Third World arenas. Far from bringing relief from ethnic, religious, military and others types of insidious duress, the one-person-one-vote franchise has often been exploited by the Third World political elite to sustain and legitimize their authority (several military dictators have been quite successful at this). At the more global level, the same forces that champion global democracy, dismiss these principles at their own selective behest, a splendid example being the voting structure within the United Nations.

The standards underlying the geopolitics of twenty-first century global, liberal democracy are reflected also in the policies of ombudsmen like the G8, United Nations and a host of international NGOs which demonstrate that Rwanda, Burundi and Sierra Leone are not Bosnia, Macedonia or Yugoslavia; and that the Third World is not part of continental Europe. As Rugumamu demonstrates in chapter 3, through mechanisms like the Lome Conventions, the 1992 Maastricht and WTO treaties, global forces use their unrivaled supremacy both to perpetuate their political and economic domination and to undermine Third World empowerment. For example, the West is systematically discarding earlier provisions of Lome as it shifts from a policy of multilateralism to a post-cold war bilateralism that is reminiscent of the British colonial divide and rule policy. The consensual partnership of the early Lome Convention period is being rapidly restructured on the basis of a shift from mutuality and respect between equals to one of mandates from the metropolitan countries. These philosophical shifts are being accompanied by a distinct shift in regional focus from the Africa-Caribbean and Pacific (ACP-countries) to the Baltic and East Europe in which the same forces that seek to integrate parts of ACP economies (South Africa, Brazil, Jamaica...) into the global system, seek also to make the system more streamlined by reneging on former commitments to the Third World.

Globalization and State-Market Relations

Proponents of globalization have transformed market freedom to a type of comparative advantage in the drive towards market liberalization and privatization in the Third World. The definition of market freedom in these neoliberal terms, covers a wide array of issues, including, market decontrol, labor decontrol and a catch-all of imperatives aimed at removing all forms of government limitations on private sector operations. To put it more vividly but less subtly, market freedom has come to mean that free-wheeling, free-dealing and fast-moving capital must have the freedom to control state policies (Bryan and Farrell, 1996; Schmidt, 1995; Horseman and Marshall, 1994; Rinehart, 1995). States that do not conform to this dogma run the risk of being blacklisted as international economic and political pariahs.

As noted in the previous section, as the state reacts to these new rules of economic engagement, it has been encouraged/coerced to withdraw from many of its traditional roles in promoting employment and social welfare. State withdrawal from these traditional purviews has led to claims that the Third World state is an extinct or nearly extinct behemoth, which cannot cope with the onslaught of globalization (c.f. Ohmae, 1990; Kennedy, 1993; Horseman and Marshall, 1994; Guehenno, 1995; Rosecrans, 1996; Cable, 1995). Suggestions that global economic activities now occur in a 'stateless' arena arise from the presumption that control over and dispensation of resources is a zero-sum game. As such, increased market freedom can come only at the expense of decreased state control in the new era of market triumphalism (c.f. Zartman, 1995).

There are those who take the contrary position that the Third World state is alive and well (Dunn, 1994; Kapstein, 1991/92) and claim that its strength is reflected in its ability to reconfigure itself in response to reconfigured capital. The viable state in the twenty-first century, is one that effectively reconfigures to meet the challenges and demands of capital by accomplishing three, highly interconnected, goals: significant withdrawal from resource allocation, market liberalization and political liberalization (democracy and human rights). In these terms, state retrenchment from economic activities, far from being a sign of weakness, is a sign of its adaptability and strength, as it grapples with its new tripartite role. Only a flexible and strong state can maneuver through the non-coincident requirements of global capital and the welfare needs of the poor. Some of the chapters recommend strategies for the state to manifest its strengths and not suffocate the market and some others describe case studies where the states has tried to achieve this objective.

Globalization and the Grand Poverty-Alleviation Project

The implications of unfolding state-market relations for poverty alleviation in the Third World are discussed in several chapters, but especially in chapter 2 by Yapa. He argues that the more positive aspects of globalization (for example, technology, information) beget a seamier side, which is globalized poverty. Globalized poverty, is integral to global political and economic success and manifests itself in a series of technical, social, cultural and political arenas over which neither the market nor the state has complete authority. This sovereignty vacuum leads Yapa to call for a theory of non-sovereign power to deal with the globalization of poverty. In this context, the exigencies of globalization can be tackled at multiple points simultaneously since no single agency (state or market) is equipped to accomplish the task by itself in a comprehensive way. These 'sites of opportunity' present themselves in a number of areas, including, academia, the media, labor movements, local NGOs and environmental movements.

   The success of the grand poverty-alleviation project would hinge, therefore, on a state-market relationship that can accomplish the difficult task of marshalling all these different forces to ensure that the twin goals of mass participation and poverty alleviation are made inseparable.

The State, the Market and the Grand Poverty-Alleviation Project

A fundamental task in the grand poverty-alleviation project, as noted previously, is to ensure enhanced or broader mass participation in the consumption of critical goods and services. Given this precondition, one may argue that even though state involvement may not be a sufficient condition for poverty alleviation, it is certainly a necessary one. The Third World state has its well-known shortcomings, which include, corruption, mismanagement, bloatedness and self-emolument. Yet, even with these problems, the state is still a necessary mechanism for redistributing wealth in economies with nascent market structures, especially as the market is not flawless. Not only does it share some of the shortcomings of the state, it also has its own problems. Although private enterprise may be more efficient and streamlined, it panders directly to the interests of the powerful by subordinating the concerns of the poor. In fact, the efficiency of the market derives directly from its ability to differentiate between need and want and to exclude the needy (those without purchasing power) from the consumption of many commodities. The uncharitableness of the global market is exemplified by two recent events. First, the Treaty on Multilateral Agreement on Investments (MAI) negotiated by twenty-nine advanced countries aims at denying states the authority to give preferences to domestic or local capital over foreign capital. Second, the IMF's attempts to negotiate an amendment of its Articles of Agreement in order to obtain the authority to require member countries to commit to more complete liberalization and restricting the power of governments to regulate the flow of currency into and out of their countries. These actions clearly do not proceed from a desire to empower the poor and to ensure that they gain greater access to their basic needs. To the contrary, they are designed to give the market more power to subsume state authority and to undermine the latter's facility to make social welfare and poverty alleviation a priority over macro economic restructuring to liberalize trade.

Under the conditions described above, the market can hardly be expected to replace the state in the grand poverty-alleviation project. The Third World state needs to stay active in resource allocation, if only as representative and advocate of the poor at the globalization table. It would be wishful thinking to expect the market to perform this role. Although the one person one vote system of the state may not accommodate a comprehensive form of mass participation, it is likely to be superior to a market representation where the poor are sometimes totally excluded from casting a vote. Since the state cannot approach its task in isolation from the market, some form of compromise relationship between the two must be devised. This issue is addressed in the next section.

Globalization, Democracy and State Options

The 1990s witnessed changes, not only in state-market relations and the character of the Third World state, but also in the bilateral and multilateral relationships between the Third World state and the West. These changes and their implications are described by Rugumamu (chapter 3), Carmody (chapter 4), Mengisteab (chapter 5) Nyango'ro (chapter 6), Walcott (chapter 7), Walker (chapter 8) and Rozo (chapter 9). Mengisteab and Nyango'ro, for example, elaborate on strategies that the state needs to adopt in order to adjust more effectively to globalization and the market. On the other hand, Walcott, Walker and Rozo provide examples of state intervention (with varying results) to counter the challenges of global capital.

Carmody takes the view that, by forcing the state to reconfigure in ways that have undercut its ability to reproduce viable social institutions, globalization has created a dysfunctional state. In Carmody's view, the Third World state is a gutted entity (the weak state perspective discussed earlier) that is being exploited as a vehicle for the globalization of underdevelopment and poverty (Yapa's globalized poverty theme). Since Third World poverty has a global dimension, the problem cannot be resolved merely by forcing Third World states to democratize. The democratization project should be global (involving multinational organizations like the UN) and should be aimed at forging consensus on improved state-market relations; on the mechanisms through which institutions like the WTO control and oversee international trade; and in the way(s) the IFIs and international NGOs participate in policy formulation and implementation in the Third World.

In chapter 5, Mengisteab argues that state democracy can be used as a starting point to combat successfully some of the negative impacts of the market. He acknowledges the complex relationship between economic globalization and Third World democracy and suggests that this relationship is best analyzed and understood in terms of process rather than of outcomes, by focusing on the impacts of market-state relationships on mass participation and democracy, on class relationships and on state-civil society relations. He notes that, at present, the market narrows the scope of democracy by alienating the poor from the political process (they do not see that they have anything to gain through political participation), widens the gap between social classes and pits the state against its own citizens (this problem is often reflected in structural adjustment programs).

A possible solution to these difficulties is to redefine democracy beyond its present rigid ideological boundary to incorporate social concerns and strengthen the role of civil society, the state and even the market in poverty-alleviation (Owusu, 1992; Zartmen, 1995; Sartori, 1991; Schmitter, 1995). This type of democracy would work on stakeholder consensus. It would seek to give representation to different agendas and constituencies (a federalism of interests and not merely of ethnicity and regions, in fact, a new regionalism as described later by Shaw in chapter 12). Mengisteab is convinced that this project can be accomplished without obfuscating the needs of the market (which the state also needs for its own survival).

In chapter 6, Nyango'ro, like Mengisteab, takes an optimistic view regarding future prospects for a viable state-market wedlock to address poverty. He believes that the state can reconfigure to address poverty while accommodating the market through a new industrial agenda. Industrialization need not be completely predatory and antithetical to the interests of the poor. To the contrary, the state needs to be flexible and pragmatic enough to be able to devise strategies to exploit the neoliberal consensus in selective ways. There is historical precedence for such state action: to support its infant textile industry during the 18th century, Britain imposed tariffs on imports from India and China and absolutely banned certain classes of competitive imports; during the 19th century, France, Germany and the United States counteracted British hegemony through nationalist economic strategies that included protective tariffs and credit facilities from state banks in order to develop national industries; similar protective policies and strong state input supported and ushered in the twentieth century industrialization in Russia, Japan and the Asian tigers. Clearly, all of these options are not available to the Third World state within the present globalization regime. Yet, Nyango'ro believes that African states, for example, can adopt a regional approach to the industrialization, using South Africa as a conduit for the transfer of capital and technology (although this may be problematic given the slow, rather spasmodic realization of post-apartheid expectations) (c.f. Adam *et al.*, 1997; Gelb, 1997; Jung and Shapiro, 1995). Whatever the obstacles that present themselves, Nyango'ro insists that the Third World state must persevere to launch an industrial agenda within the framework of a restructured international trade regime, as envisaged by Carmody. The state still has opportunities to put mechanisms in place to attract global capital while protecting the welfare of the poor. The task in to confer with different elements of capital and civil society to devise appropriate and reasonable labor, environmental and tax packages. For the outcomes of these negotiations to be beneficial to the poor, the state must consider both the industrial and the poverty alleviation projects to be complementary planks of national development.

That state-led industrialization can be part of a successful state-market relation, is underscored in Walcott's discussion in chapter 7 of science parks in China. These parks have been created by the Chinese state to attract foreign direct investment from high technology companies. The state's objective is to provide Chinese companies with access to transferable technology, while simultaneously financing their development through foreign trade profit. The state has undertaken this project as a long-term national security project, inserting itself into its design and implementation by shaping reasonable labor laws and constraints on the free flow of profit. The Chinese model demonstrates that the state and the market can develop an amicable working relationship based on mutual compromise.

In chapter 8 Walker shows that comparative advantage can be obtained in a variety of ways in the new global regime. Since 1990, Taiwan has engaged in the formal 'importation' of foreign laborers from Thailand, the Philippines and Indonesia. The importation of labor is a state-designed strategy to attract foreign direct investment, slow capital flight, retain and expand existing industries and attract new industry. Foreign workers comprise an integral part of Taiwan's national strategy for sustained industrial development. Its strategy of labor importation allows the state to continue to attract foreign investment for industrial development even in the face of high local wages, local employment shifts into the expanding service economy and reduced availability of local industrial workers.

In contrast to the benign engagement between market and state in the two Asian examples, Rozo's discussion in chapter 9 reveal some of the weaknesses of state action against the power of foot-loose capital. He shows that the adoption of export-led development, based on the availability of US capital, has led to serious setbacks in the Mexican economy on several fronts. These negative outcomes are reflected in reduced national and industrial productivity, regional polarization and social polarization.

Yapa's grass roots, multi-pronged approach, Carmody's state recapture, Mengisteab's reconceptualization of democracy and Nyangoro's new industrial agenda are all major challenges in the grand poverty-alleviation project. Unfortunately, the neoliberal advocacy for complete state exclusion in this project is unlikely to be useful. What is required is for each country or group of countries to identify a workable mix of instruments that would allow the state and the market to cooperate effectively. As the Chinese and Taiwanese case studies illustrate, this is still a possibility within the neoliberal regime; it merely requires foresight and planning from the state.

Civil Society, State-Market Relations and Poverty-Alleviation

Some attention has been directed recently at the role of civil society in facilitating state market relations. The focus on civil society is often aimed at individuals, communities, local NGOs (for example, church and community groups) and international NGOs. These various groups are seen as possible vehicles for the formulation and dissemination of strategies to tackle the rigors of democracy and neoliberalism.

In the Third World, civil society groups have made the transformation of the state their top priority. There is a sense among these groups that political transformation that empowers local communities may be the first step towards poverty-alleviation. Civil society groups have been very instrumental in forming global alliances to counteract the excesses of the state and bring about democratic change. As a result of these activities, elections are now often held under international observation, local reporters affiliated with major international broadcasting corporations are able to disseminate news about local politics and economics, more so than was possible in the 1970s and 1980s, the judiciary in many countries has obtained real independence and the state even engages in its own house cleaning by taking legal/administrative action against leading political figures. These are all laudable achievements that mark the vigor of civil society from Central and South America, through Africa, the Middle East and south and southeast Asia. More recently the same international alliance of civil society has started to turn its attention to the excesses of the market, as evidenced by a number of highly publicized activities.

1. The Jubilee 2000 Petition was launched during the 1998 G8 summit in Birmingham, England. The demonstration, reportedly involved 70,000 people linked together in a chain of arms to persuade the world leaders to provide debt relief for Third World countries.
2. The Africa Summits held in various American cities between 1998–2000 around the theme, 'Africa Matters', focused on the investment potentials of African countries. Civil disobedience at WTO meetings in 1999 and 2001 and World Bank/IMF meetings in 1999 and 2000, also drew world-wide attention to the debt burden of Third World countries and the need for debt relief for the poorest countries.
3. During the 2000 international AIDS conference in Cape Town, a global coalition linked the debt burden and its subsequent impacts on health care to the rapid rise of AIDS amongst the poor. The call for debt relief was again reissued here and at the 2000 G8 summit in Japan.

Despite some notable success at community mobilization and international political activism, there are still serious questions surrounding the ability of civil society to represent the interests of the poor effectively. For one thing, civil society covers a wide array of groups and agendas. Like the state and the market, elements of civil society tend to be self-serving and engage in a lot of turf protection to secure donor funding. Civil society organizations, either by design or by accident, tend also to promote neoliberalism, democracy and sustainable development as unproblematic projects in the third World. To that extent, elements of civil society, especially international NGOs and their local allies, may be viewed as mere extensions of, not counterfoils to, the dominant forces of globalization.

In chapter 10, Glentzer uses his five years experience as an officer of civil society organizations in Mali to explore some of these issues. He traces the chronological ascendancy of the three major actors in policy formulation in post-independent Mali, the state, bilateral and multilateral agencies and civil society represented by NGOs and emphasizes that policy formulation has become an arena of even greater contestation since the emergence of the last in the 1990s. Fundamental to the role of civil society, is the presumption that they know the needs of the poor better than anyone else and can, therefore, speak very eloquently to those needs. This logic has allowed civil society groups to obtain donor funds, which, in turn, has forced the Third World state to recognize them, however grudgingly, as central actors in the development project.

Despite their status as champions of the poor, Glenzer concludes that there are difficulties with the assumption that civil society can fill the vacuum that is being created by new state-market configurations under globalization. Civil society is often beset by a number of shortcomings: local organizations tend to be led by individuals with strong ties to the state and with agendas that are sometimes antithetical to the needs of the poor; many groups lack the managerial and organizational skills required to tackle, headlong, the grand project of poverty-alleviation; many groups lack the capacity to replace the state as provider of the basic social needs of the poor; and their reliance on the market (or agents of the market) for funding, encourage an agenda that is likely to impoverish the poor even further.

Peet examines the links between civil society and neoliberalism in chapter 11, using the South African example as a case in point. As the state, represented by the African national Congress (ANC) and civil society interact in the post-apartheid environment, the former has been encouraged or coerced to soften its radical agenda. As a consequence, following the1994 elections, the state started to move quite noticeably away from its leftist stance on poverty-alleviation towards a neoliberal, export-oriented policy, an orientation that is vigorously opposed by the labor unions and the radical wing of the party. This shift in policy is now enshrined in the government's GEAR program, which under the strong influence of civil society, aims at achieving poverty alleviation through the neoliberal market structure. Peet questions why the ANC would move so quickly towards compromise with the same forces with which it waged years of struggle. The answer is to be found in the global power of civil society, represented by what he refers to as the Academic-Institutional-Media (AIM) complexes. Unlike the infrequent, spasmodic actions associated with civil society disobedience against globalization, the elements of the AIM complex are continuously active at facilitating the performance of global capital.

AIM complexes represent a global network of ideological alliances between neoliberals and civil society at different points in the global system. These complexes legitimize prevailing ideologies and praxis on behalf of global capital and often use local units (example local NGOs) to further their goals (after all, the notion of local NGOs is not of local origin). Peet questions the commitment of the AIM complex to poverty alleviation in the Third World. Like Yapa, he believes that AIM complexes must be tackled at specific points in order for the grand poverty alleviation project to achieve some success. Unlike Glentzer, who believes that the link between elements of civil society and capital is too strong to breach, Peet takes the position that committed elements of civil society can be identified and then mobilized to infiltrate the AIM complex. On the other hand, both Peet and Glentzer agree that civil society can replace neither the state nor the market in providing for the poor (although it is possible that some civil society groups can be organized to provide basic services for the poor at a faster rate than is possible with either of the other two institutions).

Fortunately, all is not bleak concerning the role of civil society in the grand poverty alleviation project. In chapter 12, Shaw describes the formation of 'new regionalisms' by which the state and civil society are reorganizing themselves to combat the new globalization regime. He describes this as a process by which, at a number of geographic, political and social scales, different elements of civil society are cooperating with each other as a coping mechanism to counter the rigid ideological and other boundaries of globalization. These strategies take on formal and informal social, cultural and regional dimensions at several scales of operation.

At the macro, physical level, the new regionalism incorporates a wide range of novel corridor and triangle 'governance' arrangements as one form of state reaction to the failings of 'old regionalism' to address the negative effects of globalization. In southern Africa, for example, there are moves to constitute peace parks between South Africa, Zimbabwe and Mozambique in order to attract a larger global tourist market, the Lesotho Highlands Project and the Maputo Corridor Project, are also designed to exploit economies of scale that would allow the state to function more effectively in the new global environment.

At the micro, informal level, new regional groupings are taking form, some observable, others progressing without serious recognition by policy makers and scholars. The former would include, for example, local and cross national trading activities by market women, game poaching, local manufactures and remanufactures, drug and gun running and mercenary activities. The lesson that should be drawn from these emerging and uncertain alliances is that globalization is creating new configurations to which neither the literature on the state nor that on civil society is paying particular attention. Yet, the same mechanisms that allow neoliberalism its strength, also empower these new and emerging social, political and civil society organizations and agents.

Globalization, Resource Exploitation and Economic Polarization

Sustainable development (SD) has been used by the agents of globalization as the yardstick for determining the legitimacy of development projects since the mid-1980s. The application of SD to the development business takes on both conceptual and practical overtones within the broader aegis of globalization. Conceptually, SD is presented as wise resource use by the present generation in order to maintain similar quality of resources for future generations; at the practical level it is presented as the objective of development projects, especially local projects which involve environmental resources (vegetation, soil, wildlife).

From a third World perspective, the important link between SD and globalization has to do with its implications for poverty-alleviation. The Brundtland Report, which entrenched SD in mainstream discourse, discussed poverty only in vague terms, opting to avoid issues of political ecology. As SD discourse has evolved through the 1990s, it has moved even further away from deliberations of resource access, focusing instead, on problems of intergenerational equity. Within this mainstream discourse, poverty is not associated with globalization. To the contrary, it is conceived of as a localized problem, brought on by the proclivity of the poor to degrade their environment because of their high discount rates and equally high social time preferences. Poverty becomes an issue, then, only in so far as it is seen as the cause of degradation of the 'global' commons. Rather than address the structural causes of poverty, the global environmental agenda has found it easier to influence Third World policies through either the stick of possible economic and political sanctions or the carrot of schemes like debt for nature swaps and other financial inducements. With its fixation on issues like tropical deforestation and the loss of tropical megafauna, the agenda of this movement sometimes result in exacerbating Third World poverty (the CITES agreement comes to mind).

In chapter 13, Moseley pursues some of these themes at a more micro scale. He analyzes three important assumptions in the current environmental discourse: that inhabitants of the poorest countries destroy their immediate environment in order to survive; that traditional agricultural communities no longer have the capacity to deal with rapid rates of environmental change; and that the forces of economic globalization have been relentlessly transforming the African landscape. He examines these assumptions by exploring how members of Bambara agricultural communities in the Sanankoro-Djitoumou Commune of southern Mali are responding (or not responding) to changing environmental and economic conditions and the degree of tension that exists between local responses to environmental change and global prescriptions for economic production, on the one hand and environmental conservation, on the other.

In summary (chapter 14), the book explores three interrelated themes surrounding the impacts of globalization on Third World poverty: the welfare role of the state in the age of market triumphalism, the ability of civil society to fill any vacuum created by state withdrawal from its welfare responsibilities, the influence of the global environmental movement in prescribing how the poor can use their environment to obtain their most basic needs. Each chapter attempts to deal with one or a combination of these three broad issues, always with the focus on the 'globalized' rather than on the 'globalizer'.

References

Adam, H., Slabbert, F. and Moodley, K. (1997) *Comrades in Business: Post-Liberation Politics in South Africa*. Cape Town: Tafelberg Publishers.

Barnet, R. and Cavanagh, J. (1994) *Global Dreams: Imperial Corporations and the New World Order*. NY: Simon and Schuster.

Bergsten, F. (1996) 'Globalizing free trade'. *Foreign Affairs* 75 (3), 105–120.

Brodhead, L. (1996) 'Commissioning consent: globalization and global governance'. *International Journal* 51, 651–668.

Bryan, L. and Farrell, D. (1996) *Market Unbound: Unleashing Global Capitalism*. NY: John Wiley.

Cable, V. (1995) 'The Diminished Nation-State: A Study in the Loss of Economic Power'. *Daedalus* 124 (2), Spring, 23–53.

Connor, W. (1994) *Ethnonationalism: The Quest for Understanding*. Princeton, NJ: Princeton University Press.

Dunn, J. (ed.) (1995) *Contemporary Crisis of the Nation State?* Oxford, England: Blackwell.

Esping-Andersen, G. and van Kersbergen, K. (1992) 'Contemporary Research on Social Democracy'. *Annual Review of Sociology* 18, 187–208.

Gelb, S. (1997) 'South Africa's Post-Apartheid Political Economy'. In L. A. Swatuk and D. R. Black (eds) *Bridging the Rift: The New South Africa in Africa*. Boulder: Westview Press.

Gill, S. (1996) 'Globalization, Democratization and the Politics of Indifference'. In J. H. Mittelman (ed.) *Globalization: Critical Reflections*. Boulder and London: Lynne Rienner Publishers, 205–228.

Guehenno, J. (1995) *The End of the Nation State*. Translated by Victoria Elliot. Minneapolis: MN.

Hirst, P. and Thompson, G. (1996) *Globalization in Question*. Cambridge, England: Polity Press.

Horseman, M. and Marshall, A.(1994) *After the Nation State*. London: Harper Collins.

Huntington, S. (1996) 'The West unique, not universal'. *Foreign Affairs* 75 (6), 28–46.

Jung, C. and Shapiro, I. (1995) 'South Africa's Negotiated Transition: Democracy, Opposition and the New Constitutional Order'. *Politics and Society* 23 (3), September, 269–308.

Kapstein, E. (1991/92) 'We are US: the myth of the multinational'. *The National Interest* 26, 55–62.

Kennedy, P. (1993) *Preparing for the Twenty-First Century*. NY: Random House.

Mathews, J. (1997) 'Power Shift'. *Foreign Affairs* 75, 50–66.

Ohmae, K. (1990) *The Borderless World: Power and Strategy in the Interlinked Economy*. NY: Harper Business.

Ohmae, K. (1995) *The End of Nation States: the Rise of Regional Economies*. New York: FreePress.

Owusu, M. (1992) 'Democracy and Africa – A View from the Village'. *The Journal of Modern African Studies* 30 (3), 369–96.

Rinehart, J. (1995) 'The Ideology of Competitiveness'. *Monthly Review* 47 (5), October, 14–23.

Sartori, G. (1991) 'Rethinking Democracy: Bad Polity and Bad Politics'. *International Social Science Journal* (August), 129.

Sassen, S. (1998) *Globalization and its Discontents: Essays on the New Morality of People and Money*. NY: New York Press.

Schmidt, V. (1995) 'The New World Order, Incorporated: The Rise of Business and Decline of the Nation-State'. *Daedalus* 124 (2) Spring, 75–106.

Schmitter, P.C. (1995) 'Democracy's Future: More Liberal, Preliberal, or Postliberal?'. *Journal of Democracy* 6 (1), 15–22.

Sjolander, C. (1996) 'The rhetoric of globalization: what's in a wor(l)d?'. *International Journal* 51, 603–616.

Zartman, W. (ed.) (1995) *Collapsed States: The Disintegration and Restoration of Legitimate Authority*. Boulder and London: Lynne Rienner Publishers.

Chapter 2

Globalization and Poverty: From a Poststructural Perspective

Lakshman Yapa

Introduction

Globalization, the latest phase in the economic integration of the world economy, is an integral part of the older, more familiar logic of economic development. That logic presents Third World poverty as a condition of underdevelopment and naturally, regards economic development as the solution to the problem. In opposition to this, I argue that poverty and material deprivation are a form of socially constructed scarcity induced by the very process of development. By accelerating development through space and time, globalization has intensified social construction of scarcity and therefore, has aggravated problems of poor people. If that claim is true, we must ask, can poverty ever be eradicated from a world that is ruled by powerful forces of globalization.

This chapter is comprised of four sections. In the first part I argue that post-structuralism gives us useful tools not only to study the problem of poverty in the global economy, but also to provide creative solutions. In the second part I present the view that it is *not* helpful to view poverty as an economic problem; rather, it should be looked at directly as a substantive issue of why some people have difficulty obtaining basic goods such as food and shelter. In the third part I present globalization as a nexus of relations where each node of the nexus is implicated in the social construction of scarcity. We cannot address poverty as a question of low income or lack of development without understanding how scarcity is created in a diffused network of globalized production relations. Finally, I illustrate these arguments with examples taken from the sector of food and agriculture.

Elements of the Poststructural Argument

The poststructural argument is presented as four sub-themes. First is the claim that poverty in the global economy is not simply a material condition, but a discursive material formation. Second is the assertion that poverty is socially cons tructed, with academic discourse being deeply implicated in it. Third is the proposition that scarcity is socially constructed at a large number of interconnected sites, which together form a nexus of production relations diffused throughout the larger society. Fourth is the conclusion that to engage the diffused structure and power of the global economy we require a new social theory of non-sovereign power.

Poststructuralism is best explained by distinguishing it from the more familiar and better-known concept, 'postmodernism'. Scholars such as Harvey (1989), Soja (1989), Baudrillard (1993) and Jencks (1996) treat postmodernism as a material condition of the world characteristic of the closing decades of the twentieth century: Coming after the Modern Age this is a time in which the world has changed qualitatively, with acceleration in production, exchange and consumption, rapid transmission of information, high mobility of capital and new forms of art and architecture which are believed to reflect the radical transformations in the economy. In that sense, claims of postmodernity can be seen as matters of empirical verification and judgement. In fact, have these changes occurred and are they of a sufficiently large magnitude to be seen as a historical rupture with the modern? This chapter is not concerned with questions of postmodernism as rupture or a new epoch in history. In contrast to postmodernism, poststructuralism is about epistemology; it is about how we know what we know and why don't we know what we don't know. It is a body of methods about how to conduct social inquiry, how to present our findings and how to overcome the traditional dualism between the subject and object of social research. Next, I shall present a brief overview of a poststructural argument presented in four parts.

First, our words cannot simply mirror objects resident in the world because the path from word to object is always mediated by a concept. This would not pose a serious problem if such mediating concepts were single and unique, but they are not. Every 'word/object' pair has multiple mediating concepts. Meaning does not arise from essential attributes of the object but rather from the context in which one or more mediating concepts occur. Although it is true that material objects can exist independent of our thoughts about them, mediating concepts come into immediate play at the very moment an object becomes the focus of our reflection and conversation. Objects that are part of our daily life are not simply material entities, they are discursively constructed to be discursive material entities. Complex objects of our reflection such as poverty, race, development, globalization and nature can be said to be discursive material formations. This is the basis of the poststructural claim that science is not a mirror for society because reality is socially constructed.

Second, poverty is a condition where some people in society experience long-term scarcities of goods that satisfy basic needs such as food, shelter, health care and clothing. The science of economics says that scarcity exists when the demand for a good exceeds its supply. Economics claims that scarcity follows from objective conditions where human demands are unlimited but resources for satisfying them are limited. But if reality is socially constructed why should scarcity form an exception to that rule? I propose to question the objective basis of scarcity by invoking a notion called 'the end-use of a commodity' which refers to the final use of the commodity. As an example, consider an automobile as a commodity whose end-use is the journey-to-work. Next consider different ways in which that end-use can be satisfied, for example, use of public transport, bicycling, walking, or even 'telecommuting'. The history of urban transportation in the U.S. shows how the automobile became a dominant mode while different ways of getting to work were marginalized, neglected, underfunded, or even sabotaged. The increased demand for automobiles cannot be understood through the internal workings of that industry without taking into account the social construction of that demand through the evolution of the urban space economy, public subsidies for highways, suburbanization of homes, offices and jobs, government policies and massive advertising (Lewis, 1997; Jackson, 1985).

A second mechanism that increased demand for automobiles is an expansion of its end-uses beyond the journey to work. Automobiles came to be associated with symbols of success, glamor, sex and freedom (Sachs, 1992a). To summarize, the scarcity of a commodity is socially constructed by contracting alternative and complementary ways in which an end-use can be met and by expanding into other end-uses that go beyond the original use value.

Third, the process through which alternative sources of supply are contracted and end-uses are expanded occurs at several nodes of a nexus that are associated with technical, social, cultural, political, ecological and academic relations. These relations act and react upon each other in a manner such that each node is constituted from the other nodes in the nexus. The task of abstracting a technical or a social node from such a mutually constituted formation is only an academic device to enable a conversation of the entity under investigation. The world around us exists as a seamless flux. Concepts such as economy, culture and nature are discursive cuts we make into an otherwise undifferentiated reality to enable conversations about our life-world. Having discursively created such categories we must not make the mistake of investing them with distinct boundaries, coherent structures and inner laws that are really not there. It is futile to look for root causes of problems such as poverty because there is no academic theory, nor will there ever be, that can rank order the myriad relations that affect the life circumstances of the poor. Since the causes of poverty are multiple and occur in overdetermined systems we cannot address the problem through social policies that privilege one set of causes over another.

Fourth, if social problems such as poverty cannot be solved by privileging particular sets of causes, what are some useful ways of addressing such problems? Let us consider the specific example of poverty in the global economy. The material deprivations that people suffer occur at myriad sites, which are at once technical, social, cultural, political, ecological and academic. Since there is no way to rank order these sites or relations in any order of importance there can be no sovereign power or agency that can provide a solution to poverty. Indeed the very idea that poverty is an economic problem that can be alleviated through the unhindered operation of the market, or the regulation of the market by the state, are misleading metanarratives that get in the way of suggesting creative solutions. The need for a new theory of non-sovereign power is more evident when poverty is looked at in the context of the global economy.[1] Globalization is driven by a phalanx of powerful forces, which include large transnational corporations, international institutions like The World Bank and The IMF and leaders of many nation states, whose concerted actions are rationalized by a discourse of neo-liberal economics. There is no sovereign power or agency that can counter such forces of globalization. Resistance requires a theory of non-sovereign power, which conceptualizes globalization as a nexus of relations – technical, social, ecological, cultural, political and academic – diffused throughout the world economy. The myriad sites over which global forces exert their will, are simultaneously sites of opportunity for organized resistance. Change can be brought about by conscious agents exerting their will in netlike organizations of multiple sites.

Rethinking Poverty

When social scientists address social problems they begin by implicitly dividing the world into two sectors: the realm of the problem and, that of the non-problem. Consistent with that, the conventional approach to poverty defines it as an 'economic' problem resident in the poverty sector – a bounded, separate segment of the economy. It is believed that poverty can be alleviated through economic growth, increased investments, more jobs and higher income. We can call this the axiom of development. History shows that development has offered little help to the long-term resolution of poverty. Instead of asking why households do not make more income, suppose we ask the substantive question of why poor households have problems getting adequate food, nutrition, housing, transport, health care and so on. The answers we get to these questions are different from those that use the conventional approach. To the question why are over 800 million people in the world routinely hungry, I am not satisfied with the answer, 'They do not make enough money.'

By locating each basic good within a nexus of production relations we can uncover how scarcity is socially constructed at each node of a nexus of relations – technical, social, cultural and so on. The sites at which scarcity is constructed are not confined to the 'so-called poverty sector', they are diffused throughout the larger society. But each of these sites is also a locus of opportunity to resist the forces that create scarcity. Poverty has no root causes because scarcity is created everywhere. Even though the search for root causes is considered good science, I argue policy that privileges one set of factors over another aggravates problems of the poor. There can be no utopian blueprint, no revolution and no grand project of development. If poverty is created everywhere we need social theories that can teach us how to confront it everywhere (Yapa, 1996; 1998).

Globalization as a Nexus of Relations

Life in the global economy represent the best of times for some and the worst of times for many more. Alluring images of the corporate globe are no further away than a CNN commercial – images of London, Zurich, Hong Kong, Bangkok, KLM, Hertz, Holiday Inns, conference rooms, golf courses, cell phones and instant contact with business associates or family. They show success, security and the endless possibilities of one world united by capital and information. There are other images of the global economy that seldom appear on TV: this is of the world child labor, long shifts, non-union agricultural labor, sweat shops in export zones, sex tourism, rainforest destruction, shanty towns and the burden of structural adjustment borne by those least able to afford it.

In theory, the world of poverty is an aberrant, temporary condition, which could be overcome by the world of wealth through the application of science, technology and investment, in a word, through development. In practice, the permanent juxtaposition of wealth and poverty is the continuing reality. The problems of uneven development cannot be overcome through even development because there is no such thing as even development. The history of development contains within it a parallel history of socially constructed scarcity (Sachs, 1992b; Yapa, 1998). Globalization represents the newest and the latest phase of the history of economic development. That is why poverty cannot be eradicated through the economics of globalization.

Most books on the global economy define globalization as a process in which there has been an unprecedented acceleration in the movement of information, commodities and people (Anderson, Cavanagh and Lee, 2000: 4–25). However, in order to clarify how globalization is implicated in the social construction of scarcity, it is necessary to locate it at the center of a nexus of relations – technical, social, cultural and so on.

Technical

Economic globalization was made possible by new and revolutionary developments in communication technology, which allowed the rapid transmission of numeric, textual and graphic information. It is this capacity to design structures in one place and realize them in tangible forms in another far removed place which allows companies like Nike, Gap and GM to organize tightly their far flung global networks.

One result of this spatial organization of the world economy is that a third of all international trade is not between countries but between branches of the same company. Intra-company transactions allow a firm to avoid taxes by setting prices to minimize earnings in countries with high tax rates and maximize earnings in countries with low tax rates, an accounting practice known as transfer pricing. Information technology has also given capital unprecedented mobility allowing billions of dollars to move across national borders at lightening speed with little or no regulation (Barnet and Cavanaugh, 1994).

Besides traditional sources of finance to Third World countries such as governments and multilateral agencies there are also private financial flows such as direct investment, portfolio investment, commercial bank loans. Since 1980 such flows have outpaced the growth of trade flows. The total value of foreign-exchange transactions that travel across borders exceeds $1.5 trillion a day. But less than 2% of these transactions are related to trade or direct investment (Anderson, Cavanagh and Lee, 2000: 33). The remainder is about short-term investment or currency speculation (Barnet and Cavanaugh, 1994: 361–402). So central is information technology to corporate globalism that three out of the five largest firms in the world are high-tech information companies – Cisco, Microsoft and Intel.

Social

Giant firms like GM, Ford, Toyota, Exxon, Monsanto, ADM, Nestle and their counterparts in other countries are the principal drivers of the world economy. Their decisions shape the lives of most of the world's people and the directions of every national economy. They produce most of the world's goods and services, finance that production and trade more and more of it across borders. In turn, they have steered the agendas of most governments at every level and have twisted the operations of the global institutions set up to govern the global economy in their interests (Anderson, Cavanagh and Lee, 2000: 65). The big multinational firms and banks exert their influence on countries directly through investment and finance and indirectly through: business coalitions like USA*NAFTA, Business Roundtable (a club for Fortune 500 CEOs); think tanks like Heritage Foundation and Cato Institute; and public institutions like the World Bank, IMF and WTO (Korten, 1996; Mander and Goldsmith, 1996).

The emergence of corporate globalism has changed the relation between capital and labor in a most fundamental way. First, the bargaining power of labor has been considerably weakened by capital's ability to shift production from one place to another, to threaten closing of branch plants and pull out and to persuade Third World governments to regulate and control labor on behalf of global firms (Rifkin, 1996; Barnet and Cavanagh, 1994: 283–309). Second, labor has been weakened also from the viewpoint of consumption. Traditionally, capital has drawn on labor not only for its productive power, but also on labor's capacity to consume products of firms. Though it would be economically rational for a single firm to reduce wages and therefore, its production costs, it is not in the collective interests of all firms to reduce the total size of the wage bill because that reduces labor's capacity to consume and capital's capacity to accumulate. This was the basis of Henry Ford's thinking when in 1914 he paid his workers an unprecedented five dollars a day; he wanted his workers to buy his cars. Corporate globalism has weakened this compact between capital and labor because corporations do not depend on national markets alone (Luttwalk, 1998: 91–99). Even though India is a very poor country of over 900 million people for global firms it represents a market of at least a 100 million middle-class consumers.

Cultural

An important theme that appears in the literature on globalization and culture is the rapid homogenization of culture. Barnet and Cavanagh have looked at the role that the entertainment industry has played in that process. In what they have called the global cultural bazaar, satellites, cables, walkmans, videocassette recorders, CDs and other marvels of entertainment technology have created the arteries through which modern entertainment conglomerates are homogenizing global culture. The larger cultural theme under globalization is the intensified pressure to modernize, a matter that has received much attention in the work of the Swedish philosopher Helena Noberg-Hodge (1991). The cultural pressure to modernize has ramifications in production, consumption and identity formation. In the production sphere, western-style schools isolate children from their culture and local environment leaving them unable to use local resources. If they study agriculture they learn about industrial farming and commercial inputs, ignoring what the environment naturally provides. The presence of modern educated agricultural experts transforms peasant farmers into backward illiterates. Accelerated modernization and advertising have created new needs. Noberg-Hodge (1991) has described that in Ladakh there is a vicious circle in which individual insecurity contributes to a weakening of family ties which in turn further shakes individual self-esteem. Consumerism plays an important role in this because individual insecurity generates a greater desire to acquire possessions that would make you into somebody. 'This is the cultural basis of supermarket nutrition, fast food, designer clothes and so on' (Lechner and Boli, 2000: 283–368).

Political

Economic globalization has weakened national governments and undermined sovereignty and self-determination. There are several mechanisms at work. Internationalization of capital markets and the free movement of money across borders has eroded the power of governments to regulate the economy through the traditional Keynesian fiscal and monetary policy. Global firms are no longer limited by national borders and monetary policy in moving capital, which makes it harder for governments to regulate their economies. The long-term deterioration of terms of trade for Third World countries have made them more dependent on foreign investment, credit and aid. Third World governments are further weakened by their inability to repay mounting debts, which in turn allows the World Bank and the IMF to impose drastic conditions as part of structural adjustment packages. Trade and investment are coming under the governance of powerful international treaties. The most important among these is the Uruguay Round of the General Agreement on Tariffs and Trade (GATT), which liberalized the rules of trade and investment. The new World Trade Organization (WTO) was created to enforce the GATT rules. Taking the GATT rules further is the Multilateral Agreement on Investment (MAI), which would accelerate economic globalization by increasing restrictions of national governments to regulate investment (Ohmae, 1991; 1996; Lechner and Boli, 2000: 195–235).

Ecological

Production requires matter and energy as inputs and a repository to hold waste material, chemicals and heat, defining what are called ecological relations of production. Globalization has given global firms far more access to resources across borders than was possible under colonialism. Multinational companies like United Fruit, Unilever and Nestle are involved in vast portions of international production and trade. 'In fact, transnationals directly or indirectly command 80% of the land around the world that is cultivated for export crops such as bananas, tobacco and cotton' (Karliner, 1997: 17). Millions of acres that once fed poor families in poor countries are now growing fruits and vegetables for export to consumers in rich countries, a course of action that is sponsored and even paid for, by the World Bank. Among the many factors that contribute to deforestation are the activities of firms such as Georgia-Pacific and Sumitomo. The ecosystem has always acted as the repository of waste from our industrial, agricultural and transportation systems. Economic globalization has magnified, intensified and expanded the scope of transforming our life-supporting systems into repositories of waste leading to the globalization of the ecological crisis. Evidence of this comes from global warming, acid rain, air pollution, deforestation, accelerated soil erosion and salinization of irrigated land, water pollution from agricultural run-off and pesticides in food sources. Under economic globalization Third World countries have come to play a central role as repositories of hazardous waste. Nations such as Thailand, Indonesia and Mexico invite global firms with package deals of cheap non-union labor and almost non-existent environmental laws. An example is the movement by Sandoz, a Swiss company, of a large part of its pesticide production operation to Brazil and India in the 1980s after a series of chemical spills into the Rhine (Karliner, 1997). Another aspect of this is the rapid rise of an export industry in toxic waste, chemical and nuclear, to be buried in landfills of poor countries (Karliner, 1997). There is a much publicized and often quoted infamous memorandum written by Larry Summers in 1992, then the chief economist at the World Bank, who wrote that Third

World countries had a comparative advantage in less polluted air and cheaper human life leading to an impeccable economic logic for dumping toxic waste in the lowest wage countries.

Academic

The category of academic relations calls explicit attention to the role of discourse in production and the social construction of scarcity. Academic relations are of two kinds: internal and external. Internal relations refer to the general rules under which science produces knowledge. In earlier sections of the chapter I alluded to the poststructural critique of the rules under which social science produces knowledge of poverty. External relations refer to discourses that are produced at those sites in the nexus that I have already discussed technical, social, cultural, political and ecological.

There is an explicit and powerful academic discourse that drives globalization, namely neoliberal economics. The term economic neoliberalism refers to a set of ideas rooted in the ideas of Adam Smith concerning the relationship between the state and the market. 'Today's neoliberalism can be defined as including the following components: the primacy of the market, the reduction in public expenditure for social services, the reduction of government regulation and the privatization of state-owned enterprises' (Karliner, 1997: 2). There is a vast well-financed far-flung academic industry that produces and disseminates the neo-liberal discourse. This academic industry includes: prestigious institutions such as University of Chicago, Stanford University and University of Pennsylvania; public institutions such as the World Bank and the IMF with their economic research divisions and countless policy chapters; corporate think tanks such as Heritage Foundation, Brookings Institution and Cato Institute. These institutes are well financed, have resident research scholars, publish research articles and books, maintain extensive web pages and are routinely listened to by policy makers. In addition, corporations such as Mobil, Exxon, Monsanto and ADM produce and disseminate neo-liberal discourses through paid newschapter and TV advertisements.

As central as they are, globalization consists of more than modern information technology and new social relations of capital; it is simultaneously made of cultural, political, ecological and academic elements. Since globalization exerts power through all these elements, they all constitute sites at which the process can be engaged and resisted.

Food and Agriculture in the Global Economy

In this section I consider the issue of globalization and poverty. In an earlier part of the chapter titled, 'Rethinking Poverty' I suggested that instead of asking the question how can poor people obtain more money from the economy, we can ask the substantive question why do some people not have access to basic necessities like food, clothing and housing. With that in mind I shall focus on food and explore how the globalized economy is directly implicated in creating food scarcities for poor people. As I theorized at the beginning of this chapter, scarcity occurs in two forms. One is the disappearance or non-availability of alternative sources of supply and the other is increasing end-uses of a commodity beyond its original use-value. These two processes work at all sites of the nodes of the nexus of production relations through discursive and non-discursive mechanisms. I shall illustrate the argument that globalization aggravates poverty by creating food scarcity for poor people by using three examples: food production technology, export agriculture and consumption.

Food Production Technology

A major international agricultural initiative of the past three decades has been the launching of the so-called 'Green Revolution' through the introduction of high-yielding varieties of wheat, maize and rice. The effect of this was to increase dramatically the production of cereals in many countries of the Third World and the 'Green Revolution' was widely hailed as the answer to world hunger. Nevertheless, in the late 1990s there were 1.2 billion hungry people whose diets lacked in calories and protein and another 2 billion whose diets suffered from deficiency of vitamins and minerals (Gardner and Halweil, 2000: 60). How is the 'Green Revolution' implicated as a causative agent of hunger and malnutrition? The new so-called improved seeds do not reproduce well, so they have to be purchased at the beginning of each growing season. This has led to the breakdown of farmers' own efforts at preserving seeds and caused the disruption of their informal networks of seed exchanges. The new seeds are genetically uniform which makes them very vulnerable to crop diseases.

Some scientists consider the erosion of the genetic diversity of our food plants the greatest threat to food security (Fowler and Mooney, 1990; Shiva,1993). The new seeds in order to produce high yields, require large amounts of fertilizer, large amounts of pesticides because they lack natural immunity and irrigation because they need a controlled supply of water. The financial costs of growing improved seeds are much higher than those of traditional varieties which in turn lead to the exacerbation of social inequality and increased hunger by turning small peasants into landless laborers.

At a cultural level the new technology created a class of agricultural experts and another of backward peasants. It created new demands for agricultural universities and extension services and devalorized indigenous knowledge. At a political level, by creating a new dependence of farmers on purchased inputs and credit, it increased opportunities for clientism, patronage and graft. From an ecological point of view it created massive scarcities by substituting commercial industrial inputs for resources that were naturally available in the environment.

Moreover, the 'Green Revolution' has led to a progressive degradation of land and water by increasing soil erosion, reducing the organic content of soil, introducing pesticides into the food chain, contaminating water through fertilizer and pesticide runoff, taxing the ground water table and salinization and water logging of irrigated land. Academically, the new seeds created a discourse of progressive modern farming. At the same time it had the effect of dedeveloping and devalorizing the production of food in ecologically sustainable small farms (Shiva, 1991; Yapa, 1993). Many studies now show that traditional polycultural farms produce more food per unit of input than industrial monocultures. For example an experiment comparing these two systems showed that polycultures could produce 100 units of food from 5 units of inputs whereas an industrial system requires 300 units of input to produce 100 units of food (Bray, 1994). 'The 295 units of wasted inputs could have provided 5,900 units of additional food. Thus the industrial system leads to a decline of 5,900 units of food. This is a recipe for starving people, not feeding them' (Shiva, 2000: 13). All the globalizing agents that I cited in the early part of the chapter were responsible for producing, sponsoring and propagating the scarcity-creating technology of the 'Green Revolution'. Among these agents were the Rockefeller Foundation, CGIAR – the Consultative Group of the International Agricultural Institutes, the Food and Agricultural Organization of the UN, The World Bank, universities and global firms that sold inputs such as seeds, pesticides and agricultural machinery.

Biotechnology, the re-engineering of the genetic structure of living organisms, also called the 'gene revolution', is now being promoted as the lasting solution to problems of food supply and plant disease. The technology, which involves the ability to transfer genetic material from one organism to another, permits the crossing and intermixing of species to create new microbes, plants and animals. 'Many predict that the twenty-first century will become the age of biotechnology. Biocolonizing companies and governments know that the economic and political entities that control the genetic resources of the planet may well exercise decisive power over the world economy in coming decades. However, the new drive for international hegemony in the engineering and marketing of life represents an extraordinary threat to the earth's fragile ecosystem and to those living in them' (Kimbrell, 1996: 132–133).

Advocates for biotechnology argue that it will help feed the world. Such claims are an integral part of the advertising campaigns of companies like Monsanto and ADM but the technology may end up hurting the capacity of the world to feed itself. One such technology is herbicide resistant crops, an example being Monsanto's Roundup Ready soybeans, grown from transgenic seeds where genes have been inserted from other organisms. Roundup is the largest selling weedicide in the world. Farmers who use the seed must sign a contract with Monsanto allowing it to inspect farmers' fields at any time to make sure that farmers have not retained seeds for replanting. Farmers using Roundup Ready seeds use greater amounts of the herbicide throughout the growing season without fear of destroying the plants. This is why all major seeds companies have been bought or tied to chemical companies; the seeds are genetically designed to create a market for chemical inputs (Middendorf, Skladny, Ransom and Busch, 1998: 85–96). It is feared that the introduction herbicide-tolerant seeds into Third World farming systems will lead to a broad degradation of the ecosystem. What agribusiness firms consider weeds are food, fodder and medicine for Third World farmers. Women in rural India use 150 different species of plants for vegetables, fodder and medicine. In West Bengal 124 so-called weed species colleted from rice fields have economic importance for farmers. Increased use of herbicide resistant seeds will lead to the destruction of earthworms, soil bacteria and beneficial fungi. It would also undermine the soil conservation functions of cover crops and mixed crops, leading to accelerated soil erosion. There is also a fear that herbicide-tolerant genes may flow out of the field boundaries into weedy relative plants and produce 'super weeds' (Mendelson, 1998: 272–273).

Seeds from food crops have always performed two basic functions that have benefited humans and animals: they produced food and reproduced themselves naturally. The ability of seeds to reproduce themselves naturally has always been a barrier to capital in transforming the seed to a complete commodity. One answer to this has been the development of plants that are genetically engineered to produce infertile seeds. The early work was done by a company called Delta and Pine Land Company in collaboration with the US Department of Agriculture. Later this company came under the control of Monsanto. The technology of producing genetically engineered sterile seeds is now popularly called the 'terminator technology'. The seed is engineered to produce seeds of the next generation that will self-destruct by self-poisoning. Between 15 and 20% of the world's food is grown by poor farmers who save seed. These farmers feed at least 1.4 billion people. Contrary to the claims of global agribusiness feeding the world's hungry, it is clear that the general adoption of this technology will undermine the very basis of traditional agriculture (Steinbrecher and Mooney, 1998: 276–279). In one of the very few instances of its type, amidst a widespread criticism and a well-organized campaign by grassroots food activists and some scientists, Monsanto announced in late 1999 that it would not pursue the commercial development of the 'terminator technology'.

Export Agriculture

Since colonial times Third World countries had come to rely on one or two export crops for their economic mainstay, a principal legacy of the imperial division of labor and the colonial construction of comparative advantages. The production of export crops was done at the expense of growing food crops for local consumption. The Third World is a net importer of basic foodstuffs such as grain and meat, but is a major exporter of many cash crops, such as peanuts, bananas, coffee, tea, cocoa, cotton, soybeans, sugarcane and tobacco. The emphasis on export crops displaces subsistence farmers from their land and exacts substantial environmental costs though the heavy use of pesticides, chemical fertilizer, irrigation and loss of biodiversity. Recent decades have seen the rapid expansion of what are called 'non-traditional exports' such as flowers, fruits and vegetables for European, North American and Japanese markets (French, 2000). Although there are many causes of deforestation, the draw of international markets for wood products is clearly a factor as seen in the rapid expansion of this industry in Malaysia, Indonesia and Brazil (Abramovitz, 1998; Menotti, 1998; Goldsmith, 1997b). Promotion of export agriculture is an integral part of the economic logic of the World Bank's prescription for alleviating poverty.

Mexico provides a good example of the scarcity inducing logic of export agriculture. Corn is the basic food staple in Mexico where it is produced by two and a half million farmers mostly of indigenous decent. The growing of corn is an important part of the economic, social and cultural life of poor rural Mexicans. In preparation for the passage of NAFTA, Mexico eliminated whatever protections there were for small food producing farmers. North American agribusinesses moved to Mexico and took over land dedicated to subsistence agriculture and converted them to the cultivation of pesticide intensive crops such as strawberries and cantaloupes for the U.S. market. In turn they began to sell Mexicans corn and beans grown in the U.S. All this, despite the fact that Mexico's corn program had been widely regarded as a rural employment program. In a pattern widely repeated throughout the Third World displaced rural people migrate to overcrowded polluted cities in search of non-existent jobs (Lehman and Krebs, 1996). Such is the logic of export agriculture and poverty alleviation in the global economy driven by neo-liberal economics.

Increased Consumption

Creating a global economy means '...transforming the vast mass of still largely self-sufficient people in rural areas of the Third World into consumers of capital-intensive goods and services, mainly those provided by the transnational corporations' (Goldsmith, 1996: 81). For this to be possible the cultural patterns of self-sufficient life-styles must be destroyed and replaced by values of a high mass-consumption society. That task is being ably accomplished by advertising firms that employ communication technologies that made globalization possible in the first place (Goldsmith, 1997a). I shall cite a few examples of how this process is implicated in the social construction of scarcity.

Pulses are the edible seeds of crops such as peas, beans, lentils and chickpeas. Pulses provide protein of a very high quality and are referred to as the poor man's meat. They are also excellent sources of numerous micronutrients. Yet in countries such as Colombia, India and Sri Lanka the per capita consumption of pulses have declined. In many middle-income countries of the world, particularly those that have enjoyed rapid rates of economic growth in recent years there is an increased adoption of meat-based diets which require the use of land to grow feed crops for livestock (Brown, Kane and Ayres, 1993: 37). The displacement of cropland from pulses to feed crops replaced a cheap source of proteins with an expensive one. It also reduced the total availability of protein because it takes many more grams of vegetable protein to produce one gram of animal protein.

Another example is the widespread promotion by companies of expensive infant formula as a substitute for mother's breast milk. Infant formula is expensive, nutritionally inferior and harmful to health when used with improperly boiled water or under inadequate refrigeration, conditions that are altogether too common in poor Third World households. Imagine the economic, social and ecological consequences for the Chinese population if the plans of the leading automakers in the world to sell an automobile to each person that now rides a bicycle, takes a bus, or simply walks, were to materialize.

Conclusion

Despite claims of its advocates, globalization will not eradicate poverty in the world. Data shows that during the past two decades income gaps between rich and poor nations and that between rich and poor people have widened considerably. For Third World countries globalization represents the latest phase in a centuries long process of integration into the world economy, beginning with colonization and then passing through a brief period of post-colonial economic development. Even though economic development is about the expansion of production forces I have shown through examples selected from the food sector how it contains a parallel, unacknowledged history of socially constructed scarcity. In the economic sense of the term, 'scarcity' comes into being when the demand for a good exceeds its supply. Applying that idea to poverty, economists say that poor people do not have enough income to convert their needs for basic goods into effective demand. But instead of looking at this as a problem in lack of income, I asked the more direct substantive question as to why some people in particular places lack basic goods. We found that lack of basic goods is caused by socially constructed scarcity, which occurs through the operation of two parallel mechanisms. Given the end-use of a commodity (or what Marx called use value) there are processes in society which eliminate, marginalize, or de-develop alternative and complementary ways of meeting that end-use. Likewise, there are other processes, which expand the end-uses of a commodity beyond the original use value. The contraction of sources of supply and the expansion of end-uses, the twin processes of socially constructed scarcity, function through discursive and non-discursive mechanisms at all nodes of the nexus of production relations.

In this chapter I presented globalization at the intersection of a nexus of relations: technical, social, cultural, political, ecological and academic. I then applied that framework through a series of examples to look at why poor people do not have access to food in the global economy. I presented the material also as examples of a poststructural analysis of the questions under consideration. How is change to be induced in vast complex system such as the global economy? How are issues of poverty to be addressed in the global economy? I used access to food as a way of presenting a substantive view of poverty.

Scarcity of food is created at a large number of sites in an overdetermined system. There is no sovereign agency that can oppose the global system because the global economy does not exercise sovereign power. The network of global institutions – the multinational firms and multilateral agencies exert power over food and agriculture through a myriad of discursive and non-discursive practices. In such a system there are no privileged points of entry, no essential variables and there are no well-defined targets to oppose. My argument is that if scarcity of food in socially constructed at a large number of sites, then they are also sites of opportunity at which we can exercise non-sovereign power to bring about change. Non-sovereign power can be exercised at each site in the nexus of food relations in the global economy. Social change cannot come from a specified vision of a utopian society. In fact there are no separate, alternative spaces we can create called 'solution spaces'. It is not uncommon for people to say, 'We know what the problem is, please tell us how to solve it.' I do not find this to be a useful declaration. What is important is the statement of the problem as it is constituted in detail in the nexus of relations.

Solutions, if I may use that word, will flow from a detailed substantive under-standing of the problem. Actions can take place at myriad substantive sites at which the problem occurs through conscious actions of numerous agents. In poststructural theory this is what we mean by the exercise of non-sovereign power.

Note

1. For a brilliant description of non-sovereign power written for a different purpose see Foucault (1990).

References

Anderson, S., Cavanagh, J. and Lee, T. (2000) *Field Guide to the Global Economy*. NY: The New Press.

Barnet, R.J. and Cavanagh, J. (1995) *Global Dreams: Imperial Corporations and the New World Order*. NY: Simon & Schuster.

Baudrillard, J. (1993) 'Simulacra and Simulations: Disneyland'. In C. Lemert (ed.) *Social Theory: The Multicultural and Classic Readings*. Boulder, CO: Westview Press, 524–529.

Bray, F. (1994) 'Agriculture for Developing Nations'. *Scientific American* July, 33–35.

Brown, L.R., Kane, H. and Ayres, E. (1993) *Vital Signs 1993*. NY: W. W. Norton.

Foucault, M. (1990) *The History of Sexuality*. NY: Vintage Books.

Fowler, C. and Mooney, P.R. (1990) *The threatened gene: food, politics and the loss of genetic diversity*. Cambridge: Lutterworth.

French, H. (2000) 'Coping with Ecological Globalization'. In L.R. Brown (ed.) *State of the World 2000*. NY: W. W. Norton, 184–202

Gardner, G. and Halweil, B. (2000) 'Nourishing the Underfed and Overfed'. In L.R. Brown (ed.) *State of the World*. NY: W. W. Norton, 59–78.

Goldsmith, E. (1997a) 'Development as Colonialism'. *The Ecologist* 27, 69–76.

Goldsmith, E. (1997b) 'Can the Environment Survive the Global Economy?'. *The Ecologist* 27, 242–248.

Harvey, D. (1989) *The Condition of Postmodernity*. Cambridge, MA.: Basil Blackwell.

Jackson, K.T. (1985) *Crabgrass Frontier: The Suburbanization of the United States*. NY: Oxford University Press.

Jencks, C. (1996) *What is Post-Modernism?* London: Academy Group.

Karliner, J. (1997) *The Corporate Planet: Ecology and Politics in the Age of Globalization*. San Franscisco: Sierra Club Books.

Kimbrell, A. (1998) 'Why Biotechnology and High-Tech Agriculture Cannot Feed the World'. *The Ecologist* 28 (5), 294–298.

Korten, D.C. (1996) *When Corporations Rule the World*. West Hartford, CN: Kumarian Press.

Lechner, F. and Boli, J. (ed.) (2000) *The Globalization Reader*. Oxford, UK: Blackwell.

Lehman, K. and Krebs, A. (1996) 'Control of World's Food Supply'. In J. Mander and E. Goldsmith (eds) *The Case Against the Global Economy*. San Francisco: Sierra Club Books, 122–130.

Lewis, T. (1997) *Divided Highways*. NY: Penguin Putnam.

Luttwalk, E. (1998) *Turbo Capitalism: Winners and Losers in the Global Economy*. NY: Harper Collins.

Mander, J. and Goldsmith, E. (ed.) (1996) *The Case Against the Global Economy*. San Francisco: Sierra Club Books.

Mendelson, J. (1998) 'Roundup: The World's Biggest-Selling Herbicide'. *The Ecologist* 28 (5), 270–275.

Menotti, V. (1998) 'Globalization and the Acceleration of the Forest Destruction Since Rio'. *The Ecologist* 28, 354–362.

Middendorf, G., Skladany, M., Ransom, E. and Busch, L. (1998) 'New Agricultural Biotechnologies: The Struggle for Democratic Choice'. *Monthly Review* 50, 85–97.

Norberg-Hodge, Helena (1991) *Ancient futures: learning from Ladakh*. San Francisco: Sierra Club Books.

Ohmae, K. (1996) *The End of the Nation State*. NY: Free Press.

Ohmae, K. (1999) *The Borderless World*. NY: Haper Collins.

Rifkin, J. (1996) 'New Technology and the End of Jobs'. In E. Goldsmith and J. Mander (eds) *The Case Against the Global Economy*. San Francisco: Sierra Club.

Sachs, W. (1992a) *For the Love of the Automobile: Looking Back into the History of Our Desires*. Berkeley: University of California Press.

Sachs, W. (ed.) (1992b) *The Development Dictionary: A Guide to Knowledge as Power.* London: Zed Books.

Shiva, V. (1991) *The Violence of the Green Revolution: Third World Agriculture, Ecology and Politics.* London: Zed Books.

Shiva, V. (1993) *Monocultures of the Mind.* London: Zed Press.

Shiva, Vandana (2000) *Stolen Harvest: The Hijacking of the Global Food Supply.* Cambridge, MA: South End Press.

Soja, E.W. (1989) *Postmodern Geographies: The Reassertion of Space in Critical Social Theory.* NY: Verso.

Steinbrecher, R.A. and Mooney, P.R. (1998) 'Terminator Technology: The Threat to World Food Security'. *The Ecologist* 28 (5), 276–279.

Yapa, L. (1993) 'What Are Improved Seeds? An Epistemology of the Green Revolution'. *Economic Geography* 69, 254–273.

Yapa, L. (1996) 'What Causes Poverty? A Postmodern View'. *Annals of the Association of American Geographers* 86, 707–728.

Yapa, L. (1998) 'The poverty discourse and the poor in Sri Lanka'. *Trans Inst Br Geogr* 23, 95–115.

Chapter 3

Globalization and Marginalization in Euro-African Relations in the Twenty-First Century

Severine Rugumamu

Introduction

In the last two and a half decades, dramatic changes have taken place in the global political and economic order. The world has witnessed the conclusion of the Cold War, the rapid development of a global market economy and a strong trend towards regional economic bloc formation. During the same period, the European Union (EU) has undergone profound transformations in its integration and enlargement. More specifically, the 1992 Treaty of Maastricht established a common citizenship of the EU, proposed economic and monetary union including a single currency and envisaged a common foreign and security policy, including the eventual framing of a common defense policy. Most of these processes are still under way and have compelled the EU to re-assess its policies in international security, trade, investment and development cooperation with developing countries.

While Europe has been experiencing epochal transformations, the situation in Africa has been deteriorating and the 1980s were characterized as the 'lost development decade' for the continent. Of the forty-seven countries classified by the United Nations as least developed, 32 are to be found in sub-Saharan Africa (Botswana and Mauritius were the only two countries to graduate from this club of destitutes) (Harsh, 1992). The incidence and depth of poverty on the continent has been on the rise since the mid-1970s and it was estimated that 50% of the African population lived in poverty by the early 1990s. Sandstrom (1993:7) predicted that given the continent's high population growth rates (over 3% a year) and its overall poor economic performance, as many as 100 million more Africans could be living in poverty by the turn of the 21st century (see also, UNDP, 1997:2).

The purpose of this chapter is to examine the political implications and the likely responses of African economies to the challenges and opportunities of the emerging world order. More specifically, it seeks to put into a proper context the impact of unfolding Euro-Africa relations in the post-Cold War period. It is argued that, although development cooperation is accorded a 'special and privileged position' in the Maastricht Treaty, the pattern of EU's recent policies and actions towards Africa reflect the continent's reduced e geo-strategic significance to Europe. Both the quantity and quality of bilateral and multilateral aid from Europe to Africa have declined, portfolio flows and commercial lending are visibly marginalizing much of

Africa, the new international trade regime is increasingly disadvantageous to poor countries and the continent's onerous foreign debt burden has received only casual attention. In short, in the unfolding global context, the Lomé Convention arrangements are no longer a priority for the EU.

Globalization in Context

The more eloquent and extreme proponents of globalization refer to the current wave of the process as the New World Order, which encompasses a wide range of phenomena, from the internationalization of economic activities to the globalization of national cultures, politics, environment and security. The unprecedented volume and velocity of international trade flows, investment, information, culture and migration have created a more integrated world. Growth in international trade has consistently outstripped growth in global gross domestic product for almost two decades. World financial markets and capital flows have expanded rapidly, further integrating national economies. The growth of money markets has been even more spectacular, with over one trillion dollars a day traded in currency transactions. At the same time, new technologies have led to the development of increasingly knowledge-based systems of trade and production (see, Ohmae, 1990; Soros, 1997).

However, those who study the longer-term implications of globalization argue that it is a continuation of historical trends in capital accumulation. According to this perspective, although the attributes of globalization are significant, they are not unprecedented. These global transformations do not constitute a new economic system, the international economy is not yet global and markets, even for strategic industries are still far from being fully integrated. Further, capital flows are still restricted by currency and banking regulations; immigration controls and xenophobia undermine labor mobility; and multinational enterprises maintain most of their assets and strategic command centers in their home nations. These criticisms of globalization have come from trail-blazing works by Hirst and Thompson (1999), Held (1997), Hoogvelt (1997), who have argued that globalization is not a supra-human process created by abstract and unchangeable market forces, or by intangible and uncontrollable technological forces. The emerging global system is a societal construct, driven and shaped as required, by national, international and transnational players and processes. These dynamic forces are economic, technocratic and political. The emerging global order is characterized by unrelenting competition between enterprises and, politically, it is characterized by intense pressure, lobbying and financial aid by powerful corporations. Globalization is, therefore, but one of a number of distinct conjunctures of the international economy that have taken place since the 1860s. In many ways, the level of integration, interdependence and openness of national economies in the present era is less than what prevailed between 1870–1994. Hirst and Thompson (1999:9) argue that 'if the theorists of globalization mean that we have an economy in which each part of the world is linked by markets sharing close to the real-time information, then it began not in the 1970s but in the 1870s' Arrighi (1999:55) argues, further, that the spectacular economic expansion and transformation of the last two decades should not be construed as novel except for their scale, scope and complexity.

Critics of globalization argue also that capital mobility is not producing massive shifts of investment and employment from advanced to developing countries. Rather, foreign direct investment, technological capacity, industrial production and markets are highly concentrated in the advanced economies of the European Union, Japan and North America. These major economic powers have the capacity to exert significant governance pressures over financial markets. Apart from a small minority of newly-industrialized countries, Third World countries remain marginal to the beneficial impacts of many of these processes. Some studies have projected that the losses from globalization far outweigh the gains of the process for Third World countries. The least developed countries as a group are expected to lose up to US$600 million a year in the next five to eight years (Harrison, *et al*. 1995: 38–40; UNDP, 1997: 82). Thus, globalization is not without severe contradictions. Rather than benefiting all actors and all nations, they tend to produce gains for some at the expense of others. As the Human Development Report (UNDP, 1996: 59) observed, it is not a positive-sum game but rather 'a two-edged sword with winners and losers'. These inequities can be understood only in the context of the structural dynamics of capitalism and world trade.

Earlier theoretical insights, including those of accumulation on a world scale (Amin, 1974), the production of a capitalist world systems thesis (Wallerstein, 1974), the development of underdevelopment (Frank, 1978), unequal exchange (Emmanuel, 1972) and dependency theory (Rodney, 1972), have sought to provide frameworks within which the inner structural dynamic of capitalism could be interpreted. In this context, the current phase of globalization may be traced to the prolonged crisis of the 1960s and 1970s. Structural reform in advanced economies constituted a shift from the Fordist mode of production and accumulation to flexible capitalist accumulation (see Arrighi, 1994; Ohmae, 1990; Fukuyama, 1992 for analyses of capitalist transformations in the past century). The conclusion of the Uruguay Round of Negotiations and the establishment of WTO institutionalized these transformations by extending the realm of free markets beyond issues of international trade to include services, intellectual property rights, agricultural commodities and textiles (see, Sassen, 1996). These structural shifts also illuminate changing Euro-African relations.

Globalization and Euro-Africa Relations: A Brief Background

Structural changes in capitalist accumulation ushered in a new era of North-South relations at the end of the Second World War. In the search for a more effective global capitalist structure, the imperial powers relinquished their colonial possessions but put in place elaborate structures to ensure close economic and political ties with former colonies. In this respect, the 1958 Treaty of Rome establishing the European Community (EC) accorded eighteen African colonies associate status within the Community. At the Yaounde Conventions of 1963 and 1969, the associate status of the African partners, now independent states, was renewed. As associates, African countries received aid and enjoyed tariff preferences for their exports to the EC. In return, the EC received preferential treatment of its exports in the markets of the associates (Grilli, 1993; Ravenhill, 1985).

The accession in 1973 of the United Kingdom, Denmark and Ireland, to the EC changed the nature of the relations between the Community and the entire bloc of developing countries, particularly the former British colonies. Until then, most former British colonies maintained comparatively close ties with one another and with Britain through the Commonwealth. The enlarged Community initiated negotiations that led to the signing of the first Convention on February 28, 1975, between the nine members of the European Community and forty-six African, Caribbean and Pacific (ACP) states in Lomé, the capital of Togo in West Africa. The 1975 Lomé Convention has since been renegotiated five times, conveniently referred to as Lomé I, II, III, IVa and recently the post – Lomé IVb Agreement. The Conventions are the principal and most detailed instruments of the Community's development cooperation policy.

All the Lomé Conventions included provisions for co-operation in the fields of trade, aid, investment, industry and the stabilization of ACP earnings from commodity exports. This special relationship was initially considered the most complete instrument of development cooperation. In very broad terms, it encapsulated the principles of dialogue, contractuality and predictability. Indeed, the preamble to the first Lomé Convention claimed that the Convention set out 'to establish a new model of relations between the developed and developing states, compatible with the aspirations of the international community towards a more just and a more balanced economic order'. Similarly, Falk (1980: vii) claims that the Lomé Convention represents 'the most ambitious North-South experiment in international economic cooperation yet to be made'. This optimism was quickly proven wrong.

On paper, the Conventions spoke eloquently about 'partnership' and equality in Euro-Africa relations. One of the basic principles of the first Convention, is that 'ACP-EU cooperation, underpinned by the legally binding system and the existence of joint institutions, shall be exercised on the basis of the following fundamental principles: equality between partners, respect for their sovereignty, mutual interest and interdependence; and the right of each state to determine its own political, social, cultural and economic policy options'. However, as Ravenhill (1985: 2) points out, 'the Convention aroused high expectations that subsequently have not been fulfilled'. One of the primary objectives of this chapter is to explain why this is the case.

At the very heart of Euro-Africa relations are inordinate structural inequalities between the EU and African states. While the former is a community of advanced industrial economies, the latter is a collection of predominantly weak, dependent economies with fragile polities. The asymmetrical power balance between the two groups springs structurally from the aggregate economic, political and organizational resources of the EU and the overall weakness of the African states individually and collectively. It is within this context of relative power inequalities that the general and specific contents of various Lomé Conventions should be explained (Rugumamu, 1999a)

The Political Economy of the First Lomé Convention

The first Lomé Convention was negotiated under special historical circumstances. The Cold War, the activism of the Group of 77 for a New International Economic

Order (NIEO) as well as the power of OPEC provided the environment within which it was negotiated and signed. As negotiations proceeded, primary commodity producing states in the South tried to follow OPEC's example of establishing commodity cartels and were generally perceived to be on the brink of wielding commodity power. This perception was heightened in Europe by concomitant real shortages in raw materials following strong inflation in the North. These factors, together, were equally critical in European decision-making. As Kwarteng (1997) and Galtung (1976) have observed, bi-polarism and competition between the superpowers had, since the 1950s, heightened the importance of Europe maintaining the political alliance of newly independent African states. Two decades later, the anxieties of the 1970s were confirmed by the European Commission (1996: 9) which acknowledged that one of the major reason for the apparent Lomé I benevolence was. 'The concern to defend...economic and geo-political interests in the age of the Cold War...the European anxiety at the first oil crisis i.e. the fear of raw material shortages and a desire to hold on to the valued overseas markets united with geo-strategic interests.'

These conditions motivated the Europeans to make far-reaching concessions to ACP countries in Lomé 1, making this convention one of the most mutually beneficial, negotiated economic arrangements between developing countries (as a group) and a group of donors. ACP states were accorded contractual right to aid, non-reciprocal trade arrangements and export price stabilization schemes (Zartman, 1993; Grilli, 1993).

One of the most significant contributions of the first Lomé Convention was the establishment of the European Development Fund (EDF), an instrument for channeling multilateral aid from the Community directly to its developing partners. The EDF was to be complementary to bilateral aid and, it was to be stable (multi-year), non-political, negotiated with the recipients, administered in association with them, utilized to fit the recipients' priorities and free of narrow donor conditionalities. Above all, the multilateral aid program was to be given mostly in the form of grants (Grilli, 1993; Asante, 1981).

Lomé I was important also for projecting a sense of equality among the negotiating partners. During the halcyon days of Euro-Africa relations, the African 'partners' were expected, in theory, to participate effectively in the entire aid administration process: programming, project preparation, ex-ante evaluation, financing decisions, project execution and ex-post project evaluation. In this respect, at the beginning of every new Convention, EU missions visited each ACP state in order to discuss its respective National Indicative Program (NIP), an annual ritual known as the programming process.

Unfortunately, practice tended to be at variance with stated policy as the amount and disbursement dates of grants to each ACP state was decided unilaterally by the EU. In addition, over 70% of the aid returned to the Community in the form of orders and contracts. During the first Convention, about 80% of total EDF resources financed development projects and were allocated to the NIP for each of the ACP member states (Table 3.1). The problems that EDF funding addressed were highly selective and were defined by donor interests.

**Table 3.1 Financial Resources Budgeted for Lomé I to IV 1975–2000
(in mill. Ecus)**

Convention	Period	Amount
Lomé I	1975–80	3,450
Lomé II	1980–85	5,700
Lomé III	1985–90	8,500
Lomé IV a	1990–95	12,140
Lomé IV b	1995–00	14,956
Total		**44,746**

Source: European Commission (1998)

Another significant element of the first Convention was the establishment of the commodity price stabilization program, STABEX. The scheme covered 44 commodities, all of which were either unprocessed or semi-processed. Like insurance, STABEX was designed to compensate for shortfalls in commodity earnings. Application for the stabilization of export incomes had to be submitted for each commodity, which accounted for at least 6.5% of the export income of the country in the preceding year (there were two exceptions sisal, 5% and the other applied to the least developed, landlocked and island countries, for which the figure was 2%). The compensatory payment, which was to be made almost automatically rather than at the discretion of the EU, was based on the difference between the average over the proceeding four years and the sums actually received (ACP Secretariat, 1998). In practice, however, payments could be denied if, in the opinion of the donors, the decline in export earnings was caused by a trade policy that discriminated against EU interests. Mytelka and Langdon (1979) conclude that STABEX was both an incentive to maintain present levels of production in specific commodities and a disincentive to diversify commercial agriculture and other activities that would promote domestic economic linkages.[1]

The abandonment of trade reciprocity with the ACP countries was the third significant concession made by the Community. Like revenue stabilization, this was a demand by developing countries dating back to the 1950s, when the basic rules concerning international trade enshrined in GATT began to be criticized as unsuitable to their special development needs. The South's demands were aimed in two directions: the attainment of a measure of price stabilization for primary commodities and the attainment of trade preferences for their manufactured exports in Northern markets. The first Lomé Convention obligated the Community to make a regional exception to trade reciprocity. As of 2000, about 92% of the products originating from the ACP countries entered the EU market duty free. If agricultural products, which were subject to a tariff quota with zero duty, are included (protocol products such as sugar, beef, bananas and rum), this percentage rises to about 99%. The only exceptions are products, which fall under the Common Agricultural Policy (CAP) such as tomatoes, carrots and onions. While the majority of the EU's exports to ACP countries consist of manufactures and capital goods, ACP countries export largely agricultural raw materials, minerals and crude oil.

Despite the preferential access to EU markets offered under various Lomé Conventions, ACP exports to Europe deteriorated during those two decades. The share of the ACP in total EU imports fell from 6.7% in 1976 to 3% in 1998. This reflects the declining share of the ACP in world trade, which halved from 3 to 1.5% during the same period. Most ACP countries, particularly those in Africa, failed to diversify their exports into non-traditional income-elastic products and most could not manage to become competitive in the world market. Even those ACP countries that have made modest gains in diversifying into areas like garments, fresh fruit, flowers and vegetables are finding it difficult to maintain or improve their situation in the global trade system. The market niches for non-traditional exports are highly competitive and require connections to the complex international commodity networks, which continually draw new entries from countries worldwide. Moreover, products for new market niches are highly perishable. They require expensive transportation; are subject to wide-ranging price fluctuations; and entail risks for producers and are often natural to temperate rather than to tropical climates. This largely disadvantages African entrepreneurs whose knowledge is essentially of local tropical crops. These features, combined with the need for large capital investments, contribute to the dominance of large foreign firms, for which Africans only serve as low-wage labor (Klark, 1998). Other structural factors inherent in Euro-Africa relations, for example, biotechnology, are also swiftly eroding Africa's traditional comparative advantage in the current international division of labor (Clark and Juma, 1991; McQueen, 1998; Ravenhill, 1985).

Another difficulty facing ACP countries is the 'Safeguard Clause', which allows EU members to make derogations from the guarantees of free access if their markets are threatened by ACP products. Parfitt (1996) notes that the United Kingdom used the threat of the Safeguard Clause to force Mauritius to conclude a voluntary export restraint on its textile exports to the Community. Furthermore, the EU has recently put in place upward harmonization of European-wide technical standards of imports, a move that threatens to exclude African exports. In fact, the EU has constantly invoked sanitary and phyto-sanitary measures to bar African products like fish and meat products from its markets. Thus, the initial euphoria notwithstanding, Lome 1 and subsequent conventions have failed to meet Africa's development expectations. Subsequent Conventions (Lomé II, II and IV) were negotiated and concluded at the time when the geopolitical and economic conditions of the 1970s had changed significantly and ACP countries, in general, were weaker.

The Political Economy of Lomé II and III

Under the Second Lomé Convention of 1980, the EU succeeded in negotiating favorable investment regulations with all ACP countries. It extended the application of bilateral investment protection agreements concluded between an EU member state and an ACP country to all EU investments. It also secured special agreements relating to investments in mining with all ACP countries. The investment protection agreements covered the transfer of profits, the provision of prompt and adequate compensation when foreign companies were nationalized and arbitration in the event of disputes.

The only significant innovation in Lomé II was the System for Promotion of Mineral Production and Exports (SYSMIN), essentially an insurance against reductions in mineral output in ACP countries. Introduced as an alternative to the ACP proposal to extend STABEX to mineral exports, it covered copper, phosphates, manganese, aluminum and tin as well as iron ore from 1985 onwards. SYSMIN, unlike STABEX, was designed to ensure mineral supplies to EU consumers rather than to stabilize or increase export revenue for ACP countries.

The Third Lomé Convention was negotiated between September 1983 and November 1984. By the time the treaty was finally concluded and signed, EU anxiety over Southern commodity power had completely dissipated. Furthermore, the 'blame-the-victim-thesis' had been deeply internalized in EU circles. The recommendations of the famous Berg Report (World Bank, 1981) were considered sacrosanct. Africa's colossal failure to improve its exports, inefficient use of foreign aid, lack of economic diversification and inability to attract investment were all blamed on the failure of pervasive state interventionism. The 'Washington Consensus' was firmly embraced by Brussels, which argued that the removal of government-engineered distortions and increased internal economic efficiency, were requisite for long-term productivity in Africa.

Lomé III introduced strong conditionalities, cumbersome administrative procedures and allowed for EU intervention into the fine operational details of developmental programs. The tradition of low conditionality combined with the principle that Southern partners should retain their 'acquis' (that is the rights and privileges that they have attained under previous Lomé Conventions) were eroded significantly by these new and complex set of conditions. The principle of co-management became more a concept than reality. Development priorities and projects came to be largely influenced by donor objectives. The new regime created considerable administrative delays and miscommunication in program implementation and STABEX was the first major victim. It lost its traditional automatic character and gradually became so under-funded that the EU unilaterally reduced the compensation paid to ACP countries (Parfitt, 1996: 53). African governments began to experience strict EU control over the use of funds including those of STABEX. The previous practice of automatically financing economic diversification with STABEX funds now had to be justified to the Commission. Above all, Lomé III introduced the concept of 'policy dialogue'. negotiations on the use of funds between the Directorate General for Development in the Commission (DG8) and respective ACP member countries on the argument that EDF funds were being grossly misused. The policy dialogue was designed to exert pressure on African governments to focus not only on efficient economic management, but, more importantly, to address issues of democracy and good governance.

Further Changes Under Lomé IV

While the fourth Lomé Convention was being negotiated, the communist system disintegrated, marking the beginning of the end of the Cold War. This historic event undermined the ideological, military and political foundations of the post-Second World War international order (Sagasti, 1999; Rugumamu, 1997; Griffin, 1991). With the conclusion of the Cold War, the rationale for development cooperation disappeared (the record suggests that the imperatives of human solidarity, democratization and human rights do not possess the same mobilizing power, as the Cold War). For two decades preceding the 1990s, net disbursement of Official Development Assistance (ODA) consistently amounted to around 0.35% of donors' combined gross national product (GNP). Subsequently, there has been a sustained fall in aid levels. Between 1990 and 1997, for example, net ODA fell by one third in real terms and the anticipated peace dividend for development has failed to materialize. Furthermore, the share of net ODA in the GNP of the Development Assistance Committee (DAC) declined to 0.22% compared to 0.35% in the mid-1980s. Only four countries (Denmark, The Netherlands, Norway and Sweden) exceeded the UN target of 0.7% of GNP in 1997 (OECD, 1998: 55).

The composition and direction of the flow of aid resources has been changing in line with other global changes. The immediate post-Cold War period has witnessed extraordinary civil conflicts, new challenges to development and new demands on dwindling aid budgets. Following the collapse of the Soviet bloc, it became increasingly apparent that the former communist countries would need substantial assistance to help manage their transition to market economies. These new demands on the EU have reduced drastically the funds available for Africa.

Additionally, donors have shifted their focus from aid to domestic issues like cutting national deficits, stimulating trade and improving social welfare. New conditionalities, especially those pertaining to democracy have also been used against ACP countries. In 1991, the EU adopted a resolution, which stated unequivocally that in the future, democracy and respect for human rights would be conditions for receiving aid from Western Europe (Resolution, 10107, 1991). Again, in Council Resolutions in 1992 and 1993, the European Commission confirmed its commitment to the promotion of human rights and the rule of law in developing countries. These arguments were later included in the Maastricht Treaty of 1992 (Article 130U section 2) and in the Lomé IV (1995–2000) Article 5 of Revised Lomé IV Convention:

> ... Respect for human rights, democratic principles and the rule of law, which underpin relations between the ACP states and the Community and all the provisions and governs the domestic and international policies of contracting parties, shall constitute an essential element of this Convention.

Undemocratic and dictatorial regimes, which were prominent in Africa during the Cold War era, have either collapsed or are under increasing pressure from the North to democratize. With the East-West ideological conflict no longer a motivating factor, the EU has no reason to tolerate authoritarian regimes in the South (Kirkpatrick, 1982). As a consequence, fifteen of fifty-four African countries (roughly 28%) are now described as either maintaining or having ensured a successful transition to democratic governance, as compared to only 5 (9%) democracies in 1990. Regimes that fail to abide by the new political conditionalities are threatened with potential diplomatic isolation and economic sanctions (Lancaster, 1993; Olsen, 1998).

Unfortunately, the EU has not developed a set of objective criteria against which to measure performance in this sensitive and contentious area and it has failed to consult with relevant ACP bodies on how best to operationalize the new policy. The Article on democracy and human rights, therefore, has been subject to different interpretations. During the 1990s, development cooperation was fully suspended in eight cases: Burundi, Liberia, Nigeria, Rwanda, Somalia, Sudan, Haiti and Turkey. In other cases, aid for new projects was suspended, while current projects remained unaffected. Such partial measures were taken in the Gambia, Mali, Niger, Togo and Zaire (Crawford, 1998).

Central to emerging Euro-Africa relations in the post-Cold War era, is the issue of economic performance as one of the conditionalities for accessing EU resources. Traditionally, aid allocations were based on objective criteria related to the needs of a country, such as size, population growth, GNP per capita and poverty levels. After the 1995 mid-term review of Lomé IV, the system of aid entitlement was partially abandoned, with the introduction of a phased programming system. The European Commission's Green Paper (EU, 1996) called for a more selective and incentive-based approach for future aid allocations, based on both quantitative needs criteria and qualitative merits, or performance and good management criteria. The NIP was now to be paid in two tranches: the first 55% automatically and the second 45% conditional on the country's performance as well as the 'political situation in each ACP state'. These open-ended performance criteria have raised many concerns with African partners (Bossuyt, 1994: 3).

Summarizing Globalization and Post-Cold War Euro-Africa Relations

Since the end of the Cold War, Europe has downgraded its interest in Africa and the region has become unattractive to foreign investors. Unable to improve its participation in international trade, the region (except for a few countries) has become a non-player in international decision-making and increasingly unable to elicit the interest of other regions. Ake (1996) and Chole (1997) have concluded that whatever aspect of global economy one considers – security, aid, investment, trade and the information revolution – Africa's prospects give no cause for jubilation.

As the world strives to organize itself into major economic and security blocs, Africa appears to become increasingly isolated. Indeed, the prospects of Fortress Europe created shock waves through the rest of the world. Despite the protestations of the EU that it would meet the requirements of the General Agreement on Tariffs and Trade (GATT), the United States reacted by forming the North American Free Trade Area (NAFTA). Japan also reacted by forming the Association of South-East Asian Nations (ASEAN), which in 1992, was transformed into the Asian Free Trade Area (AFTA). No pragmatic steps of this nature have been adopted in Africa.

At the same time, Africa is becoming increasingly marginalized in foreign direct investment (FDI). Widely considered to be the engine of growth in the globalization process, FDI is shying away from Africa at the same time that it is growing substantially in other world regions. Global flows of FDI in 1995 reached $315 billion, a nearly six-fold increase over the level of 1981–85 period. This growth reflects the development of new technologies, falling transport costs and the emergence of global production systems under the auspices of transnational corporations. As Gunder Frank (1991) points out, the real struggle is between the

United States, the EU and Japan. These three power blocs are not only the major global investors, but are also major recipients of investment. By contrast, FDI flows to Africa increased only by 5% between 1995–1996 to $5 billion, the smallest amount for any developing region (south east Asia received $81 billion in 1996, China, $16 billion and Singapore $9 billion) (UN, 1997: 21–23). Paradoxically, this low rate of foreign investment flows has coincided with various aggressive African attempts to liberalize investment policies and sign bilateral investment promotion and protection treaties.

It has been suggested that African governments must bear responsibility for the exclusion of their economies from the main dynamics of globalization. Collier and Pattillo (2000) argue in their study of the investment climate in Africa that, until recently, most governments were unambiguously capital-hostile, altering public policy at will and threatening the security of property rights. A 1994 World Bank survey of 150 foreign executives in East Africa concluded earlier that investing in Africa was a highly risky venture even for the most daring capitalist. Some of the major factors cited in the survey include an unreliable investment environment, lack of production and commercial infrastructure, economic policies that penalize exports and investment for the sake of local business interest and lack of human capital (World Bank, 1994).

Africa is also becoming increasingly marginalized in international diplomacy. The current international political arena is marked by a visible inattention to issues of particular concern to Africans (UN action in the Baltics versus Liberia, Sierra Leone or the DRC is instructive of this tendency) (Hutchful, 1991). Fantu Cheru (1996: 150) notes that Africa's marginalization at these important meetings was further compounded by the inability of its delegates to organize themselves effectively at a caucus level in order to articulate their demands.

Relatedly, the post-Cold War era has seriously undermined Africa's importance and relevance in global strategic issues. As Barry Buzan (1991: 435) argues, Africa's geo-strategic significance has become marginal to the vital interests of the West in general and to those of Europe in particular. Europe seems to be gradually diverting its attention away from Africa in favor of those regions of the world to which it bears closer cultural, economic and strategic connections. The Soviet threat, no longer a calculus in EU foreign policy, several foreign military bases on the African continent are being closed down and Africans are constantly counseled to fend for themselves.

Following the end of the Cold War, it was widely hoped that the UN would be able to adopt a more balanced and enhanced role as the world peacekeeper and peacemaker. This optimism seems to have been vindicated by the successful US-led UN operations in Kuwait. Since then, the West has been clearly reluctant to become directly involved in African conflicts. For example, instead of the familiar blue UN helmets, peacekeepers in Sierra Leone fought under the banner of the Economic Community of West African States (ECOWAS). By the same token, when the warring parties in the Democratic Republic of Congo gathered in Lusaka, Zambia, in 1999, they endorsed a cease-fire agreement initiated and mediated by the Southern African Development Community (SADC), with the UN playing a secondary role. In fact, Africa is the only continent being called upon by its former Cold War allies to set up its own international force for peace keeping and humanitarian assistance (Clever and May, 1995).

In a similar pattern, France is slowly but inexorably disengaging herself from Africa. Historically, one of the strategic roles of Paris in Africa was the provision of military support to the French-speaking African countries. In fulfilling her 'gendarme role' on the continent, France maintained security and defense agreements and stationed troops in several African countries. This elaborate network of agreements and logistical support structures enabled the French army to intervene at least thirty times in Africa in the last four decades. However, as the Cold War has thawed, France is slowly withdrawing her forces from the region and from the use of her soldiers in Africa's domestic problems (Olsen, 1998; Guy, 1995). In some ways, this may be a welcome development, as African countries may be forced to muster the courage to terminate the paralytic weaknesses of individual national security systems and embrace the Abuja Treaty on African Economic Cooperation and Integration.

Perhaps, above all else, existing Euro-Africa relations has been marked by the EU's casual attention to Africa's debt crisis. Africa's total external debt rose from US$111 billion in 1980 to US$310 billion in 1997; and debt service payments, from US$12 billion in 1980 to US$23 billion in 1997. Africa's low capacity to service its debts is vividly reflected not only in the massive build-up of arrears and high service ratios, but most importantly, by the number and frequency of rescheduling. Unsustainable debt has created serious foreign exchange constraints in most African countries and the accumulation of arrears has contributed to an unsustainable debt stock, which deters investment and undermines economic stability. Apart from diverting domestic financial resources, debt servicing has resulted in the diversion of development assistance, with bilateral aid from the EU being used to finance the debt owed to the IMF and the World Bank. It has been estimated that around one-quarter of bilateral aid – some $9 billion annually – is currently being used directly to finance debt repayments (Oxfam, 1998; World Bank, 1999; ECA, 1989; UNDP, 1996).

Africa's position in science and technology paints an equally gloomy picture. Over the past two decades, the world has witnessed radical innovations in micro-electronics, biotechnology and new materials. Production has become more and more knowledge-intensive, as investment in intangibles such as research and development, software, design, engineering and management have come to play a greater role in the production of goods and services. Not only has the nature of production changed, competition has also become more innovation-based. As knowledge has become more important in the modern economy, the knowledge gap between Africa and the EU has widened. WTO agreements on intellectual property rights have been used to legitimize the further marginalization of Africa in this important area. Under the recently concluded Uruguay Round, the protocols relating to the so-called trade related investment measures (TRIMS) and trade related intellectual property rights (TRIPS) have severely circumscribed the sovereign rights of states, making it impossible for poor countries to regulate the activities of multinational corporations (see, WTO, 1996).

Besides unfavorable terms of trade, technology and finance, Euro-Africa relations are characterized by unfavorable terms in the flow of people. EU countries have all recently introduced very strict immigration policies that affect Africans disproportionately. Most Africans can now enter the EU only if they possess special skills. This accelerates the brain drain from the region, further contributing to its development woes. Unfortunately, unlike other regions, which suffer from the brain drain, sub-Saharan Africa has not been able to marshal economic remittances purposefully. The UNDP report (1999: 89) notes that Egypt obtained US$4.7 billion in remittances in 1995, close to the US$6 billion earned from the Suez Canal receipts, oil exports and tourism combined. Similarly, the Philippines received US$7 billion in remittances in 1996 (see also Dearden, 1999) The negative impacts of African migration to the EU is further compounded by the fact that the financial requirements for obtaining a legal 'stay' in many EU can be met primarily by those Africans who have been engaged in looting their countries' treasuries

Conclusion

Africa is currently being portrayed as a lost continent of civil conflicts and wars, AIDS, famines, natural disasters and unwanted immigrants. One of the extreme variants of Afro-pessimism has even pleaded for a benign colonization of some parts of the continent (Pfaff, 1995). In the immediate future, grand development expectations seem to be out of the question. What is required are assessments of the continent's capabilities and vulnerabilities in confronting the new global order; the identification of various factors that will be decisive in shaping its future; and a sober analysis of their likely impact. Instead of unproductive rants about economic and social marginalization, African policy makers need to combine their energies to evolve an indigenous development agenda that expresses the aspirations of its people and can, therefore, elicit their support. Ake (1996) proposes that the best strategy for Africa's development in the present epoch is not to seek rapid close integration in the globalizing world economy, but rather to renegotiate with the major global actors selective modalities of integration, or what is commonly called 'strategic integration'. In other words, nations and regional groupings should be actively integrated in the global economy only to the extent and in the direction in which it is beneficial for them to do so. In several respects, this is the vision of the Pan-Africanists who fought for the creation of the Organization of African Unity (OAU).

African political economies need more than the consolidation of democratic practices, preferential market access and foreign investment from Europe. They must also undertake comprehensive national and regional economic reforms as well as negotiate a fairer international environment in order to arrest and reverse the processes of marginalization. To accomplish these goals, it will be imperative to transform Africa's political mind-set to articulate, prioritize and defend the objectives and priorities of sustainable development nationally and regionally. Above all, Africa will need to engage Europe proactively. Africa must not only seek to maintain a strong physical presence of capable and committed missions in Brussels and Geneva but should also quickly learn how to negotiate and lobby actively, in order to make visible actual and future interdependencies that will work to its best advantage.

Note

1. Although within the previous four Conventions the objectives of enhancing processing, marketing, distribution and transport were considered fundamental goals of cooperation,

very little progress was made in this area. Only 7% of ACP commodities were processed before export and less than 5% were ready for marketing and distribution. For details on the subject see Wolf (1999).

References

African, Caribbean and Pacific General Secretariat (ACP). Technical Notes on Economic and Trade Cooperation. ACP/00/001/98 Rev.2, Brussels, 1998.

Ake, C. (1996) *Democracy and Development in Africa.* Washington, D.C: Brookings Institution.

Amin, S. (1974) *Accumulation on a World Scale.* NY: Monthly Review Press.

Amin, S. (1989) 'Europe and North-South Relations'. *Contemporary European Affairs* 2 (3), 120–135.

Arrighi, G. (1994) *The Long Twentieth Century: Money, Power and the Origins of Our Time.* London: Verso.

Arrighi, G. (1999) 'Globalization, State Sovereignty and the Endless Accumulation of Capital'. In D. Smith *et al.* (eds) *States and Sovereignty in the Global Economy.* London: Routledge, 53–74.

Asante, S. (1981) 'Lomé II: Another Machinery for Updating Dependency'. *Development and Cooperation* 3, 15–28.

Barnet, R. and J. Cavanaugh (1994) *Global Dreams: Imperial Corporation and the New World Order.* NY: Simon and Schuster.

Bossuyt, J. (1994) 'Phased Programming of Lomé Funds: Lessons from Current EU and ACP Experiences'. *ECDPM Policy Management Brief* No. 2 July.

Buzan, B. (1991) 'New Patterns of Global Security in the Twenty-first Century'. *International Affairs* 67 (3), 431–452.

Cheru, F. (1996) 'New Social Movements: Democratic Struggles and Human Rights in Africa'. In J. Mittelman (ed.) *Globalization: Critical Reflections.* Boulder, CO: Lynne Rienner, 145–164.

Chole, E. (1997) 'Prospects for Economic Recovery in Africa'. *Eastern Africa Social Science Research Review* 13 (1),1–16.

Clark, N. and C. Juma (1991) *Biotechnology for Sustainable Development.* Nairobi: ACTS Press.

Clever, G. and R. May (1995) 'Peacekeeping: The African Dimension'. *Review of African Political Economy* 22 (66), 485–495.

Collier, P. and C. Pattillo (2000) 'Investment and Risk in Africa'. In P. Collier and C. Pattillo (eds) *Investment and Risk in Africa.* London: Macmillan Press, 3–30.

Crawford, G. (1998) 'Human Rights and Democracy in EU Development Cooperation: Towards Fair and Equal Treatment'. In M. Lister (ed.) *European Union Development Policy.* New York: St. Martin's Press, 131–178.

Dearden, S. (1999) 'Immigration Policy in the European Union'. In M. Lister (ed.) *New Perspectives on European Union Development Cooperation.* Boulder, CO: Westview Press, 59–83.

Economic Commission for Africa (ECA) (1989) *Africa Alternative Framework to Structural Adjustment Program for Socio-Economic Recovery and Transformation.* UNECA: Addis Ababa.

Emmanuel, A. (1972) *Unequal Exchange: A Study of Imperialism of Trade.* NY: Monthly Review Press.

European Commission (1996) *Green Paper on Relations between the European Union and ACP countries on the Eve of the 21st Century.* EC: Brussels.

European Commission (1998) *Project de Communication de la Commission au Conseil, Recommendations de decision du Conseil Autorisant la Commission a negotier un Accord partenariat pour le development avec les ACP.* EC: Brussels, 28 January.

Falk, R. (1980) 'Introduction'. In Frey-Wouters. *The European Community and the Third World*. NY: Praeger Publishers.

Frank, A. (1978) *Dependent Accumulation and Underdevelopment*. London: Macmillan.

Frank, A. (1991) 'No Escape for the Laws of World Economics'. *Review of African Political Economy* 50, 20–31.

Fukuyama, F. (1992) *The End of History and the Last Man*. NY: Free Press.

Galtung, J. (1976) 'The Lomé Convention and Neo-Colonialism'. *African Review* 6 (1), 33–42.

George, S. (1993) 'Uses and Abuses of Africa's Debt'. In A. Adedeji (ed.) *Africa Within the World*. London: Zed Press, 59–72.

Griffin, K. (1991) 'Foreign Aid After the Cold War'. *Development and Change* 22 (4), 645–685.

Grilli, E. (1993) *The European Community and Developing Countries*. Cambridge: Cambridge University Press.

Guy, M. (1995) 'Continuity and Change in Franco-Africa Relations'. *Journal of Modern African Studies* 33 (1), 1–20.

Harrison, G. *et al.* (1995) 'Quantifying the Outcome of the Uruguay Round'. *Finance and Development* 32 (4), 38–41.

Harsh, E. (1992) 'More African States as Least Developed'. *Africa Recovery* 6, 11.

Held, D. (1999) 'Democracy and Globalization'. *Governance* 3 (3), 251–265.

Hirst, P. and G. Thompson (1999) 'The Problem of "Globalization": International Economic Management and the Formation of Trading Blocs'. *Economy and Society* 21 (4), 357–396.

Hoogvelt, A.(1997) *Globalization and Post-Colonial World: The New Political Economy of Development*. Baltimore: Johns Hopkins University Press.

Hook, S. (1996) 'Introduction: Foreign Aid in a Transformed World'. In S. Hook (ed.) *Foreign Aid Toward a New Millennium*. Boulder, CO: Lynne Rienner, 1–18.

Hutchful, E. (1991) 'Eastern Europe: Consequences for Africa'. *Review of African Political Economy* 50, 51–59.

Kirkpatrick, J. (1982) *Dictatorships and Double Standards*. New York: Simon and Schuster.

Klark, T.A. (1998) '13 Theses on Globalization and Neo-Liberalism'. In T. Klark (ed.) *Globalization and Neo-Liberalism: The Caribbean Context*. Lanham, MD: Rowman and Littlefield, 1–28.

Kwarteng, C. 1997) *Africa and the European Challenge: Survival in a Changing World*. Avebury: Ashgate Publishing.

Lancaster, C. (1993) 'Governance and Democracy: The View from Washington'. *IDS Bulletin* 24 (1).

McQueen, M. (1998) 'ACP-EU Trade Cooperation After 2000: An Assessment of Reciprocal Trade Preferences'. *Journal of Modern African Studies* 38, 669–692.

Mytelka, L. and S. Langdon (1979) 'Africa in the Changing World Economy'. In C. Legum (ed.) *Africa in the 1980s: A Continent in Crisis*. NY: McGraw-Hill, 123–213.

Ohmae, K. (1990) *The Borderless World*. London: Collins Press.

Olsen, G. (1997) 'Europe and the Promotion of Democracy in Post Cold War Africa: How Serious is Europe and What Reason?'. *African Affairs* 388, 343–367.

Organization of Economic Cooperation and Development (OECD) (1998). *Development Cooperation Report*. Paris: OECD.

Oxfam (1998) *International. Making Debt Relief Work: A Test for Political Will*. Oxfam: London.

Parfitt, T. (1996) 'The Decline of Eurafrica? Lomé's mid-term Review'. *Review of African Political Economy* 67, 53–66.

Pfaff, W. (1995) 'A New Colonialism: Europe Must Go Back into Africa'. *Foreign Affairs* 74 (1), 2–6.

Raffer, K. (1999) 'Lomé or Not Lomé: The Future of European-ACP Cooperation'. In M. Lister (ed.) *New Perspectives on the European Union Development Cooperation*. Boulder, CO: West view Press, 125–142.

Ravenhill, J. (1985) *Collective Clientelism: The Lomé Conventions and North-South Relations*. NY: Columbia University Press, 1985.

Rodney, W. (1972) *How Europe Underdeveloped Africa*. London: Bogle.

Rugumamu, S. (1997) *Lethal Aid: The Illusion of Socialism and Self-Reliance in Tanzania*. Trenton, N.J: Africa World Press.

Rugumamu, S. (1999a) 'Globalization, Liberalization and Africa's Marginalization'. *AAPS Occasional Paper* 4 (1) .

Rugumamu, S. (1999b) 'EU-ACP Partnership: An Appraisal'. *Cooperation South* 2, December: 45–56.

Sagasti, F. (1999) *Development Cooperation in a Fractured Global Order*. Ottawa: IDRC.

Sandstrom, S. (1993) 'The Learning Curve'. In J. Bannatyne *et al.* (eds.) *The World Bank and Poverty Reduction*. The Hague: Ministry of Foreign Affairs, 5–14.

Sassen, S. (1996) *Losing Control? Sovereignty in an Age of Globalization*. NY: Columbia University Press .

Soros, G. (1997) 'The Capitalist Threat'. *The Atlantic Monthly* 279 (2), 45–58.

United Nations Conference on Trade and Development (UNCTAD). *World Investment Reports* 1995, 1996, 1997. UNCTAD: Geneva.

United Nations Development Program (UNDP). *Human Development Reports*. NY: Oxford University Press, 1996, 1997 and 1999.

UNRISD (1995) *States of Disarray: The Social Effects of Globalization*. UNRISD: Geneva.

Wallerstein, I. (1974) *The Modern World System*, Vol. 1. NY: Academic Press.

Wolf, S. (1999) 'The Future of EU-ACP Relations'. In M. Heidheus and J. Braun (eds) *Development Economics and Policy*. Frankfurt: Peter Lang, 23–41.

World Bank (1981) *An Accelerated Development in sub-Saharan Africa: Agenda for Action*. Washington, D.C: The World Bank.

World Bank (1994) *Adjusting Africa: Reforms, Results and Road Ahead*. NY: Cambridge University Press.

World Bank (1999) *Africa Development Indicators 2000*. Washington, D.C: The World Bank.

Zartman, I .W. (1993) 'Introduction'. In I.W. Zartman. *Europe and Africa*. Boulder, CO: Lynne Rienner Publishers, 1–6.

Chapter 4

The Liberalization of Underdevelopment or the Criminalization of the State? Contrasting Explanations of Africa's Politico-Economic Crisis under Globalization

Padriig Carmody[1]

There are today South of the Sahara virtually no examples of social or political relations devoid of clientelistic calculations or considerations of identity (Chabal and Daloz, 1999, p. 30).

Neopatrimonialism and rent seeking are among the most abused and ultimately limiting concepts in the study of contemporary Africa. Surely a concept that is capable of explaining everything ultimately explains nothing (Olokushi, 1999, p. 465).

Introduction

There is widespread agreement that the state is heavily implicated in Africa's current development impasse. For neoliberals it has been an over-bearing state, supported by an urban coalition of rent-seekers, which has stiffled entreprenuerialism and distorted the effective operation of markets (e.g. Bates, 1981).[2] On the other hand, for structuralists it is colonial legacy of state authoritarianism, the creation of dependent economies and the subsequent internationalization of the state, which have prevented more autocentric development (e.g. Mamdani, 1991; 1996).

The structural adjustment programs (SAPs) under which most African countries have labored for the past twenty years were meant to redefine, fundamentally, the role of the state in Africa. Initially the international financial institutions (IFIs – World Bank and International Monetary Fund) sought not merely the retraction of the state from economic affairs, but also its weakening, through cut-backs in central government administration and the devolution of power to local government. However, with the failure of SAPs in the 1980s to arrest Africa's economic decline, the World Bank redefined its position on the role of the state in economic development. In its 1989 report, the Bank argued not just for trimming back the state, but also for its selective reconstruction so that it could serve those functions necessary to market development. During the 1990s, particular attention was paid to what were seen as the nerve centers of government through the implementation of training programs for bureaucrats in Ministries of Finance and Central Banks in particular (Grindle, 1996).[3] The aim was to establish a slim but strong state, which was insulated from popular pressure and devoid of clientelistic ties and to construct a new hegemony in rural areas (Mengisteab and Daddieh, 1999; Reno, 1998).

In its 1997 World Development Report, the World Bank further revised its conception of the state. According to Moore (1999, p. 65):

> Its prime conceptual innovation is its recognition that yes, states should do things the market cannot, but only if they have the capability to perform these roles. Thus states must match capability and role.[4]

While there is debate about the extent to which the World Bank is committed to state reconstruction in Africa, state crisis continues unabated in much of the continent. States continue to collapse and the era of military coups is not yet over, as demonstrated in Côte d'Ivoire.[5] For many neoliberals, further state decline in Africa is evidence of the inability of SAPs to destroy the clientelistic networks, which impede market development and destroy economies. Rather, they argue that economic liberalization has led to the reconfiguration, rather than the destruction, of clientelism and corruption (Boone, 1994a).[6] The World Bank (1997 cited in Moore, 1999) continues to blame traditional forms of governance for state failure, ignoring the ways in which its own policies are heavily implicated in state decay.

This chapter argues that state decay in Africa, rather than being primarily an outgrowth of traditional or clientelistic relations, must be situated in the context of structural adjustment and the current round of global economic restructuring. State decay is primarily a symptom and only secondarily a reinforcing cause, of Africa's economic crisis (Riddell, 1999). However, it is in part through contests over the terrain of the state that solutions to Africa's socio-economic crisis are likely to emerge.

State Crisis in Africa

Africa's current development impasse is multidimensional, but is primarily a crisis of institutions. It is a crisis of both the state and the market, which are mutually reinforcing (Mengisteab and Logan, 1995). Weak markets (or underdeveloped capital and labor) mean insufficient resources are generated to support strongly bureaucratized and meritocratic states. The underdevelopment of domestic capital is largely a result of Africa's colonial legacy and the fact that at independence the post-colonial state assumed the previous role of merchant capital, appropriating surpluses for both investment and distribution (Kitching, 1981).

While both state and market crises in Africa are, to some degree, mutually constitutive, the question is which is prior? Is it the structure of the state itself, which is hostile to the global economy, or are state decay and collapse symptoms of wider processes of economic restructuring and marginalization under globalization?

State and economic crises in Africa take place at different spatial scales. Economic crisis may generate what Callaghy (1990) calls the trough factor, which may foster movements for state renewal. After coming to power the National Resistance Movement government in Uganda managed to increase revenue collection by 800% (Reno, 1998). International donors may support such efforts, but to date the economic policies they promote have militated against sustainable state renewal, with external debt burdens increasing dramatically in successful adjusters (see Bello, 1994). Recent debt relief initiatives do not appear to be sufficient to prevent this from remaining a major problem for almost all African states.

Criminalizing the State

Some authors, example Chabal and Daloz (1999) believe that Africa's current development impasse has its roots in the lack of structural differentiation between the state and society. They argue (p. 12–13) that this in turn is related to the fact that colonial bureaucratic institutionalization never managed to overcome the strongly instrumental and personalized characteristics of traditional African administration. In common with modernization theorists, they see traditional institutions as inappropriate to the tasks of development. However statements about traditional African administration cannot be generalized. For example, pre-colonial Africa ranged from highly developed state-societies, such as Ashanti, to acephalous societies (Herbst, 2000). Amongst the Oromo in Ethiopia power was vested in leaders for only eight years (Alemaheyu, 2000). However, the phenomenon of indirect rule under colonialism did introduce similar institutions throughout much of rural Africa, generating important similarities and continuities (Boone, 1994b; Mamdani, 1996).

For Berman (cited in Bonne, 1994b: 131) both colonial and post-colonial states were caught between the contradictory demands of accumulation and political control and consequently resisted the transition to fully marketized social relations of production. It is not that African states were insufficiently structurally differentiated from their societies, but that given the unchanged material conditions, which they faced at independence, they had to embed themselves to retain social control (Boone, 1994b). However, the nature of this embedding was different in that the state could no longer rely as heavily on repression and had to engage in substantial legitimation expenditures in a way that the colonial state did not. Thus post-colonial social control retained elements of clientelism, combined with a new social contract (Laasko and Olokushi, 1996).

Chabal and Daloz's (1999) recent book is one of a number that see the African state as the continent's principal problem. They argue (p. 158) that it is clear in many African countries (like Côte d'Ivoire, Mozambique, Senegal or Guinea Bissau) that ruling parties were returned to power in part simply because they were perceived to be more able to deliver on expected patrimonial promises than their competitors. However, the majority of the population cannot be co-opted into clientelistic networks. If that were the case the state would be hegemonic, rather than clientelistic. The point of clientelism or patrimonialism is its particularism. Given limited resources, clientelism has to be selectively deployed to co-opt local notables and opposition is then repressed or disrupted. Thus Chabal and Daloz conflate patrimonialism with legitimation expenditures on social services and electoral democracy.

Another argument that Chabal and Daloz make is that in the face of declining resources for patrimonialism, in order to try to maintain control of their societies,

African states have instrumentalized disorder. However, they do not explore the reasons for these declining resources, such as deteriorating terms of trade and reduced aid flows. While acknowledging that structural adjustment is flawed, they suggest that Africa's problems are fundamentally rooted in African culture.[7] They raise the possibility that what Africa really requires is a cultural adjustment program. While this exonerates outside actors of responsibility, it ignores the extent to which Africa's current economic crisis is a consequence of globalization. Many economic and social indicators showed substantial improvement through the late-1970s (Barratt Brown and Tiffen, 1992) and African culture was hardly responsible for the debt crisis.

In another recent book, Bayart *et al.* (1999) discuss the criminalization of the state and of the sub-continent.[8] However, in contrast to Chabal and Daloz, Bayart (1999: 47) argues that the criminalization of the African state largely stems from Africa's colonial legacy:

> The colonial legacy of indirect rule, perpetuated in the way in which the bureaucracy acquires habits of command in a specified territory and the networks of influence and clientelism which constitute the post-colonial state like a rhizome in its tangled complexity, in all probability makes African political societies predisposed to criminal activity.

This argument appears overly deterministic. As Olokushi (1998) notes, networks of mutual obligation and trust are celebrated as social capital in Western contexts, but are criticized as neopatrimonial, or in Bayart's formulation – criminal – in Africa. It is important to note that how social capital gets deployed depends on incentives created by both the state and embedded market conditions.[9] In this sense, Bayart may be correct that criminal activities are one of the few areas of comparative advantage left for Africa in the global economy. Africa's position in the international political economy mirrors that of the informal sector internally. Both are defined by a lack of regulation, as a result of the general weakness of bureaucratic institutionalization. Although this s not acknowledged in the international political system given the imperatives of maintaining juridical statehood (Jackson and Rosberg, 1982).

Elsewhere in the same book, Bayart argues that the social capital he identifies as forming the basis of criminal networks is an epiphenomenon of the historical trajectory of the sub-continent, which has resulted in deepening dependence (p. 42). This argument is not fully developed. In some places Bayart argues that the state has literally imploded under the combined effects of economic crisis, neo-liberal programmes of structural adjustment and the loss of legitimacy of political institutions (p. 19). Later though, it is argued that distinctions between military dictatorships, multi-party activity, or periods of economic nationalism or liberalization are relatively insignificant, in that all systems in Africa are dependent on the trade of influence (p. 47). Thus, whilst acknowledging the maelstrom of globalization (p. 116), one of the main arguments is for the primacy of patrimonialism and the exceptionalism of the African state.

For Bayart, as for Chabal and Daloz, one of the principal problems is the way in which the African state is connected to society. Again, this is again open to question on the basis of comparative evidence. For example, there has also been a spectacular growth of organized crime in Eastern Europe (Reno, 1999), another region of the world experiencing dependent reintegration into the global economy as its manufacturing industry is displaced by overseas competition (see Castells, 1996).[10]

Bayart also argues (p. 44) that war has become the main mode of state formation in Africa. However, as Martin (2000: 3) notes this does not resist closer scrutiny particularly if one takes into account the (relatively peaceful) progress of democratization in such countries as Benin, Botswana, Ghana, Libya, Mali, Mauritius and Niger. Primitive accumulation generates attempts to assert social control over capital (Olokushi, 1998) and this explains the contradictory movements in Africa towards anarchy/order. In any event, it is inter-state, rather than intra-state, wars, which are more likely to contribute to the identity formation, associated with nation building.

In neither Bayart *et al.* or Chabal and Daloz's accounts is there a substantial discussion of the impacts of poverty and stark inequality on the incidence of crime or corruption. While Hibou (1999 in Bayart *et al.*) does explain how SAPs have undermined state capacity and legitimacy, echoing Boone (1994a), she argues that the reforms have failed in large part because of the nature of the rhizome state, which has implemented them. This largely ignores the economic illogicality of the reforms themselves (see Carmody, 2001).

Reno (1998) argues that the rise of warlordism in many parts of Africa has been an outcome of and rational response to, the economic crisis generated by globalization. For example, he notes in relation to Sierra Leone, that conflict was related to cut-backs in patronage opportunities for local strongmen under SAP and that it represents an attempt by them to strike out on their own (1995 cited in Hoogvelt, 1997). Thus, for Reno, cutbacks in resources for distribution under SAP resulted in the dissolution of the patrimonial glue, which had previously prevented civil war.

According to Reno states have adopted new survival strategies, using mercenaries to suppress internal disorder in exchange for mining rights, for example. Thus state officials and nominally private networks have manipulated state prerogatives in global society to combine the alliance's capacity to create disorder for rivals with its private business acumen to expand its commercial reach (Reno, 1998, p. 22).

Contested Terrain: the African State

The problems of African states are real. Corruption undoubtedly is a major problem in many countries. For example, in Congo-Brazzaville some estimates suggest that as much as 30% of the government budget has been stolen in recent years (Blancq 1994 cited in Van de Walle, 1999). However, that means that 70% was still used legitimately on public services, administration, or on other government expenditures, such as the military and debt repayment. To talk of the criminalization of the state and warlord politics tends to ignore or downplay the fact that many African states continue to supply public services and to fulfill many of their legitimate functions, despite the threat of virtuality. It also serves to essentialize the state and contributes to an anti-statist agenda, rather than seeing the state as both a problem and part of a potential solution (Evans, 1995). It may also further contribute to an image of the coming anarchy in Africa and may thereby serve, unintentionally, to justify policies of policing exclusion on a global scale.

In a recent book on Botswana, Abdi Samatar (1999) argues that some African states are effectively institutionalized. He argues that the key to Botswana's success has been the development of awareness amongst traditional leaders that the collective gains from institutionalization out-weighed the individual gains from patrimonialism and corruption. In this way these leaders became a class for themselves rather than simply a class in themselves. Thus, in Botswana, the fact that political leaders straddled both economic and political roles did not militate against effective institutionalization. With globalization, the challenge of developing that type of class-consciousness is made more difficult as proto-capitalists may easily expatriate the proceeds of primitive accumulation, rather than investing them locally. Also, Botswana's broadly neoliberal development strategy may not be replicable given the importance of receipts from diamond exports its Exchequer.

Structural Adjustment Programs (SAPs) and the African State

In order to understand the current (under)development of African states it is necessary to contextualize properly their situation within the international political economy. SAPs have direct and indirect impacts on African states. Expenditure reduction in terms of reduced civil service employment and cutbacks in public services, for example, have direct impacts on the legitimacy of the state. On the other hand, expenditure switching through trade liberalization and currency devaluation exposes African economies more completely to the forces of globalization.

Some scholars have noted the paradox that the implementation of SAP requires a strong state, but that cutbacks undermine these capacities (Hoogvelt, 1997). Cutbacks in civil service pay under SAPs, with two-thirds of Mozambique's civil servants now below the poverty line, for example, serve as an invitation to corruption and reduced work effort (Hanlon, 1996). Many civil servants are forced to spend much of their productive energy in the informal sector to reproduce their livelihoods. The huge gap between the wages paid to expatriate development officials and those of the local state further incite corruption (de Sardan, 1999). Given that SAPs are also highly demanding of administrative capacity, they absorb attention which needs to be devoted to long-term development planning (Green and Khadani, 1986).

As state resources have been retrenched under SAPs, stateness is further weakened, generating increased incentives for corruption and undermining of the state's legitimacy. State weakness also deter development by making it impossible for policy makers to recapture the policy initiative away from international donors with their own economic and geo-strategic goals.

As SAPs erode the post-colonial social contract which had previously formed the basis for social order, people of different social backgrounds search for a set of anchoring values through which they might cope with change (Laasko and Olukoshi, 1996: 8).[11] These include ethnicity and religiosity, which may challenge the basis of the nation state. The expression of these identities in the formal political realm is facilitated by political liberalization.

It is often the combination of economic and political liberalization, which results in disorder in Africa (Nyangoro and Shaw, 1998). For example, increased poverty and inequality in Rwanda resulting from SAPs, inflamed ethnic tensions (Chossudovsky,

1997), while the Habaryimana regime promoted ethnic mobilization to deflect the threat of competitive elections (Longman, 1999).[12]

Shaw (1997) notes a global dialectic between economic integration and political fragmentation. It is the disaffection with the majority of the population as state expenditures are cut back, unemployment and poverty increase and reduced patrimonial expenditures, which create the conditions for ethnicized elite/popular coalitions against the state. Economically, the state is further challenged by reductions in import and export taxes under SAP and the informalization of the economy, which erode its revenue base.

SAPs are meant to facilitate rapid capital accumulation. Neoclassical economics assumes that the market will mobilize resources for investment. However, the market cannot mobilize resources for investment. Only concrete actors, such as the state or social classes can do that. Underdeveloped capital and labor mean the market is weak and simply freeing it will not generate investment (Mamdani, 1991). In a context of weak markets and a liberal capital regime, profits derived in the market are not locally reinvested.

Capital accumulation is an inherently conflictual process, initially through the struggle to privatize resources and subsequently because of struggles over the relative sizes of wage versus profit share. In a capitalist institutional setting, the legitimacy of the state is dependent on negotiating a balance between accumulation and legitimation. Legitimation is tied to accumulation, as without productive accumulation, the economy will stall. The deleterious impacts of unbridled accumulation must be kept in check, however, if the social formation is to retain its cohesion. As many analyses have shown (e.g. Mkandawire and Soludo, 1999), SAPs undermine productive accumulation and hence one of the most important bases of the state's social legitimacy – job creation. Without productive accumulation, the ability of the state to legitimatize itself either indirectly, or directly through social expenditures, is undermined. In this context, given the absence of capitalist hegemony and cutbacks in state resources for distribution, the state faces tough choices over the retention of social control.

Adams *et al.* (1999) argue that most states have responded with a mix of coercion and compromise with the social forces opposed to SAP. Particularly in the case of strong adjusters coercion and political repression have been much in evidence (see Okuatey-Kodjoe, 1999). Another option is to try to build corporatist arrangements (Shaw, 1997). Given the opposition of labor to market reforms, however, these often prove unstable. Furthermore, the state is often ill-equiped to resist challenges to its authority (Gallagher, 1994 cited in Herbst, 2000).

The African state faces simultaneously subjective political and objective economic crises. Economic collapse in many African countries has resulted in an intra-elite, inter-ethnic fight over spoils, as avenues of productive capital accumulation have been closed off. In most cases, those social groups, which gained in the past from dependence, are again reaping the gains of reintegration into the global market (Laasko and Olokushi, 1996).

Globalization and the African State

Globalization, to which African economies are exposed largely through SAPs, has had a profound impact on the (under)development of African states. Susan Strange

(1986 cited in Dicken, 1998) argues that globalization has resulted in a shift in power from states to markets and from weak developing country states to strong industrial states. These power shifts are much in evidence in Africa, where the international financial institutions, controlled by the major industrial states, largely determine economic policy and the global market is the most powerful institution determining the fate of the continent.

In the past thirty years, the global economy has undergone profound changes. In particular, the gap between developed and developing countries in terms of economic development has yawned, notwithstanding the much-vaunted exceptions of the East Asian newly industrialized countries (NICs). For Reno (1998) warlord states resemble network firms such as Nike, rather than the older models of industrial organization like General Motors. Hollowed-out states are more than just analogous to hollowed-out corporations, the two are intimately connected. As global deregulation has made certain types of capital more footloose, state functions have been cut back in order pay back debt and attract international capital through low tax rates. In Africa, the cutbacks are sometimes so large as to leave the state a virtual entity.[13] For example, from 1990 and 1993, Zambia spent 35 times more on debt servicing than it did on education (Knippers Black, 1999).

Global capital is restructuring rapidly in both its liquid and embedded forms. Manuel Castells (cited in Hoogvelt, 1997) talks of Sub-Saharan Africa's structural irrelevance to the global system, as the informational economy in the core requires fewer raw materials and flows of capital implode inwards within the triad of North America, Europe and East Asia. Competition in the global economy is now so intense that many African countries are suffering the effects of competitive displacement even in their traditional primary exports (Barratt Brown *et al.*, 1992). For Castells (1996) Sub-Saharan Africa, with the exception of South Africa, is becoming one of the black holes of informational capitalism.

For some authors, the rise of deregulated finance capital associated with these developments is unproblematic. According to business guru Kenichi Ohmae (1996) we are currently witnessing the end of the nation state, as transnational capital becomes the primary actor in the international political economy. Ohmae welcomes the abolition of social restrictions on the movement of capital, while not appreciating that it may be implicated in state collapse and disorder. Ohmae argues that those regions that reject the redistributionist tyranny of modern democracy and invite in the global economy (multinational capital) prosper. Thus, he argues for the autonomy of regions in economic development. If this is correct, it is somewhat surprising, then, that African regions, many of which are virtually independent (Bayart *et al.*, 1999) are not prospering. However, as institutionalists have long recognized, in an unrestrained market economy, everything, including the rule of law, is for sale.[14] Ohmae, like the World Bank (1999), argues, for deeper integration into the global economy as the solution, despite the fact that both acknowledge the growing gulf between developed and (under)developing countries.

African economies are now amongst the most liberal in the world, but international capital has conspicuously refused the invitation to invest.[15] As capital has sought to detach itself from labor (Webber and Rigby, 1995) and accumulation increasingly takes place in the webs of the global informational economy, Africa, not the internet, is becoming the invisible continent (Wangwe and Musonda, 1998;

Ohmae, 2000). In many cases liberalization has resulted in increased capital flight, which has not been offset by new inflows. South Africa, with the biggest and most diversified economy in the sub-continent, provides an interesting case study with respect to the relationship between capital flows, economic development and state capacities.

South Africa: Corporate Delinking and Future Governance

The rhetoric coming from the South African government makes it very clear that it seeks to make the country a node in the global economic network. It is not clear, however, exactly how this is to be achieved. A press release from the South African tri-partite alliance (ANC, SACP and COSATU) argued recently that much is still needed to be done for South Africa to become part of the capital flow process, in comparison with countries such as Canada, Columbia and South Korea (ANCLIST, December 13th 1999). South Africa attracted $1.7 billion in foreign direct investment (FDI) in 1997, although much of this was the result of one privatizations and corporate unbundling.[16] However, South African firms made $2.3 billion of outward investments as they race to delink selectively from the continent and become internationalized transnationals (Adelzadeh, 1999). Thus, in South Africa, globalization has had both internal and external drivers (see Marais, 1998).

The South African government's neo-liberal economic strategy (Growth, Employment and Redistribution – GEAR), adopted in response to the rapid depreciation of the rand in 1996, was itself the outcome of a tight monetary policy, which resulted in the development of a speculative bubble (Roberts, 1997). GEAR, justifications to the contrary, is implicated in a substantial slowing of economic growth (Weeks, 1999). Despite the government's commitment to economic orthodoxy and the achievement of investment grade on South African government bonds, foreign investors remain aloof and the rand continues to depreciate (South Africa's Economic Lament, 2000). Many argue that there is no choice but to be integrated into the global economy, with the state retaining some social democratic commitments, sometimes called progressive restructuring (Koeble, 1998). Incredibly, since the end of apartheid, income inequality in South Africa has risen as hundreds of thousands of jobs have been lost (Bond, 2000; Statistics South Africa, 2000). Between 1997 and 1998, South Africa lost 4% of its formal sector jobs. Further cuts of up to 1% of the labor force were announced in July 1999 (Mnyanda, 1999).

Increased unemployment and inequality are likely to have important political implications. Already, crime has reached frightening proportions, with the country having one the highest murder rates in the world. Whether this anarchy at street level (Knippers-Black, 1999) or results in ungovernability remains to be seen. Habib and Padayachee (2000) already detect a shift towards delegative democracy in South Africa, as formal political power is increasingly centralized in order to implement neoliberal economic policies. The result of neoliberalism in South Africa is likely to be involuntary delinking and this, in turn, will likely forebode political instability, as has happened in Zimbabwe.

Global Reform or Local Control?

Given the instability and inequality unleashed by neoliberalism in the global economy some scholars have argued for a new Bretton Woods agreement, where social and political controls on the movement of capital are reasserted (e.g. Michie and Grieve Smith, 1995). If globalization is driven by capital over-accumulation (Harvey, 1982), but flows of capital are becoming more geographically concentrated within Western Europe, North America and Asia, then should not global economic crisis be imminent? If so, might that open up the possibility of African countries seizing the chance to pursue more self-directed development? The question whether or not recent crises in Asia, Russia and Latin America will be replicated in Europe and North America is currently open to speculation. Rapid productivity growth in the US as a result of new technology temporarily, buoyed stock prices, despite a massive trade deficit. Investors from other countries remain willing to finance this trade deficit because so much of the world's private savings are held in dollars (Ohmae, 2000). Whether this can be sustained remains to be seen. Recent turbulence in the US stock market may forebode worse to come.

Already the French and Canadian parliaments have supported the introduction of a Tobin tax on international currency transactions (Round, 2000). If the US stock market declines dramatically, political support for global capital controls (Michie *et al.*, 1995) may increase in the core countries. However, international capital will still attempt to engage in regulatory arbitrage by shifting economic activity to those areas with least regulation.

Given the current power of international capital, many scholars have noted the importance of pursuing more autocentric development strategies. Some, such as Cheru (1989), argue that there has been a silent revolution in Africa where much of the peasantry has delinked from the formal market and, consequently, the state. There are also many examples of popular initiatives (see Barratt Brown, 1995). However, in the absence of strong central states, or effective local control, African populations are still subject to the depredations of globalization and its inclusionary/exclusionary dialectic. The fact that the state continues to be the most important potential mediator of engagement with the global economy makes it an important actor in any structural reformulation (Leys, 1996).

If more autocentric development is a necessity, why are developing country governments so reluctant to pursue more self-directed strategies? Part of the answer may lie in the failure of earlier experiments with delinking from the global economy. Negotiated engagement, as in the Asian NICs or Cuba, has sometimes been more successful (see Amsden, 1989; Monreal, 1999).[17] The concern of governments over globalization is that any attempt to constrain transnational capital will result in involuntary delinking because international capital resists tends to use the exit option to resist restrictions on its field of valorization. Once the genie of globalization is out of the bottle, it is hard to put back in, as Zimbabwe has learnt to its cost.[18]

What then are the potential forces for progressive economic change on the continent? The newly instituted structural adjustment participatory review, whereby civil society groups pressure/cooperate with the international financial institutions to be more accountable, will perhaps have some impact (www.igc.org/dgap/saprin/). It will also be up to African governments to push the limits of the new IFI emphasis on poverty reduction and the potential space opened up by the rhetorical abandonment of SAP by the World Bank and the introduction of Comprehensive Development Frameworks (CDFs) in their stead (World Bank, 2000).

Historically, there have been three primary social forces, which have pressed for economic transformation: the state, capital and labor. In Japan, the impetus for more self-centered development came from a modernizing Èlite within the state itself (Sandbrook, 1993). In Africa, there have been examples of state renewal, as in Ghana and Uganda. Unfortunately, these have not been translated into broader development efforts because of the constraints imposed by SAPs, the dynamics of globalization and, to some degree, the politicization of ethnicity. African states are currently too internationalized and beholden to international capital and the IFIs to implement more autocentric policies (Agnew and Corrbridge, 1995).

In Africa, domestic capital is too insufficiently developed to pressure the state to promote its interests, or where it is developed, more interested in globalizing, as in the South African case. However in many industrial countries, such as Sweden, labor has played a progressive role in helping formulate economic development policy (Weiss, 1998). Given that (non-professional) labor is a much more locally embedded social force than the African state or capital, it might appear to be potentially more inclined to push forward national/regional development projects.

In Zimbabwe, the leadership of the Zimbabwe Congress of Trade Unions was instrumental in setting up the Movement for Democratic Change, although as the recent election campaign wore on its economic policy became increasingly neoliberal, in order to garner international support. In South Africa, the Congress of South African Trade Unions is increasingly disquieted over the neo-liberal course and there have been a number of recent large-scale strikes. Even when labor has been instrumental in the election of particular parties, such as the Movement for Multi-Party Democracy in Zambia, the state has subsequently been more responsive to international forces (Laasko and Olokushi, 1996). Also, organized labor is relatively weak in most African countries.

Samatar (1999) argues for a developmental project between the state, national capital and the popular classes a new triple alliance. The challenge then, is to build institutions, which force the state to be accountable to domestic constituencies, particularly those that are locally embedded. Thus, in contrast to Tendler's (1997) emphasis on the internal, in Africa, a synergy between the state and civil society must be developed so that external relationships can be renegotiated.

Africa's engagement with the global economy must become more selective. The long-term imperative of sustainability requires a reduction of scale in economic systems to reduce energy consumption and stop the core drawing unsustainably on the periphery's natural resources (Daly, 1996). The aim should not be to achieve economies of high mass consumption, but economies that sustain people (see Korten, 1995).

Selective engagement in the global economy appears to be increasingly difficult for Africa. The fact that its economies are, in general, so specialized means that the incentive is to trade. Economic diversification is then imperative. The liberation of South Africa, with its diversified economic base might have opened up the possibility of greater regional cooperation, however the South African government is, at the moment intent on greater global integration, signing a free trade deal with the European

Union, for example.[19] This suggests the importance of local economic diversification.

Given the extent of the internationalization of the state, it is local communities, which must assert control of their own development along the lines suggested by Shuman (1998). Africa cannot play by the rules of neoliberal economic competition when the rules are stacked against it. One important tool might be the use of community currencies, which restrain the impacts of global competition and retain income within the community, rather than it being extracted by international finance capital. Conceivably in Africa, internal state weakness may thus be of potential benefit to local initiatives, although it also allows for the rise of warlords. Thus in the longer term the aim must be to reform the state so that it can provide for public order and support heterodox local economic development initiatives. Such initiatives will be imperative to prospects for survival and deglobalization in Africa.

Notes

1. Many thanks to the conference participants and to Ikubolajeh Logan for his helpful comments.
2. Mkandawire (1992) notes that these 'urban coalitions' never existed and that the project of import-substitution industrialization was driven by nationalism.
3. The World Bank was also instrumental in other initiatives, such as underwriting the African Capacity Building Foundation, based in Harare, Zimbabwe.
4. He continues that 'this sleight of hand allows the Bank to caution weak states to do very little until, somehow, they gain the capability to regulate and, sometimes, even make industrial policy'.
5. The coup was related to dramatic falls in world cocoa prices and conseuent non-payment of military salaries ('Chance for West Africa's Jewel to Regain its Sparkle', Financial Times, January 6th, 2000, p. 8).
6. Pederson and McCormick (1999) argue that structural adjustment has increased the importance of the 'economy of affection' as the poorer segments of population increasingly dependent on family networks. and patron-client ties.
7. With the failure of structural adjustment, this culturalist argument is again gaining wider acceptance, from the Economist for example (*Hopeless Africa*, 2000). Christopher Clapham argues that neopatrimonialism is the most salient type [of authority] in the Third World as it corresponds to the normal forms of social organization in precolonial societies (quoted in Bratton and Van de Walle, 1997, p. 62). In this way the entire history of colonialism is conveniently erased.
8. According to Chabal and Daloz (1999, p. 154) to talk of the criminalization of the state in Africa is a misnomer because what would be considered to be criminal in a Western context is actually tied up with notions of legitimacy and political accountability. That is that, they argue that in Africa technically illicit activities are morally sanctioned as long as a share of the spoils are distributed to followers.
9. For a brilliant discussion of the relationship between capitalist (under)development and politics in Africa see Lemarchand (1991).
10. Chabal and Daloz (1999) argue that South Africa is structurally distinct from the rest of Africa because it has been more thoroughly Westernised, but by all accounts crime is as prevalent in South Africa as in many other countries, if not more so (see Ellis 1999 in Bayart *et al.*).
11. Bratton and Van de Walle (1997) also note the correlation between structural adjustment and mass civil unrest, although for them it is because African populations are insufficiently

sophisticated to distinguish between the effects of economic crisis and structural adjustment. They also argue (p. 107) that 'many protest participants seemed to view democracy instrumentally: Rather than being an end in itself, it was a political means to bring about improvements in livelihood and well-being' – the implication, perhaps, being that people should be happy to have a vote even as their standards of living decline.

12. Longman (1999) argues in contrast to most accounts of the genocide, that it was an outcome of state strength, as it was an enormous logistical operation organized by the state, rather than of state weakness. However, in many places the paradox of the post-colonial state has been that it has tried to project strength to deflect its underlying weakness.

13. This terminology draws on the idea of 'virtual democracy' elaborated by Richard Joseph (1999).

14. Interestingly Ohmae (1996, p. 2) identifies the problem of capital over-accumulation, arguing for example that in Japan there is the equivalent of $10 trillion stored away and that the problem is that suitable and suitably large- investment opportunities are not often available in the same geographies in which this money sits. The pressure to valorize the financial surplus is largely what accounts for the globalization of finance.

15. The NAFTA for Africa or the African Trade, Growth and Opportunity Act is unlikely to result in substantial foreign investment given the advantages already offered by Mexico for US-based TNCs.

16. Unbundling refers to the selling off of non-core businesses.

17. Cuba and the Asian NICs are seemingly contradictory examples, however, in both cases strong authoritarian states have responded to the potenial authoritarianism of unregulated capital by disciplining or constraining markets to meet socio-economic goals. Discipling may require authoritarianism. The challenge is the transformation of the market.

18. Zimbabwe's structural adjustment program resulted in economic calamity, while attempts to reimpose selective controls have been punished by international capital (Bond, 2000).

19. This is understandable given that South Africa's trade with the rest of the continent is only a very small proportion of the total. However, studies by economists in the South African government predicted the free trade deal to be detrimental to South Africa's economy (Teljeur, 1998). It was adopted nonetheless, perhaps in expectation of increased foreign investment.

References

Adams, F., Dev Gupta, S. and Mengisteab, K. (1999) 'Globalization and the Developing World: An Introduction'. In F. Adams, S. Dev Gupta and K, Mengisteab (eds) *Globalization and Dilemmas of the State in the South*. NY: St Martins Press, 26–36.

Adelzadeh, A. (1999) 'The Costs of Staying the Course'. In *Ngqo! An Economic Bulletin* published by the National Institute for Economic Policy. Johannesburg (on the web at www.niep.org.za).

Agnew, J. and Corbridge (1995) *Mastering Space: hegemony, territory and international political economy*. London and NY: Routledge.

Alemayehu, M. (2000) *Industrializing Africa: Development Options and Challenges for the Twenty First Century*. Trenton, NJ: Africa World Press.

Barratt Brown, M. (1995) *Africa's Choices: After Thirty Years of the World Bank*. London: Penguin.

Barratt Brown, M. and Tiffen, P. (1992) *Short Changed: Africa in World Trade*. London: Pluto.

Bates, R. (1981) *States and Markets in Tropical Africa*. Baltimore: Johns Hopkins.

Bayart, J., Ellis, S. and Hibou, B. (1998) *The Criminalization of the State in Africa*. Bloomington and Indianapolis: Indiana University Press, James Currey.

Bello, W. with S. Cunningham and B. Rau (1994) *Dark Victory: The United States, Structural Adjustment and Global Poverty*. San Francisco: Food First.

Bond, P. (2000) *Elite Transition: From Apartheid to Neoliberalism in South Africa*. London and Pietermaritzburg: Pluto Press and University of Natal.

Boone, C. (1994a) 'Trade, Taxes and Tribute: Market Liberalizations and the New Importers in West Africa'. *World Development* 22 (3), 453-467.

Boone, C. (1994b) 'States and Ruling Classes in Africa: the enduring contradictions of power'. In J. Migdal, A. Kohli and V. Shue (eds) *State Power and Social Forces: Domination and Transformation in the Third World*. NY: Cambridge University.

Bratton, M. and van de Walle, N. (1997) *Democratic Experiments in Africa: Regime Transitions in Comparative Perspective*. NY: Cambridge University Press.

Callaghy, T. (1990) 'Lost Between State and Market: The Politics of Economic Adjustment in Ghana, Zambia and Nigeria'. In J. Nelson (ed.) *Economic Crisis and Policy Choice: The Politics of Adjustment in the Third World*. Princeton, New Jersey: Princeton University Press.

Carmody, P. (2001) *Tearing the Social Fabric: Neoliberalism, Deindustrialization and the Crisis of Governance in Zimbabwe*. Portsmouth, New Hampshire: Heinemann.

Castells, M. (1996) *The Network Society*. Oxford: Basil Blackwell.

Chabal, P. and Daloz, J. (1999) *Africa Works: Disorder as Political Instrument*. Bloomington and Indianapolis: Indiana University Press, James Currey.

'Chance for West African Jewel to Regain its Sparkle' (2000) *Finanacial Times*, January 6th, p.8.

Cheru, F. (1989) *The Silent Revolution in Africa*. New York: Zed.

Chossudovsky, M. (1997) *The Globalization of Poverty: Impacts of IMF and World Bank Reforms*. NY: Zed Press

Daly, H. (1996) *Beyond Growth: The Economics of Sustainable Development*. Boston: Beacon Press.

De Sardan, O. (1999) 'A moral economy of corruption in Africa?'. *The Journal of Modern African Studies* 37 (1), 25–52.

Dicken, P. (1998) *Global Shift: Transforming the World Economy*. NY: Guilford.

Evans, P. (1995) *Embedded Autonomy: States and Industrial Transformation*. Princeton, NJ: Princeton University Press.

Green, R. and Kadhani, X. (1986) 'Zimbabwe: Transition to Economic Crisis, 1981-83: Retrospect and Prospect'. *World Development* 14 (8), 1059–1083.

Grindle, M. (1996) *Challenging the State: Crisis and Innovation in Latin America and Africa*. NY: Cambridge University Press.

Habib, A. and Padayachee, V. (2000) 'Economic Policy and Power Relations in South Africa's Transition to Democracy'. *World Development* 28 (2), 245–263.

Hanlon, J. (1996) *Peace Without Profit: How the I-M-F Blocks Rebuilding in Mozambique*. Portsmouth, New Hampshire: Heinemann and James Currey.

Harvey, D. (1982) *The Limits to Capital*. London: Verso.

Herbst, J. (2000) *States and Power in Africa: Comparative Lessons in Authority and Control*. Princeton, New Jersey: Princeton University Press.

Hoogvelt, A. (1997) *Globalization and the Post-Colonial World: The New Political Economy of Development*. Baltimore: Johns Hopkins University Press.

'Hopeless Africa' (2000) *The Economist*, May 13th-19th, p.17.

Jackson, R. and Rosberg, C. (1982) *Personal Rule in Black Africa: Prince, Autocrat, Prophet, Tyrant*. Los Angeles and Berkeley: University of California Press.

Joseph, R. (1999) 'The Reconfiguration of Power in Late-Twentieth Century Africa'. In R. Joseph (ed.) *State, Conflict and Democracy in Africa*. Boulder: Lynne Rienner.

Khadiagala, G. (1995) 'State Collapse and Reconstruction in Uganda'. In W. Zartmann (ed.) *Collapsed States: The Disintegration and Restoration of Legitimate Authority*. Boulder: Lynne Rienner.

Kitching, G. (1981) *Class and Economic Change in Kenya*. Princeton, NJ: Princeton University Press.

Knippers Black, Jan (1999) *Inequity in the Global Village: Recycled Rhetoric and Disposable People*. NY: Kumarian Press.

Koeble, T. (1998) *The Global Economy and Democracy in South Africa*. New Brunswick, NJ: Rutgers University Press.

Korten, D. (1995) *When Corporations Rule the World*. NY: Kumarian Press.

Laakso, L. and Olukoshi, A. (1996) 'The Crisis of the Post-Colonial Nation-State Project in Africa'. In A. Olukoshi and L. Laakso (eds) *Challenges to the Nation-State in Africa*. Uppsala: Nordiska Afrikainstitutet.

Lemarchand, R. (1991) 'The Political Economy of Informal Economies'. *Africa Insight* 21 (4), 214-221.

Leys, C. (1996) *The Rise and Fall of Development Theory*. London: James Currey.

Longman, T. (1999) 'State, Civil Society and Genocide in Rwanda'. In R. Joseph (ed.) *State, Conflict and Democracy in Africa*. Boulder: Lynne Rienner.

Mamdani, M. (1991) 'Uganda: Contradictions in the IMF's Programme and Perspective'. In D. Ghai (ed.) *The IMF and the South*. London: Zed Press.

Mamdani, M. (1996) *Citizen and Subject: Contemporary Africa and the Legacy of Late Colonialism*. Princeton, NJ: Princeton University Press.

Marais, H. (1998) *South Africa: The Limits to Change*. London: Zed Press.

Martin, G. (2000) 'Book review of J. Bayart, S. Ellis and B. Hibou 1998'. *The Criminalization of the State in Africa*. Bloomington and Indianapolis: Indiana University Press, James Currey.

Mengisteab, K. and Daddieh, C. (1999) 'Why State Building is Still Relevant in Africa and How it Relates to Democratization'. In K. Mengisteab and C. Daddieh (eds) *State Building and Democratization in Africa*. Westport, Connecticut: Praeger.

Mengisteab, K. and Logan, B. (eds) (1995) *Beyond Economic Liberalization in Africa: Structural Adjustment and the Alternatives*. Cape Town: SAPES and London: Zed Press.

Michie, J. and Grieve Smith, J. (1995) (eds) *Managing the Global Economy*. NY: Oxford University Press.

Mkandawire, T. (1992) 'The Political Economy of Development with a Democratic Face'. In G. Cornia, R. van der Hoeven and T. Mkandawire (eds), *Africa's Recovery in the 1990s*. NY: St. Martin's Press.

Mkandawire, T. and Soludo, C. (1999) *Our Continent, Our Future: African Perspectives on Structural Adjustment*. Trenton, NJ: CODESRIA, IDRC and Africa World Press.

Monreal, P. (1999) 'Sea Changes: The New Cuban Economy'. *NACLA Report on the Americas* XXXII (5), 21–29.

Moore, D. (1999) 'Sail on , O Ship of State: Neoliberalism, Globalization and the Governance of Africa'. *Journal of Peasant Studies* 27 (1), 61–96.

Mnyanda, L. (1999) 'Spiralling job crisis besets economy'. *Business Report* July 12, 11.

Nyango'ro, J. and Shaw, T. (1998) 'The African State in the Global Economic Context'. In L. Villalón and P. Huxtable (eds) *The African State at a Critical Juncture: Between Disintegration and Reconfiguration*. Boulder: Lynne Rienner.

Ofuatey-Kodjoe, W. (1999) 'Ideology, Politics and Public Policy in Ghana'. In F. Adams, S. Das Gupta and K. Mengisteab (eds) *Globalization and Dilemmas of the State in the South*. NY: St. Martins Press.

Ohmae, K. (1996) *The End of the Nation State: The Rise of Regional Economies*, NY: Free Press.

Ohmae, K. (2000) *The Invisible Continent*. NY: Harper Business.

Olukoshi, A. (ed.) (1998) *The Politics of Opposition in Contemporary Africa*. Uppsala: Nordiska Afrikaininstitutet.

Pederson, P. and D. McCormick (1999) 'African business systems in a globalizing world'. *The Journal of Modern African Studies* 37 (1), 109–135.

Reno, W. (1998) *Warlord Politics and African States*. Boulder: Lynne Rienner.

Reno, W. (1999) Mafiya Troubles, Warlord Crises. Paper presented at 'Beyond State Crisis? The Quest for the Efficacious State in Africa and Eurasia'. Madison, Wisconsin, March 11-14th.

Riddell, B. (1999) 'Symptoms or Causes of the Crisis in the Third World: Beyond the Coming Anarchy'. *Canadian Journal of Development Studies* XX (1), 182–188.

Roberts, S. (1997) 'Monetary Policy within Macroeconomic Policy: An Approach in the Context of Reconstruction and Development'. *Transformation* 32, 54–78.

Round, R. (2000) 'Time for Tobin'. *The New Internationalis* 320, 19–20.

Samatar, A. (1999) *An African Miracle: State and Class Leadership and Colonial Legacy in Botswana Development*. Portsmouth, New Hampshire: Heinemann.

Sandbrook, R. (1993) *The Politics of Africa's Economic Recovery*. NY: Cambridge University Press.

Shaw, T. (1997) 'Prospects for a New Political Economy of Development in the Twenty-First Century'. *Canadian Journal of Development Studies* XVIII, (3), 375–394.

Shuman, M. (1998) *Going Local: Creating Self-Reliant Communities in a Global Age*. NY: Free Press.

'South Africa's Lament: With Things Looking up, foreign Investors Remain Aloof' (2000) *New York Times*, November 11, B1-2.

Statistics South Africa (2000) *Measuring Poverty in South Africa* Internet; available at www.statssa.gov.za, accessed September 24, 2000.

Teljeur, E. (1998) 'Free Trade: Does South Africa Gain? Impact of Free Trade Agreement between South Africa and the European Union'. *Trade and Industry Monitor*, July, 1–6.

Tendler, J. (1997) *Good Government in the Tropics*. Baltimore: Johns Hopkins.

Wangwe, S. and Musonda, F. (1998) 'The Impact of Globalization on Africa'. In A. Bhalla (ed.) *Globalization, Growth and Marginalization*. NY and Ottawa: St Martin's and IDRC.

Webber, M. and Rigby, D. (1995) *The Golden Age Illusion: Rethinking Postwar Capitalism*. NY: Guilford Press.

Weeks, J. (1999) 'Stuck in low GEAR? Macro-economic policy in South Africa, 1996-98'. *Cambridge Journal of Economics* 23, 795-811.

Weiss, L. (1998) *The Myth of the Powerless State*. Ithaca, NY: Cornell University Press.

World Bank (1989) *Sub-Saharan Africa: From Crisis to Sustainable Growth*. NY: Oxford University Press.

World Bank (1999) *World Development Report: Entering the 21st Century*. NY: Oxford University Press.

World Bank (2000) Background and Overview of the Comprehensive Development Framework; available from http://www.worldbank.org/cdf/overview.htm; Internet; accessed 27 July 2000.

Chapter 5

Does Globalization Advance or Hinder Democratization in Africa?

Kidane Mengisteab

Introduction

The principal objective of this chapter is to examine how the post-Cold War phase of the global capitalist order (economic globalization) has impacted the demo-cratization struggle in Africa. The relationship between globalization and democracy is rather complex since globalization tends to promote and hinder democratization. Determining the relationship between the two is also complicated by the fact that they are processes that take considerable time to develop. The relationship cannot be meaningfully established by simply correlating outcomes, but by analyzing how the structural and institutional changes associated with globalization: impact on the scope of democracy; impinge on the relationships among social classes; and alter state-society relations (the latter being indirect but critical indicators of democratization). Absence of consensus over what globalization entails further complicates efforts to distill the relationship between democracy and globalization.

The chapter is divided into five parts. The first section discusses the essence of globalization. Section two examines the scope of democracy as conceived and projected by globalization forces. Section three discusses the impacts of globalization on relations among social classes in the African context. Section four examines the impacts of globalization on state-society relations in Africa and the final section draws conclusions about the implications of globalization for Africa's struggle for democratization.

Conceptualizing Globalization

Globalization is a highly complex and controversial concept. The debates are not only about what it is, but also about whether it is taking place at all. Three contrasting views can be identified. One is that, although the process is at an initial stage, a fundamental restructuring of the global system is underway and a new global socioeconomic system is unfolding (Ohmae, 1990; Horseman and A. Marshall, 1994; Giddens, 1996/97; Harris, 1998/99 and T. Friedman, 1999). A second view is that there is little that is new in the global system and that globalization is largely a myth (Hirst and Thompson, 1996). Marshall (1996), for example, argues that globalization appears to be little more than the re-labeling of the dynamics associated with capital accumulation on a world scale. He adds that capitalism can be interposed with globalization whenever the word globalization appears in the literature. A third view recognizes the intensification of interdependence among countries but contends that the changes are not fundamental (Underhill, 1994; Holm and Sorenon, 1995; Boyer and Drache, 1996; Weiss, 1997).

Given the crisis of socialism, the near end of the Keynesian welfare state (Skidelsky, 1997), the reconfiguration of the distribution of global power following the collapse of the Soviet Union and changes in the global economic system manifested by rapid integration of production and financial markets, it is difficult to deny that the global system of the last half a century has undergone some notable changes. However, as Wood (1998) notes, there needs to be a clarification of whether the changes represent an epochal rupture in the essential logic of capitalism or merely indicate the maturation and universalization of capitalism. Since the new order is still in its formative stages, the magnitude of the changes it represents, its characteristics and its implications cannot yet be fully captured. Nonetheless, several key aspects of globalization are already identifiable.

1. Marked integration of global production and the global market. As Holton (1998) notes, the tyranny of distance has been obliterated by the technological and communication revolutions. The resulting rapid decline in transportation and communication costs has contributed to the emergence of an integrated and knowledge-based system of production. Integration of global production is, at least, partly manifested in the fact that about one-third of merchandise trade is now composed of shipments among affiliates of a single company (Sachs, 1998). In this integrated system of production, capital, labor, raw materials and management are organized on a global scale and linked through informational networks largely replacing the spatially fixed and technologically less flexible Fordist system of production of the post-Second World War era. Integration of production has also been accompanied by rapid integration of financial markets, made possible by the growing deregulation of exchange rates and capital flows.
2. Integration of global production has been accompanied by growing integration of the global elite and marginalization of the popular masses. Even in poor countries, one can witness the connection of the elite with the global system through satellite dishes, while the poor masses are disconnected and fragmented.
3. The rise to prominence of a neoliberal ideology, which, in conjunction with the growing power of capital, has transformed market-state relations. With the disintegration of the Soviet Union and the crisis of socialism and statist economic systems, capitalism has shed its defensive posture of the era of the welfare state and has entered an aggressive phase. (Neo)-liberalism, which advocates significant reductions in state involvement in income redistribution, has risen to prominence.
4. A surge in the perception that national economies have converged into a single global economy and that there is only one appropriate form of social organization. Although a single world community is far from being a reality, there has emerged a powerful advocacy for and greater awareness of such a perspective. In other words, as Giddens (1996/97) notes, globalization is not just an analytical notion, it is also an ideological one, expressing a certain orientation toward the future. A global regime of economic governance with identifiable rules of behavior in

trade, finance, taxation, investment policy, intellectual property rights, currency convertibility and foreign investment policy all crafted along neo-liberal principles is taking shape. New institutions have been created and old ones have been reconstituted to manage this new global regime

5. A surge in the power of global capital over other social entities and interests. With liberalization of the flow of capital across borders and advances in communication technology, capital has obtained the power of exit. By contrast, labor's ability to organize and to maintain collective bargaining has been weakened by deregulation of the labor market along with technological change and deregulation of capital mobility. Aspects of the state that are not capital-friendly, for example, trade or labor regulations, have been weakened. The emergence of a transnational legal system and supranational world trade organizations has eroded state sovereignty, especially in developing countries. Contrary to claims by its proponents, globalization is shaped by governments and not by markets (T. Friedman, 1999)

The characteristics described above represent significant changes in the global system that predominated over the last seven or so decades. However, these changes do not constitute a fundamental shift in the essential logic of capitalism. Rather, they signal a new phase of capitalism, which is more universal, more unchallenged, more pure and more unadulterated, than ever before (Wood, 1998). There are those who dispute this position, arguing that the current global system has not even attained the level of integration that existed during the pre-World War I era (Waltz, 1999; Wade, 1996; Zevin, 1992). There are also those who claim that governments now intervene much more than they did in the pre-World War I era (Waltz, 1999). The points raised in this argument, are valid. However, they do not repudiate the globalization tendency of capitalism which was regulated by the last seventy or so years and has resumed in full force. The levels of integration of the global system of production and state disengagement from economic activity may not have exceeded the levels of 1910, but they are rapidly intensifying and are likely to surpass those levels.

The financial crisis, which has sprouted in different countries, may have shaken confidence in the validity of neoliberalism. For example, the World Bank, in stark contrast to the minimalist state advocacy of the 1980s, now accommodates a significant role for the state in protecting and correcting markets (World Bank, 1997). Following the financial crises experienced by many counties, there has also been a growing realization that unfettered financial flows, especially from advanced countries to emerging markets can create profound instability in the latter (Stiglitz and Squire, 1998). Some proponents of globalization have even admitted that Keynes skepticism about financial mobility may still be relevant (Sachs, 1998). Yet, advocacy for globalization remains strong.

The Conception of Democracy Projected by Globalization

Democracy has become accepted as a universal dictum under globalization (Sen, 1999). Like globalization, it also has various conceptions. One is that democratization must allow the general population to control public decision-making on an ongoing basis (Beetham, 1992). A much narrower conception limits democracy to the procedures by which the general population selects its leaders (Schumpeter, 1976).

Both conceptions face the difficult problem of demarcating the sphere of public decisions from that of private decisions. In the Marxist tradition, where the means of production are publicly owned, for example, the sphere of private decisions is rather narrow as economic decisions largely fall in the public sphere. In liberal democracy, by contrast, private ownership of the means of production and the liberal ideology of a limited state, impose constraints on the sphere of public decisions and expand the sphere of private decisions.

Despite these broad differences, however, the degree of limitations of the state and, thus, the appropriate line of demarcation between private and public decisions are neither clear nor rigid, even in liberal democracies. This flexibility allows significant variations along a continuum within liberal democracy. As Bowles and Gintis (1986) note, liberals have both supported and opposed the welfare state and state intervention in economic activity. At one extreme, within this school, are the minimalists who largely adopt the narrow definition of democracy and argue that only a free market economy, in which the state is restricted to its core tasks, creates conditions for sustainable democracy. At the other extreme are the maximalists who view a laissez faire market system as incompatible with democracy and, thus, incorporate a great deal of economic decisions, including regulations, into the public sphere (Keynes, 1936; Lindblom, 1982; Dahl, 1993).

Unlike minimalists, maximalists do not rigidly restrict, *a prior* the range of issues subject to public decision. The maximalist view is flexible in demarcating the boundaries between private and public decisions. As a result, it allows for the existence of a welfare state to provide basic resources for all citizens through government-operated or government-financed services. In less developed countries, such as those of Africa, this flexibility would allow a developmentalist state to pursue more vigorously, resource access for its subsistence peasantry, marginalized ethnic groups and other deprived segments of society. In this way, the developmentalist state can facilitate the transformation and incorporation of these segments of society into an integrated exchange economy.

Liberal democracy has risen to prominence in the post-Cold War era with the surge in the power of capital over other social classes and with the crisis of socialism. For some, liberal democracy no longer has a rival;

> [a]s we enter the last decade of our century liberal democracy suddenly finds itself without an enemy. Whatever else had laid claim on the word democracy, or had been acclaimed as real democracy, has fizzled out almost overnight (Sartori, 1991: 1).

Sartori goes on to assert that non-liberal systems also are, by the same token, non-democratic. There is little doubt that with the crisis of socialism, the socialist conception of democracy has been decimated. Moreover, with the unfolding phase of capitalism, liberal democracy has gravitated to its minimalist form (Schmitter, 1995). The discussion in the next section outlines the ways by which globalization tends to narrow the scope of democracy in the Third World, in general and in Africa, in particular.

Globalization Narrows the Definition and Scope of Democracy

Several attributes of globalization tend to narrow the scope of democracy. Capital's current dominance over other social classes is one such attribute. Since different social classes advance different socioeconomic arrangements, the relative size of the spheres of public and private decisions are related to the balance of power among social classes. As capital becomes more dominant, the sphere of private decision expands and the sphere of public decision shrinks. Conversely, as the power of labor and other lower classes increases, the sphere of public decision expands. A number of studies have established the relationship between the strength of unions and the development of the welfare state and the parliamentary fortunes of social democratic parties in western countries (Western, 1995; Esping-Andersen, Gosta and van Kersbergen, 1992).

With its new power and mobility, capital's influence over governments has increased although the magnitude of its leverage over different governments varies considerably. Fear that they might lose competitiveness in attracting capital has increasingly pressured governments to extract concessions from labor and to make their policies increasingly capital-friendly. As Wilber (1998) notes, under pressure from the internationalization of capital markets, many countries have overhauled their tax and expenditure policies, leading to tax cuts and cut-backs on social expenditures. Presently, policies on taxes, trade, interest rates and regulations of financial markets and the environment are increasingly determined by the logic of international capital rather than by popular will.

The pressure that capital exerts on governments is much greater in less developed countries. Debt ridden African countries have been unable to resist the conditionalities of the IMF and the World Bank (IFIs) even when they are very onerous. The inability of the government of the African National Congress of South Africa to implement significant redistributive policies to rectify the gross inequalities of the apartheid system is a good example. The transformation of market-state relations, which is evident by the growing disengagement of the state from economic activity and regulatory mechanisms, is another development, which has narrowed the scope of democracy. With globalization and the imposition of structural adjustment programs, African states have curtailed their regulatory, redistributive and resource allocation roles. The more the state disengages, of course, the narrower the scope of public decisions becomes.

The Positive and Negative Aspects of State Disengagement

Reducing state intervention in the economy can be positive since it gives space to civil society to mobilize resources towards poverty-alleviation. Reduced state direction of economic activities also creates the potential development of an economic elite that would be relatively autonomous of the state, in some ways reducing the severe competition for government positions among the elite. Unfortunately, the market mechanism, by itself, does not necessarily create a positive space for civil society and a vibrant economic middle class, if one does not already exist. The market also, does not bring about internal interdependence among the different segments of society where such interdependence does not exist. State disengagement may, thus, curtail the potential role of the public sector in creating these conditions in countries where they are absent.

Global institutional changes culminating in the emergence of a regime of economic governance with a transnational legal system and supranational world trade, finance and banking organizations is yet another factor that narrows the scope of democracy. Organizations such as the Group of 7, the Organization for Economic Cooperation and Development, the World Trade Organization, the International Monetary Fund, the World Bank, the Basle Committee on Banking Supervision and the International Organization of Securities Commissions, have all become major players that author international rules that hold together the unfolding global system. African countries are grossly under-represented in these international organizations. As these organizations and their technocrats co-opt for themselves the reins of global and local policy formulation, they disenfranchise African populations, which can no longer use the power of their votes to comment on their support for policy makers. This situation leaves the African state vulnerable from the top (global policy makers) and the bottom (local populations) a situation, which has often led to political instability and the institution of draconian, undemocratic reforms by the state. The present situation in Zimbabwe is a telling example of this. Caught between the dictates of structural adjustment, urban unrest over inflation and rural unrest over land availability, the Mugabe regime has become increasingly dictatorial.

Many from the liberal tradition celebrate state withdrawal from economic activity. Samuel Brittan (1977), for example, contends that limiting the state reverses the Keynesian economic system, which, in his view, represented the most self-destructive tendencies of democracy. Claiming that state involvement in economic activity constitutes the transfer of control from the people and the market, to politicians and coercive interest groups, Hut (1979) also asserts that state disengagement from resource allocation enhances democracy. Hayek (1978), arguably the most notable critic of the welfare collectivist system, also views state disengagement positively. He argues that it is impossible for a government which has unlimited powers to confine itself to serving the agreed view of the majority of the electorate or to promote their general interest since it buys its authority by handing out special favors to particular groups.

Undoubtedly, state involvement can be self-serving and governments often reward the most powerful interest groups or social classes. However, the claim that the domination of powerful interest groups over social (general) interest would be less under a pure market system is unfounded. As Gamble (1996) notes, the reality in market-dominated societies is a hierarchical system in which the majority of individuals are subordinated to the power of giant transnational corporations and with increasing disengagement of the state, social inequalities have become more pronounced. Liberalism, in its zeal to protect individuals from the state, can easily subject society to the tyranny of the economic elite against which it provides little protection.

Under the one-person-one-vote system of existing democracies, the masses obtain some power from their numbers, provided that the domain of public decisions is significant. In this light, among the potential value of democracy to African peasants is that it could enable them to express their interests in public policy making. They can use their franchise to recall self-serving politicians. To the contrary, an unregulated market system with a devitalized sphere of public decisions provides no mechanism for recall of self-serving dominant elites. The masses also lose any advantage from their size in a 'market democracy' where voting is on the basis of purchasing power. 'Market democracy' is, thus, inherently oligarchic, especially under conditions of egregious inequality, a characteristic of many African economies, most notably, South Africa, Nigeria, Ivory Coast, Zimbabwe. This characteristic is present even in the poorest Africa states, including those in political chaos like Sierra Leone and Liberia, where diamonds perpetuate serious class inequalities.

Despite the limitations of existing democracies in Africa, therefore, the dictatorship of the elite can be controlled only through the sphere of public decisions. Excessive retrenchment of the state in resource allocation narrows the sphere of public decisions without creating any viable democratic alternative. Narrowing the scope of democracy in this way, has the potential to strip capitalism of much of the human face and social justice it had progressively obtained in the era of the welfare state and to turn it back to the worst excesses of the early industrial revolution. In the African context, where problems of social inequality are more severe and state building is still nascent, this narrower re-conceptualization and implementation is particularly worrisome. Recent events in Cote d'Ivoire, for example, underline this point. The rule of democracy, orchestrated by a vibrant economy and a thriving middle class, has been overturned and both political democracy and the market are imperiled.

Globalization and State Building

Historically, state building was achieved initially, largely by means of force, before it was consolidated through the integration of economic and political infrastructures. It is clear that African countries cannot accomplish state building through force (although some, like Ethiopia and Somalia have tried). In general, African states are not strong enough to suppress rebellions; either internal or external territorial threats and only a few can afford the human and material costs of protracted conflicts. The more promising option for African states, therefore, is to integrate their different ethnic and regional groups by democratizing their socioeconomic systems. This option involves determining the terms of integration of different groups through negotiated compromises. This fusion of state building and democratization implies that the levels of centralization (decentralization) of power and the demarcation between the spheres of the private and public decisions have to be settled by popular consent and not *a priori* by ideology.

In this context, it seems imperative that African countries devise a democratic system compatible with their own conditions. In other words, the conception of democracy cannot be separated from the aspirations of citizens. By and large, what Africans expect from the state is markedly different from the expectations of citizens in the advanced countries. It is, thus, highly unlikely that a conception of democracy imported from the advanced world would be appropriate for Africa. Claims such as those made by Sartori may be valid, but the victory of the minimalist liberal democracy does not necessarily mean that it is relevant to Africa or that African societies should not strive to adapt democracy to their own conditions.

It stands to reason that African countries should tap into the rich traditional consensual decision making institutions that prevail in many African communities, instead of simply relying on imported institutions. So far, African countries have made little headway in these regards. It is hardly surprising that the democratization attempts in the continent, which have largely been reduced to electoral contestations, have been disappointing. Elections, where they have taken place, have essentially failed to empower the general population. Instead, they have largely been used as a mechanism for legitimizing the rule of an elite in power or as device by which a contending elite attempts to capture power (Lumumba-Kasongo, 1998) (Zambia, Zimbabwe, Togo and Kenya provide good examples). Recent political changes in Cote d'Ivoire have not been smooth and the elections in Ghana, though unproblematic as a process, still has to demonstrate that it has brought real empowerment to the larger population.

Globalization and Class Relations

At the global level, state disengagement, in conjunction with deregulation of the labor market, de-unionization of workers and decentralization of wage bargaining, have increased inequality between classes. Inequality among social classes was already a serious problem in Africa before globalization and the implementation of structural adjustment programs. African countries are characterized by gross inequalities between rural and urban areas as well as among social classes and ethnic groups in terms of access to different forms of resources. Such disparities are reflected in literacy rates (over three-fourth of Sub-Saharan African countries have illiteracy rates of over 50%); and national poverty headcounts as percentage of total population ranges from 30%–70% in many countries (World Bank, 1998). Under such conditions, it would be difficult to achieve stability and genuine democracy. Democratic institutions are unlikely to survive and even if they do, they are likely to remain empty shells, existing in form only and devoid of real significance Mayor (1999).

Many neo-liberals view increased inequality and poverty following on the heels of deregulation and state disengagement as a short term problem and argue that economic efficiency brought about by the free market via globalization is certain to be more successful than the welfare state in alleviating poverty. Rapid growth, it is argued, will bring about more comprehensive and lasting economic change than the public sector can ever expect to accomplish. Some neo-liberal thinkers, like Hayek, largely dismiss concerns of social inequality since they view them as mere vestiges of the bygone era of primitive communalism. According to Hayek, these primitive instincts need to be weeded out and replaced by individual freedom and responsibility, irrespective of the problems of inequality and poverty. In Hayek's (1973) view, the morals of the market order are essential for the creation of wealth that would sustain civilization. However, there is little empirical evidence and theoretical justification to support claims that the market mechanism reduces inequality.

There is, little doubt that severe inequality can destroy democracy by either reducing it to hollow procedures or by generating destabilizing social conflict. Many African countries presently find themselves engulfed by various types of conflicts mostly related to problems of deprivation of segments of their populations. In this context even the process of state building by integrating different ethnic entities is unlikely to be successful without accompanying market reforms that mitigate poverty and inequality.

Globalization and State-Society Relations

The impacts of globalization on the state are a highly controversial issue. Recent widespread disengagement of the state from economic activity has led many observers to view the state as a victim of globalization. It has become fashionable to assert that the era of the nation state is passing by and that national-level governance has become ineffective in the face of globalized economic and social forces (Horseman and Marshall, 1990; Ohmae, 1990). Others have argued that the state has facilitated, if not authored globalization (Panitch, 1996; Weiss, 1997).

Undoubtedly, globalization has undercut the conventional economic as well as political authority of the state. Transnational corporations and other supra-state and sub-state regional and multilateral organizations, including the international financial institutions, have all infringed on the sovereignty of the state, especially in developing countries. Yet, the role of the state in globalization needs to be reexamined since not all states play the same role or are impacted by globalization in the same manner.

As an overarching organization of citizens, the state is ideally expected to have an organic relation with the community of citizens and to serve the interests of society at large. Given the plurality of interests among citizens and given the marked differences in the power and influence of different segments of society, the state rarely represents or advances the interests of all social classes equally. Often, it serves the interests of dominant interest groups or classes. At other times it becomes self-serving. Yet, as Rueschemeyer and Evans (1985) note, the state is ultimately an organization of citizens and is capable, depending on the balance of power between the state and civil society and among the different interests within civil society, to serve as a corporate actor or as an agency for promoting the common good. Under a genuinely democratic system where imbalances between social classes are mitigated, the state can be expected to act on behalf of common social interests.

At the present time, while capital advocates less regulations, labor, environmentalists, small businesses, the poor and many other groups generally prefer a more engaged state. In this struggle the state has become more responsive to the interests of capital, which is more powerful and often more organized. This explains why the state in the powerful countries of the North, where the hegemony of capital over other social classes is well established, has largely joined hands with MNCs in promoting globalization and has entrusted the multilateral financial institutions to do the same. The liberal economic order, which was championed by the hegemonic state in previous phases of capitalism, is now projected by the collective consensus of the states of the North.

The capitalist class in Africa, unlike that in the countries of the North, has not yet established a clear hegemony over other classes. Whatever the African state does in promoting globalization is, thus, primarily as a result of external influence and not necessarily a reflection of domestic social interests. Most African states implement structural adjustment programs with considerable reluctance in order not to be denied assistance from the IFIs. The post-independence state, which often inherited the characteristics of the colonial state, was largely ineffective in advancing the interests of society. Its failure in this regard is well documented (Ayoade, 1988; Bates, 1981; Keller, 1991; Young, 1994). Dependency on the former colonial powers and the ideological rivalry of the Cold War limited the African state's ability to pursue independent policies that advance social interest.

Globalization has further undermined the limited sovereignty and control African states were able to muster following decolonization in the 1960s. Pressure and conditionalities from the IFIs and donor countries have forced the African state to adopt openness and other capital-friendly policies. Often, these policies are incompatible with African realities and detrimental to African social interests, including state building, transformation of marginalized regions, ethnic groups and social classes. The South African state is a good example of these difficulties. Under pressure from capital and external actors, it has not yet been able to implement policies of land reform and redistribution despite the widespread popular demand by former victims of apartheid. With strong support from the IFIs, policy makers in that country have avoided aggressive land reform. The longer they take to implement land reform, the more difficult it will become, as many African elites will join the ranks of the landowners. Zimbabwe's current experience should be a telling lesson for South Africa.

The characteristics discussed above exemplify the African state's increasing disconnection from its society. In other words, the African state, like the African economy, is extroverted and highly disarticulated. It is important to emphasize that the disarticulation of the African state was not brought about by globalization. However, globalization, in conjunction with the current hegemonic liberal ideology, has legitimized and intensified the disarticulation of the African state.

Conclusion

As noted at the beginning of this chapter, the impacts of globalization on democratization in Africa cannot yet be fully assessed. Since African countries have rarely attempted genuine democratization, it is difficult to demonstrate empirically the constraints globalization places on the democratization process. The conclusions of this chapter are thus rather tentative. Nevertheless, the analysis suggests that the structural and institutional changes represented by globalization, project a narrow conception of democracy. As Latham (1997: 54) notes, '...globalization which has created barrier-free global space for market networks to operate, has also erected a rigid ideological boundary. Its homogenizing ideology reduces the scope of national and regional decision-making and blocks the development of any alternatives'. By advocating the disengagement of the state from selected activities, such as development planning and income redistribution, globalization has shifted these critical issues from the realm of public decision-making.

In the African context where the process of state building is still underway and problems of poverty and social inequality are rampant, a broader conception of democracy and an actively engaged state are indispensable. It is highly unlikely that the free market mechanism, by itself, will be able to overcome these problems.

Needless to say, a distinction needs to be drawn between the existing disarticulated state and a state that advances social interest. The failure of the existing state does not render the state irrelevant since there are different types of states. The democratization struggle that is presently underway on the African continent, if not thwarted by globalization forces, has the potential to lead to the creation of a more desirable state mechanism (at least from the perspective of the larger majority of the local population). To the contrary, as long as such a democratic state remains illusive or democracy is narrowed to become irrelevant, Africa's general crisis (economic and political) is likely to continue.

References

Amin, Samir (1985) *Delinking: Towards a Polycentric World*. London: Zed Books.

Ayoade, John A.A. (1988) 'State Without Citizens: An Emerging African Phenomenon'. In Donald Rothchild and Naomi Chazan (eds) *The Precarious Balance: State and Society in Africa*. Boulder: Westview Press, 100–118.

Barber, Benjamin (1995) *Jihad vs. McWorld*. NY: Random House.

Bates, Robert H. (1981) *Markets and States in Tropical Africa*. Berkeley: University of California Press.

Beetham, David (1992) 'Liberaal Democracy and the Limits of Democratization'. *Political Studies*, Special Issue 40, 40–53.

Bienefeld, Manfred (1994) 'The New World Order:Echoes of New Imperialism'. *Third World Quarterly* 15 (1), 31–48.

Bowles, Samuel and Herbert Gintis (1986) *Democracy and Capitalism*. NY: Basic Books.

Boyer, Robert and Daniel Drache (1996) 'Introduction'. In Robert Boyer and D. Drache (eds) *States and Markets: The Limits of Globalization*. London and NY: Routledge, 1–27.

Brittan, Samuel (1977) 'Can Democracy Manage an Economy?'. In Robert Skidelski (ed.) *The End of the Keynesian Era: Essays on the Disintegration of the Keynesian Political Economy*. NY: Holms and Meier.

Callaghy, Thomas (1988) 'The State and Development of Capitalism in Africa: Theoretical, Historical and Comparative Reflections'. In Donald Rothchil and Naomi Chazan (eds) *The Precarious Balance: State and Society in Africa*. Boulder: Westview Press, 67–99.

Cox, Robert W. (1994) 'The Crisis in World Order and the Challenge to International Organization'. *Cooperation and Conflict*, 29/2, 99–113.

Dahl, Robert (1993) 'Why All Democratic Countries Have Mixed Economies'. In John W. Chapman and Ian Shapiro (eds) *Democratic Community*. NY: New York University Press, 259–82.

Duncan, Alex and John Howell (1992) 'Assessing the Impact of Structural Adjustment'. In Duncan and Howell (eds) *Structural Adjustment and the African Farmer*. London: Overseas Development Institute, James Currey and Heinemann, 1–13.

Esping-Andersen and Gosta and Kees van Kersbergen (1992) 'Contemporary Research on Social Democracy'. *Annual Review of Sociology* 18, 187–208.

Friedman, Thomas (1999) *The Lexus and the Olive Tree*. NY: Farrar, Straus, Giroux.

Gamble, Andrew (1996) *Hayek: The Iron Cage of Liberty*. Boulder: Westview Press.

Gibson-Graham, J. K. (1996/97) 'Querying Globalization'. *Rethinking Marxism* 9 (1), 1–27.

Giddens, Anthony (1996/97) 'Anthony Giddens on Globalization: Excerpts from a Keynote Address at the UNRISD Conference on Globalization and Citizenship'. *UNRISD News* Autumn-Winter, 15.

Hardy, Chandra (1992) 'The Prospects for Intra-regional Trade Growth in Africa'. In Frances Stewart, Sanjaya Lall and Samuel Wangwe (eds) *Alternative Development Strategies in Sub-Saharan Africa*. NY: St. Martin's Press, 426–44.

Harris, Jerry (1998/1999) 'Globalisation and the Technological Transformation of Capitalism' *Race & Class* 40 (2–3), October–March, 21–35.

Hayek, F.A. (1973) *Law, Legislation and Liberty: A New Statement of the Liberal Principles of Justice and Political Economy* (1) Chicago: University of Chicago Press.

Hayek, F.A. (1978) 'The Miscarriage of the Democratic Ideal'. *Encounter* 50, 14–17.

Hazel, Johnson (1992) *Dispelling the Myth of Globalization: The Case for Regionalization*. Praeger.

Hirst, Paul and Graham Thompson (1996) *Globalization in Question*. Cambridge: Polity Press.

Holm, Hans-Henrik and Georg Sorensen (1995) 'Introduction: what Has Changed?'. In Holm and Sorensen (eds) *Whose World Order?*. Boulder: Westview Press, 1–17.

Holton, Robert (1998) *Globalization and the Nation-State*. London: Macmillan Press.

Horseman, M. and A. Marshall (1994) *After the Nation State*. London: Harper Collins.

Hut, W. (1979) *The Keynesian episode; A Reassessment*. Indianapolis, IN: Liberty Press.

Keller, Edmund J. (1991) 'The State in Contemporary Africa: A Critical Assessment of Theory and Practice'. In Dankwart A. Rustow and Kenneth Paul Erikson (eds) *Comparative Political Dynamics: Global Research Perspectives*. NY: Harper Collins, 134–59.

Keynes, John M. (1936) *The General Theory of Employment, Interest and Money*. London.

Latham, Robert (1997) 'Globalization and Democratic Provisionism: Re-reading Polanyi'. *New Political Economy* 2 (1), 53–63.

Lindblom, Charles E. (1982) 'The Market as Prison'. *Journal of Politics* 44 (2), May, 324–36.

Lumumba-Kasongo, Tukumbi (1998) *The Rise of Multipartism and Democracy in the Context of Global Change*. Westport, Connecticut and London: Praeger.

Marshall, Don D. (1996) 'National Development and the Globalization Discourse: Confronting 'Interpretive' and 'Convergence' Notions'. *Third World Quarterly* 17, 875–901.

Mayor, Federico (1999) 'Myths and Illusions: Misapprehensions regarding Democracy and Poverty'. *UNESCO Courier* 52 (3), March, 9.

Ohmae, K. (1990) *The Borderless World: Power and Strategy in the Interlinked Economy*. NY: Harper Business.

Panitch, Leo. (1996) 'Rethinking the Role of the State'. In James H. Mittenbaum (ed.) *Globalization: Critical Reflections*. Boulder and London: Lynne Rienner, 83–113.

Piven, Frances Fox and Richard A. Cloward (1998) 'Eras of Power'. *Monthly Review* 49, January, 11–23.

Rueschemeyer, Dietrich and Peter Evans (1985) 'The State and Economic Transformation: Toward an Analysis of the Conditions Underlying Effective Intervention'. In P.B. Evans, D. Rueschemeyer and T. Skocpol (eds) *Bringing the State Back In*. NY: Cambridge University Press, 44–77.

Sachs, Jeffrey (1998) 'International Economics: Unlocking the Mysteries of Globalization'. *Foreign Policy* 110, Spring, 97–111.

Sachs, Jeffrey and Andrew Warner (1995) 'Economic Reform and the Process of Global Integration'. *Brookings Papers on Economic Activity* 1, 1–118.

Saghal, N. (1995) 'The Myth Reincarnated'. *Journal of Commonwealth Literature* 31 (1), Winter, 23–28.

Sartori, Giovanni (1991) 'Rethinking Democracy: bad Polity and bad Politics'. *International Social Science Journal* 43, August, 437–450.

Schmitter, Philippe C. (1995) 'Democracy's future: More Liberal, Preliberal, or Postliberal?'. *Journal of Democracy* 6 (1), 15–22.

Schumpeter, Joseph A. (1976) *Capitalism, Socialism and Democracy*. NY: Harper and Row.

Sen, Amartya (1997) 'Democracy as a Universal Value'. *Journal of Democracy* 10(3), 3–17.

Skidelsky, Robert (1997) *The End of the Keynesian Era*. NY: Holmes and Meier Publishers INC.

Stiglitz, Joseph and Lyn Squire (1998) 'International Development; Is It Possible?'. *Foreign Policy* Spring 138–151.

Underhill, Geoffrey R.D. (1994) 'Conceptualizing the Changing Global Order'. In Richard

Stubbs and Underhill (eds) *Political Economy and the Changing Global Order*. NY: Martin's Press, 17–44.

United Nations (1998) *World Investment Report 1998*. NY and Geneva: the United Nations.

UNCTAD (1998) *Trade and Development Report, 1998*. NY and Geneva: the United Nations.

UNDP (1994) *Human Development Report 1994*. NY: Oxford University Press.

UNDP (1997) *Human Development Report 1997*. NY: Oxford University Press.

Waltz, Kenneth N. (1999) 'Globalization and Governance'. *PS: Political Science and Politic*, 32 (4), December, 693–700.

Weiss, Linda (1997) 'Globalization and the Myth of the Powerless State'. *New Left Review* 225, September/October, 3–27.

Western, Bruce (1995) 'A Comparative Study of Working-Class Disorganization: Union Decline in Eighteen Advanced Capitalist Countries'. *American Sociological Review* 60 April, 179–201.

Wilber, K. Charles (1998) 'Globalization and Democracy'. *Journal of Economic Issues* 32 (2), (June).

Wood, Ellen Meiksins (1998) 'Capitalist Change and Generational Shifts'. *Monthly Review* 50 (5), October, 1–10.

World Bank (1994) *Financial Flows and the Developing Countries*. Washington, D.C.: The World Bank.

World Bank (1998) *African Development Indicators 1998/99*. Washington D.C.: The World Bank.

World Bank (1998) *World Development Indicators 1998*. Washington D.C.: The World Bank.

Young, Crawford (1994) *The African Colonial State in Comparative Perspective*. New Haven and London: Yale University Press.

Zevin, Robert (1992) 'Our World Financial Market Is More Open? If so, Why and with What Effect?'. In Tariq Banuri and Juliet B. Schor (eds) *Financial Openness and National Autonomy: Opportunity and Constraints*. New York: Oxford University Press.

Chapter 6

Globalization, the State and Economic Development in Africa

Julius Nyango'ro

Introduction

From the beginning, the discourse on 'development' in Africa has been a discourse on how Africa compares to the rest of the world in terms of basic, conventional indicators like levels of education, infrastructure, social services, industrialization and urbanization. In this regard, the various approaches to development, whether of the 'modernization' variety (Rostow, 1960), 'dependency' (Leys, 1975; Amin, 1977), or 'post-imperialism' (Warren, 1980), are quite similar. They all note that, compared to other regions, Africa has fared poorly in all social and economic indicators. Africa is reported to be lagging behind other world regions in education and literacy, two important requisites for access and use of information technology, a cornerstone of the present global system. Education and literacy are also important because they tend to correlate closely with industrialization, which, as Gerschenkron (1962) observed, is an inescapable indicator of development. Education and literacy are important for assessing the ability of a population to respond to the demands of an industrial society, whether in terms of working machines or engaging in other activities, which perpetuate wealth in an advanced economy. This modernization perspective (Preston, 1985; Bloomstrom and Hettne, 1984) is certainly open to debate, as shown in the literature. However, that debate is more about the details of particular development strategies than about the broad parameters of what constitutes development. It is in the context of this broad understanding of development that the debate on globalization, particularly as it relates to Africa, must be framed and the historic role that states have played in harnessing the development effort must be understood. This is especially so in Africa.

Since the early 1980s, the debate on the African state has been dominated by pessimism about its capacity to mobilize development. Indeed, the state was condemned as the principal obstacle to development because it was perceived to have failed in its various attempts at managing the economy (World Bank, 1981). Another critique during the same period, was that compared to other regions, the African state has been an ineffective vehicle for mobilizing domestic and global investment (Deyo, 1987).

It is now accepted wisdom that, without the state, the newly industrialized countries (NICs) would not have achieved their present economic status so rapidly. Given the pivotal role played by the state in the industrial development of the NICs and to a lesser extent in Latin America, I would posit the following argument as a preliminary working hypothesis: 'while the current discourse on development and globalization is about the declining (and diminishing?) role of the state, the context of development in Africa must be that of the enhanced role of the state, albeit a different and transformed one'.

State Capacity and Economic Development in Africa

Evans (1995: 3) reminds us that 'the state lies at the center of solutions to the problem of order. Without the state, markets, the other master institution of modern society, cannot function.' This suggests that a discourse on development, which attempts to draw a sharp contrast between 'the state' and 'the market', is actually a presentation of false choices. Since the publication of *Accelerated Development* in 1981, even the World Bank has adopted a less strident insistence on the supremacy of the market over the state in economic organization. This is important because the World Bank has become such a critical policy player in African development that, in many African countries, the World Bank country office is the de facto Ministry of Finance and Planning.

The control over African economic policy by the international financial institutions (IFIs) must be viewed from a number of dimensions. First, the basic question of state sovereignty and the ability of the state to undertake policies that it perceives to be in the 'national interest' are severely constrained by the reliance of the African state on external funding to pursue economic development. The state can hardly adopt policies that run contrary to the basic philosophies of the IFIs. Second, the de facto control over African policies by the IFIs raises concerns about traditional areas of state control like 'security' and sovereignty. For newly independent states, sovereignty over economic policy took on a renewed sense of urgency when it became clear that the international political and economic system would constrain the options available to them in pursuing their development objectives. The Tanzanian example underscores the tensions between the post-independent African state and the IFIs. In one of his many confrontations with the World Bank, Julius Nyerere, the late President of Tanzania, retorted that nobody appointed the World Bank to be the finance ministry of the world and by implication, of Tanzania (see Pauly, 1997). The obvious point of contention between Nyerere and the World Bank was whether Tanzania could pursue social welfare policies, example, free medical services and universal primary education, while also engaging in deficit spending. The World Bank argued that it was first and foremost important to balance the books through demand management. The Tanzanian government argued that it was more important to have a healthier and better educated population than having balanced books, although the latter was clearly important. Nyerere retired in October 1985 and Tanzania immediately embraced most of the policies demanded by the IFIs. Prompting some critics to suggest that, like most other countries undergoing structural adjustment, it has ceded its sovereignty to international finance (Campbell and Stein, 1991).

The sovereignty difficulty is not restricted to developing economies. Rather, it is a problem of all 'open' economies. The underlying principle under the Bretton Woods institutions is free trade and open economies. Standard economic literature under the

Mundell-Fleming model has demonstrated that the governments and central banks of open economies cannot give simultaneous priority to maintaining the independence of their internal monetary policies, stabilizing their exchange rates and permitting unrestricted inward and outward capital flows (Kenen, 1994). The financial crisis that engulfed the NICs in the late 1990s exposed the extent to which they have become vulnerable to IFI manipulations. Demonstrations in the streets of Seoul and Jakarta against the IMF made clear what most people thought of the IFIs.

A third dimension of IFI control over African development is the appropriateness of their policies for long-term, strategic development on the continent. The Berg Report (World Bank, 1981) severely criticized earlier government policies in Africa for diverting resources from the agricultural sector to manufacturing, a charge repeated often by Africanist scholars in the 1980s (see for example, Bates, 1981; Berg and Whitaker, 1986). The World Bank summarized the African development crisis by noting that African states had undermined agriculture by concentrating too much on import substitution industrialization (ISI), which could not be sustained because of limited markets and the high import content of inputs. To compensate for this basic weakness in the manufacturing sector, African governments squeezed out rural producers for the necessary surplus to keep the manufacturing sector operational. The net result was diminishing investment on the part of cash crop producers, leading to the decline of both the manufacturing and agricultural sectors.

While it is true that African agricultural policy was misguided in the sense that producers were overtaxed to finance inefficient state bureaucracies, it does not necessarily follow that the drive towards industrialization was misguided. As noted earlier in this chapter, historically, industrialization has been a key ingredient in the development process of other regions and its absence has been understood to be a basic characteristic of underdevelopment. Consequently, instead of outright condemnation of industrial development, there is a need to devise a suitable industrial policy for African countries, either individually or collectively as regional groups.

Industrialization is a central theme and current in globalization. Developing countries that have succeeded in industrial development, especially the NICs, are also those that have succeeded in integrating themselves into the global capitalist system. In the current world order, industrialization provides the surest means by which a developing country can demarginalize itself and become an active participant in the global economic system. As globalization continues to put pressure on companies to be competitive in more than one country or region, sites for new production centers are chosen on the basis of capacities of local economies to supply inputs. Accessibility of production sites via rapid transport, communication and easy connection to other sites of production is crucial for 'just in time' production. A critical factor in all of this is an economy that is industrialized, or rapidly industrializing (Gereffi and Wyman, 1990).

This discussion inevitably leads to the conclusion: that, for an economy to engage effectively in the contemporary global political economy, it must have a strong industrial and manufacturing base. This stricture guides post-apartheid era industrial policy in South Africa. The country has made a concerted effort to expand its manufacturing base in its drive to become the premier industrial power on the continent; although this objective has been constrained by a sluggish economy that is poorly connected to world markets (Marais, 1998). South Africa's poor performance in this regard is an indication of the difficulties that are likely to face other African countries that attempt to pursue an industrial policy. Yet, the fact that the possibilities are daunting does not mean that the strategy should be completely abandoned.

Perhaps, the most difficult aspect of any potential African drive towards industrialization would be demands by the IFIs that the countries avoid deficit spending and abide by their conditionalities. Curiously, deficit spending was never seen to be a major hurdle to development in the late 1960s and early 1970s as the NICs were pursuing their industrial programs. In fact, deficit spending was regarded as an expected outcome of the massive investment outlays required by these countries to import industrial technology and by the early 1980s, Brazil, Mexico and South Korea all had large debts resulting from their industrialization efforts.

State Capacity and Industrial Development

Any discourse on contemporary globalization, if it is to make sense in the case of Africa, must bring to the fore the role of the state. This is a lesson that seems to have eluded critics of state participation in Africa's potential industrialization (see Evans, 1995). Although less concerned with globalization and more interested in political stability and institutionalization, for the past two decades, the discourse on the African state has been dominated by notions of state incapacity (see for example, Rothchild and Chazan, 1998; Hyden and Bratton, 1992 and Harbesom, *et al.* 1994). The inability of the state to govern effectively has been an overriding theme in these studies, many of which have been unable to make an effective case that this inability must be linked to larger structural problems (many of them external and not of the state's making) that are manifested in the inability of the state to engage in meaningful industrialization. Most analyses of the African state have, thus, been primarily at the superstructural level and have taken little note of the economic substance of African societies.

To a great extent, state incapacity reflects economic incapacity. This also means that at the core of the governance crisis (corruption, lack of legitimacy, etc.) is the inability of the state to facilitate economic development. Analyses that are overwhelmingly superstructural usually miss this point, although for a decade now, the World Bank (1989) to its credit, has explicitly acknowledged the connection. Economic incapacity in Africa can be explained by a single major factor, namely, structural underdevelopment. Although it is less fashionable now to talk about dependency and underdevelopment than it was during the 1970s and 1980s, the heyday of 'dependency theory', the reality of underdevelopment has changed only minimally in Africa in the last three decades. If anything, structural under-development has become more severe as a result of two major factors: the large debt overhang, which resulted from the economic crisis of the 1970s and the widening technological gap between the developed world and Africa, as manifested especially by access to information and communications. For example, internet use in Africa was 0.5 per 1,000 persons in 1995, compared to 17.9 for industrial countries (UNDP, 1999). These numbers have undoubtedly changed in the last few years but the trend in industrial countries has been towards more access while that for Africa has remained static. Given the fact that access to information technology is key to global interconnectivity, this gap does not bode well for Africa's integration into the global economy. The seriousness of the situation was noted at the first International Telecommunications Union (ITU) meeting held in Johannesburg, South Africa, May 4–10, 1998. A statistical analysis of Africa's telecommunications system revealed the following: only 14 million phone lines have been installed in sub-Saharan Africa, fewer than in Tokyo, the average waiting time for the installation of a telephone in Africa is five years; fewer than 1 in 50 Africans has direct telephone access; at a minimum, US $50 billion would be required to make African telecommunications competitive with other regions (*Africa Recovery*, August 1998: 38).

I propose that as we engage in a discussion of globalization, the realities of political economy must be acknowledged lest we get swept away by the illusions of global benefit. In this case, therefore, we must start our analysis by noting the reality that, unlike all other regions in the global economy today, Africa still suffers from the most acute problems of underdevelopment. After two decades of structural adjustment, it is generally accepted that the 1980s was a lost decade for Africa in terms of socio-economic development. While in a few cases the 1990s may seem to have brought a little relief (Uganda, Mozambique), the sub-Saharan region as a whole experienced further economic regression up to the mid to late 1990s. The regression has been steepest in war-torn polities like the Democratic Republic of Congo, Liberia, Sierra Leone, Congo-Brazzaville, Angola and Sudan. Looking back, the annual mean rate of growth of per capita income in the region was 0.8% in the 1970s; it slumped to negative 2.2% per year from 1980 to 1989; and in the last decade, there has been a slow recovery which by no means comes close to compensating for earlier declines (Ravenhill, 1993: 19; World Bank, 1999).

The Mid-Term Review of the United Nations New Agenda for the development of Africa in the 1990s (UN-NADAF, 1996) actually notes that many of the problems the region faced half a decade earlier have become more acute, while most of the region's potential has yet to be realized. UN-NADAF outlined the elements of the continuing crisis in the following way.

1. In the 1990s, Africa's GDP accounted for less and less of world output (about 2.04% on average) even though its share of world population increased (to about 12% in 1995). While Africa's GDP grew by 2.3% in 1995, its population increased by 2.9%, resulting in an actual per capita decline of 0.06%.
2. Africa's total external debt is now widely acknowledged to be unsustainable. It rose from US$289 billion in 1991 to over US$314 billion in 1995.
3. Africa was using 31% of export earnings to service its debt in 1991. Although this ratio fell to 23% in 1994, it climbed to 31% again in 1995. Sub-Saharan Africa's arrears on debt-service payments nearly doubled from US$32.6 billion to US$62 billion in the 1984–94 period. Essentially, debt service claims nearly one-fifth of Africa's savings and over 4% of GDP.
4. Heavy indebtedness has been identified as a disincentive to foreign direct investment (FDI). In spite of the political and economic reforms implemented across the region, it is being bypassed by the boom in investment flows. For all developing countries, net FDI inflows rose remarkably from US$22.6 billion in 1991 to US$60 billion in 1995. But the story was very different for Africa, with net FDI increasing from US$1.8 billion in 1991 to US$2.9 billion in 1994, before

falling by 27% in 1995 to US$2.1 billion. Africa's share of total FDI to developing countries fell from 10% in 1987–91, to 5% 1992–4 and to merely 3.6% in 1995.

5. Africa's continued reliance on a handful of primary commodities for the bulk of its export earnings, together with growing competition from Asia and Latin America in a shrinking market for many raw materials, resulted in the region's share of world trade declining from 3% in 1990 to 2% in 1995 (Brown and Tiffen, 1994: 28–40). In order to be competitive under globalization, it is generally held that there must by diversification of commodity exports. Yet, African countries continue to rely on the same commodities they did thirty years ago. Primary commodities accounted for approximately 75$ Africa's total foreign exchange earnings over the first half of the 1990s and some African countries relied on a single commodity for more than three-quarters of their total exports.

While some other developing regions have been able to profit from increasing levels of trade by diversifying production and trading partners, Africa for the most part has not. The region essentially has been bypassed by the conspicuous transformation in commodities traded globally (i.e., manufactures and information technologies). This can be demonstrated by the fact that between 1990–95, the region's share in the trade of developing countries fell from 10.9% to 6.4%, while its share with the European Union (EU) fell from 3.3% in 1992 to 2.8% in 1995.

All these factors point to an important conclusion. While it is now fashionable to talk about Africa's need to be part of globalization, it is also obvious that Africa generally is having a difficult time coping with the demands of globalization. There is little comfort to be gained from a World Bank statement that notes that in 1999, for the fourth year in a row, most African economies continued to grow – that growth comes on the heels of two decades of either stagnation or negative growth. Indeed, the 1999 World Bank annual report notes that although growth in Africa in 1998 was significant (5% growth in 13 countries) and stronger than in many other parts of the developing world, it was lower in 1997 due to weaker international commodity prices and barely enough to keep up with population growth. Africa's overall GDP growth in the 1990s was only 2%, reflecting slow-progress, or none at all, in large countries like South Africa, Nigeria and the Democratic Republic of Congo (World Bank, 1999).

What is remarkable about these World Bank observations is that while the current discourse on globalization in centered on new technologies and systems of production, Africa's economy is still heavily dependent on traditional primary exports, which continue to face the vagaries of global price fluctuation. Thus, structurally, Africa of the new millennium (2000) may not be too different from Africa of the year 1960, the year that became known as Africa year because of the large number of African countries that became independent.

An underdeveloped state therefore, needs to address the challenges of globalization and the demands of an expanding capitalist system. The question for us is whether in their present condition, states in Africa are capable of meeting this challenge. To answer this question, we must identify those features of the state that may fit the profile of a dynamic state.

State Dynamism and Industrial Development

The principal feature of a dynamic state would be its capacity to create a niche in the global division of labor. Niche creation is both a result of understanding the attributes with which an economy is 'naturally endowed' and the ability to seize opportunities created by global interaction. In addressing this question Evans (1995:8) asked: 'Are positions in the international division of labor structurally determined or is there room for agency? Put more simply, can countries deliberately change the position they fill in the international division of labor?'

The overwhelming evidence from South East Asia and Latin America suggests that niche creation is actually a result of a concerted effort by the state to help determine an advantageous position in global production. In order to arrive at a position in which the state is capable of helping to make that determination, it must fulfill several preconditions, the first of which is legitimacy. A legitimate state is better poised to institute policies that may seem draconian and even authoritarian and yet resistance to the policies may be minimized by the benefits that the population may see accruing from those policies. For example, while it is generally acknowledged that the states in South Korea and Singapore were less than democratic in the 1970s and 1980s, their policies on mass education, infrastructure development and industrialization had clear and tangible benefits. A legitimate state is also capable of insulating itself from inter- and intra-class competition within the country and, thus, able to institute policies that are egalitarian. This aspect of the state allows it to engage international capital much more effectively and actually gives the state a 'comparative advantage' in negotiating deals.

Much of the available evidence suggests that the features, which make for competitive and comparative advantage in global interaction, are not possessed by African states. Even states in the historically better-off economies in the region, such as Kenya and Zimbabwe, have now lost any ability to engage effectively international capital and have succumbed to IFI conditionality. The essential political point to be made is that the state in these countries could not put itself above inter- and intra-class competition. The state was clearly seen as a tool of very specific factions, which completely undermined any claims it may have to legitimacy. In worst-case scenarios, the competition has led to violent conflict as in the DRC, Liberia and Sierra Leone.

Globalization and Regionalism: Contradictory or Complementary?

Traditional theory of regional integration had at its core, actions of the state and attempts at creating regional economies under the direction of states. The earliest attempts at integration in Africa: the East African Community (EAC); the Economic Community of West African States (ECOWAS); the Southern African Development Coordination Conference (SADCC); and its successor, the Southern African Development Community (SADC); all reflected this conviction. These structures remain in one form or another and SADC is involved in further expansion with the admission of new members DRC, Seychelles and Mauritius. There is also a suggestion that, given the weakness of African economies in general, perhaps the best way for Africa to engage the global economy would be through joint action within regional organizations.

Regional integration, exclusively understood as state action, is seriously inadequate given new developments in economic interaction among actors other than the state. Regionalisms – ongoing linkages among states, companies and civil societies (including communities, cultures, ecologies informal sectors) at the intermediate level between national and continental – are quite transformed not only in Africa, but globally. The new regionalism is characterized by the advocates of new integration, which involve private, non-state actors rather than states, especially companies and less exclusively economic concerns. Thus, states have become less important, particularly with the seeming triumph of the neo-liberal ideology. Given this development, one wonders what will become of the African Economic Community (AEC) initiative as reflected in the Abuja Declaration. AEC's main features are highly statist and would seem to be at best, ECOWAS and EAC writ large.

There is an inherent contradiction in the parallel developments of globalization and regionalism in Africa. Globalization, as I have argued, is affecting Africa negatively because of the latter's inability to cope with the demands of global production and the inability of African states to create niches in the global economy. This would suggest that state capacities need to be enhanced to allow for the evolution of strong, competent institutions. The old state-centric regionalism might seem to be a natural growth from state interaction in the region, but economic interaction at the sub-national level is almost out of reach for states. So both the analytic and practical question is how to merge trends at both the regional and global levels with strategies to change the state's historical inability to engage regionalism at the intermediate levels and below. It will be some time before this seeming contradiction is resolved.

The existing situation of regional integration and industrial development in Southern Africa reflect some of these difficulties. It is realistic to expect that the Republic of South Africa (RSA) represents the means by which regional industrial development and global integration can occur. Yet, the new political dispensation in the RSA comes at a time when the operative word from the IFIs is 'restraint' on demand. In practical terms, this means that the RSA is not being afforded the possibility of deficit spending as a means to industrial development, as was the case with the NICs. The adoption of the Growth Employment and Redistribution (GEAR) strategy implemented in June, 1996 by the RSA government, essentially signaled the end of any pretense that the country is pursuing a strategy other than structural adjustment (Marais, 1998). Since 1994, the RSA has had a net loss of 500,000 jobs, negating any benefits that may have accrued from the liberalization of the economy and the abolition of formal apartheid institutions (Cape Times, December 2, 1999). Most of the job losses have come from the industrial and mining sectors, traditionally the fulcrum of South Africa's economic engine and also the basis upon which the country and, possibly, the whole region could become competitive in global markets.

There is an irony in the way South Africa's economic difficulties reflect the difficulties of the continent in general. One of the arguments against apartheid by 'liberal' ideologists was that without apartheid, South Africa's economy would be more dynamic, attract foreign investment and become a base for the penetration of global capital into the rest of the region (Lipton, 1985). Indeed, the shift of the South African economy from mining and agriculture to manufacturing and services was seen as a harbinger to much that has now come to pass as the basic elements of globalization: information technology, skilled labor and less restriction in the movement of national capital. However, it would seem that the range and quality of South African expansion in the rest of the sub-region has been confined to a few sectors, particularly in services: South African Airways, hotels and tourism, food products and beverages (Nyango'ro, 1997). Further, it is not clear whether the limited range of this interaction will actually enable other economies in the region to become active players in global integration or simply be reduced to the status of a periphery of and a market for a much more powerful RSA.

The latter question is important because it reflects on a fundamental difficulty of industrial development in Africa: countries cannot industrialize individually because they lack markets and capital; as a result, countries need to pool their resources together both to industrialize and to compete effectively with other global regional blocs; yet, countries seem to be incapable of negotiating mutually beneficial policies. These problems manifest themselves in several dimensions. First, there are concerns over the ability of South Africa to play the role of conduit for international capital into the region. In order for South Africa to be effective in this role, it must have the capacity to integrate new technological innovations into its own domestic industry and to disseminate them to surrounding countries. Years of economic boycott by the international community slowed down the transformation of South Africa's industry in this regard. The disadvantages of this legacy are reflected in a fairly shaky Johannesburg Stock Exchange (JSE), which has performed poorly in the last decade. On the other hand, post-apartheid economic activities in the region, for example, in telecommunications, gives her neighbors fodder to speculate that developments would be concentrated in the RSA for the benefit of the RSA.

Some members of the Southern African Development Community (SADC), particularly Zimbabwe, have voiced concerns that the RSA's economic domination of the union may have negative effects on the rest of the region by undermining the industrial and manufacturing growth of other members. The flood of South African products into regional markets over the past decade has only amplified these misgivings. SADC members are worried that RSA's industrial dominance would effectively undermine the long-range goals of independent industrialization in each country. These tensions are affecting the ability of SADC as a community of states, to develop a coherent strategy to deal effectively with the challenges of globalization.

Similar tensions spill over into other areas that may seem peripheral to economic issues (such as the military conflicts in Lesotho and Angola) but whose effects are felt in the economic realm. For example, the continued constitutional crisis in Lesotho and the role of SADC in its resolution is hindered by the inability of members to agree on a joint program. In a much more serious sense, the current conflict in the Democratic Republic of Congo (DRC) has revealed the sharp divisions that exist among SADC members. The DRC is now a member of SADC but has not carried out the expected tasks of a member state because of a raging internal conflict that is threatening to undermine the capacity of the state to operate in a 'normal' fashion. SADC members, including Angola and Zimbabwe, are active participants in the ongoing war, complicating an already dangerous situation.

Southern Africa is more economically advanced and integrated than other regions of sub-Saharan Africa. The fact that it faces the problems that it does in terms of negotiating a regional industrial policy emphasize the difficulty of the problem in the whole continent.

Conclusion: Globalization the Savior; Globalization the Menace

In the 1990s, the discourse on African development had two primary camps, the Afro-Pessimists and Afro-Optimists (Chege, 1997). The Afro-pessimists argued the hopelessness of the African case and saw no way out of the economic crisis. Afro-Optimists saw a silver lining at every turn. Obviously the African crisis has been far much complex than either side could present, especially in light of the recent resurgence in civil society activism. The fact, however, remains that Africa is still a seriously underdeveloped continent caught in civil conflict and in some respects having non-functional states. Under these conditions, it will be difficult for the benefits of globalization to accrue to the continent. Critics of structural adjustment have presented a credible case that continued adjustment fundamentally weakens the state, the vehicle, which must be an important player in the globalization process.

Given the uncertainties involved in Africa's economic transformation, perhaps it is best to suggest that the way in which contemporary African economies will effectively globalize will be different from both the original globalization of primary commodity production (under colonialism and immediate post-independence era) and that of recent globalization by South East Asian countries. For the globalization of contemporary Africa to occur (assuming this to be the current development goal) policy makers in the region need to learn lessons from the experiences of other regions. They also need to ask the tough, uncomfortable question, why am I in trouble? What elements of my environment can I control; which elements are beyond my reach? A realistic assessment may lead us to a middle of the road solution that is both less global and more practical. This middle of the road solution cannot be without some element of industrialization, unless, of course, globalization is repudiated as the current development objective.

References

Amin, Samir (1977) *Imperialism and Unequal Development*. NY: Monthly Review Press.
Bates, Robert H. (9181) *Markets and States in Tropical Africa: The Political Basis of Agricultural Policies*. Berkeley: University of California Press.
Berg, R.J. and Whitaker, J. (eds) (1986) *Strategies for African Development*. Berkeley: University of California Press
Blomstrom, M. and Hettne, B. (1984) *Development Theory in Transition: The Dependency Debate and Beyond; Third World Resources*. London: Zed Press.
Campbell, H. and Stein, H. (eds) (1991) *The IMF and Tanzania: The Dynamics of Liberalization*. Harare: SAPES Books.
Chege, M. (1997) 'Paradigms of Doom and the Development Management Crisis in Kenya'. *Journal of Development Studies* 32, 4 April, 552–567.
Deyo, F.C. (ed.) (1987) *The Political Economy of the New Asian Industrialization*. Ithaca: Cornell University Press.
Evans, P. (1995) *Embedded Autonomy: States and Industrial Transformation*. Princeton: Princeton University Press.

Gereffi, G. and Wyman, D. (eds) (1990) *Manufacturing Miracles: Paths of Industrialization in Latin America and East Asia*. Princeton: Princeton University Press.

Gerschenkron, A. (1962) *Economic Backwardness in Historical Perspective: Essays by Alexander Gerschenkron*. Cambridge, MA: The Belknap Press.

Harbeson, John W. *et al.*(eds) (1994) *Civil Society and the State in Africa*. Boulder, CO: Lynne Reinner.

Hyden, Goran and Bratton, M. (eds) (1992) *Governance and Politics in Africa*. Boulder, CO: Lynne Reinner.

Kenen, P. (1994) *The International Economy*. 3rd edition. Cambridge: Cambridge University Press.

Leys, C. (1975) *Underdevelopment in Kenya: The Political Economy of Neo-Colonialism, 1964–1971*. Berkley CA: University of California Press.

Lipton, M. (1985) *Capitalism and Apartheid: South Africa, 1910–84*. Totowa, NJ: Rowman and Allanheld.

Marais, H. (1998) *South Africa, Limits to Change: The Political Economy of Transition*.

Nyango'ro Julius E. (1997) 'Post-Apartheid Kenya-South Africa Relations'. In Larry A. Swatuk and David R. Black (eds) *Bridging the Rift: The New South Africa in Africa*. Boulder, CO: Westview 171–187.

Nyango'ro, J. E. (1999) "Hemmed In' The State in Africa and Global Liberalization'. In David Smith *et al.* (eds) *State and Sovereignty in the Global Economy*. London: Routledge, 264–277.

Pauly, L. (1997) *Who Elected the Bankers?* Ithaca, NY: Cornell University Press.

Preston, P.W. (1985) *New Trades in Development Theory: Essays on Development and Social Theory*. London: Routledge & Kegan Paul.

Ravenhill, John (1993) 'A Second Decade of Adjustment: Greater Complexity, Greater Uncertainty'. In T. Callaghy and J. Ravenhill (eds). *Hemmed In: Responses to Africa's Economic Decline*. NY: Columbia University press, 18–53.

Rostow, W.W. (1960) *The Stages of Economic Growth: A Non-Communist Manifesto*. Cambridge: Cambridge University Press.

Rothchild, Donald and Naomi Chazan (eds) (1988) *The Precarious Balance: State and Society in Africa*. Boulder, CO: Westview Press.

Warren, W. (1980) *Imperialism: The Pioneer of Capitalism*. London: New Left Books.

World Bank (1981) *Accelerated Development in Sub-Sahara Africa: An Agenda for Action*. Washington, D.C. World Bank.

Chapter 7

Science Parks as Magnets for Global Capital: Locating High-Tech Growth Engines in Metropolitan Shanghai

Susan Walcott

Introduction

Transnational companies act as economic development growth engines for China's leapfrog into the 21st century network of global capitalism. Beijing's post-1978 modernizers use foreign companies as the fastest way to gain access to transferable Western technology and to finance the development of local companies. Foreign-investments also improve employment conditions in the country at the same time that bloated state-owned enterprises (SOE) are dismissing workers due to restructuring. Chinese workers employed by foreign enterprises receive better pay and generally better working conditions than they would with the government or with a Chinese company. On their part, foreign companies benefit when they invest in China by gaining a foothold in what is perceived to be a potentially vast, 1.2 billion person market and presently serves as a large, inexpensive labor pool for simple assembly operations.

Despite these mutual benefits, both sides operate warily against the backdrop of a long history of engagements, from silk for 1st century Caesars in the Han Dynasty, to Marco Polo and Mateo Ricci, marauding merchants and missionaries and multiple invasions in the twentieth century. The Self-Strengthening Movement in the 1890s featured bureaucrats embroiled in the Di-Yung Controversy: how could China learn the useful techniques (*yung*) of the West, while keeping her own soul (*di*)? China remains determined to set the pace and limits of change in any sphere, opting in all cases for stability.

In 1990, metropolitan Shanghai was selected by central government planners as a location to be modernized into an industrial, tertiary and high tech economic center (Tian, 1996; She, *et al.*, 1997; Walcott and Xiao, 2000). The main objective of the government is to attract foreign high technology companies to spur the rapid regeneration of metropolitan Shanghai as a means of pulling the country as a whole into the 21st century (Tan *et al.*, 1996). Since 1990, Shanghai has established six official High Tech Parks (Table 7.1) whose specific purpose is to attract foreign companies with advanced processes and products into China.

Table 7.1 One District, Six Parks

Date	Development District
March, 1999	Caohejing High Tech Development District
July, 1992	Zhangjiang High Tech Park
January, 1994	Shanghai Manufacturing University Science and Technology Park
February, 1994	International Fabric Science and Technology City
March, 1994	Jinqiao Manufacturing and Exporting District
Mid-1994	Jianqding Science and Technology Park
OTHER	
1985	Minhang Economic and Technological Development Zone
May, 1994	China Singapore Suzhou Industrial Park

Source: China High Tech Statistical Abstract (2000). Beijing: China Statistical Press

This chapter examines company relationships in four of Shanghai's six science parks: 1) Shanghai-Minhang Economic and Technological Development Zone, established in 1985 in a satellite city southwest of Shanghai, 2) Shanghai-Caohejing Hi-Tech Park, founded in 1988 close to Hongqiao Airport within central Shanghai, 3) Pudong's Zhangjiang Hi-Tech Park, begun in 1992 and 4) China-Singapore Suzhou Industrial Park (CSSIP), opened in 1994 to the west of the historic town 80 kilometers from Shanghai. The analyses are based on fieldwork conducted in the summers of 1999 and 2000, which involved 25 interviews, surveys collected between the two trips and statistical data from national and municipal level sources, development park authorities and companies. These data are used to explore the networking strategies driving growth in the science parks. Although the government is a central actor in the location decision-making, a more interesting question concerns the symbiotic dynamic in which companies employ certain advantages to exploit their location in the science parks while policy makers also employ certain strategies to exploit what the companies have to offer to the Chinese economy.

Globalization and Science Parks in Theoretical Context

A key question with which to preface a discussion of the links between global capital and Chinese industrial development is whether Shanghai's science parks represent a unique model or a mere replication of the export processing zone strategy. This question does not have a simple and straightforward answer. Use of high tech parks as a growth engine is an outcome of the present stage of capital accumulation and organization. The global capitalist economy has structured a hierarchical network within which regions closest to innovation sites garner the greatest profit from modernization and production. These incomes reduce progressively down to regions of routine, low-cost labor, which are marginal to the high technology production chain.

Traditional Marshallian analyses do not quite get to the heart of the raison d'etre for science parks. Such analyses suggest that industrial districts are perpetuated through the utilization of shared pools of geographically fixed inputs such as labor, infrastructure, tax breaks, tertiary services, low transportation and transaction costs and a local culture of cooperation. Certain economic advantages may accrue in general from spatial proximity of similar companies utilizing the pooled labor, information networks and physical infrastructure resources of a technopole planned development (OECD, 1987; Castells and Hall, 1994). This is particularly the case when such districts are set within the orbit of a large metropolitan area, which allows them to benefit from urbanization and localization economies due to proximity to firms with similar production or distribution affinities (Malecki, 1997).

A general case can be made that China's city-regions function differently. The concept of neo-Marshallian districts (Amin and Thrift, 1992) may, therefore, be more suitable for examining its development zones as nodes in the global economy, that is, as local industrial districts set within geographically expanding global corporate and urban networks. Particular cities – in the case of Shanghai, a globalizing rather than fully integrated global point – serve as major capital accumulation and transaction points (Scott, 1999; Yeoh, 1999).

Scale is a key consideration, with city-regions replacing (but not immune from the influences of) the nation-state. While one school of periphery development popular in the late 1970s predicted the continuing dependency of former colonized nations on the more developed world, the success of the so-called Asian Tigers reveals that national government policy could play a significant role in shaping the outcome of this relationship such that less developed countries could still craft a successful way out of trade dependency (Applebaum and Henderson, 1992). Theorization of high tech development within a new international division of labor framework and the sequenced process of structuring global commodity chains (Gereffi *et al.*, 1994) remains a task emerging from empirical studies such as this one.

Various new theoretical types have been proposed to characterize these industrial districts. Park (1996) envisions them as satellite high tech industrial hub and offshore spokes, emphasizing the predominance of transnational companies in these development zones. This modification of Markusen's (1997) concept of hub and spoke districts introduces the effects of long distances between headquarters and branches in another culture and many time zones removed. In her examinations of Beijing's Zhong'guancun region, which is characterized by university-affiliated entrepreneurs, Wang (1998; 1999) refers to high and/or new technology industries along the lines envisioned by another government agency hoping to engender districts configured to encourage the growth of indigenous enterprises. The science parks examined in this chapter represent attempts to blend both models, with new native ventures attempting to learn via technology transfer how to manage in a new type of economy – even as foreign firms attempt adaptations to China's evolving market and production structures.

Development districts in Shanghai can be classified along a continuum constituted of both of these tendencies, with CSSIP typifying the former and Caohejing the latter. Parks reflect a unique institutional and cultural context, as well as generally recognizable features (Yeung, 1997). Local and national governments seek to energize a network of suppliers, deliverers, service providers and buyers from foreign corporations kindling the sparks which planners hope to fan into a forest fire. Western high tech firms serve as the focus of this inquiry into the suitability of science parks to serve as economic engines, since Western technology is reputedly more available for sharing and compatible with China's level of absorptive capacity (Young and Ping, 1997).

Questions arise as to whether foreign firms keep technopole functions overseas while utilizing China for low cost labor, or use China's scientists for breakthrough ideas but then obtain a substantial share of the profits through partnership arrangements. Metro Shanghai's tech parks test the hypothesis that spatial clustering is an especially effective strategy for developing countries and other regions where barriers to access exist; yet information exchange constitutes a key production element. China's technopoles function as a national variant of the model, with distinct characteristics due to China's centrally controlled political economy and early stage of transition development (Wang *et al.*, 1998). Transnational corporations (TNCs) function to spread an internal corporate and organizational culture into the local economy through transfer of knowledge (Malmberg *et al.*, 1996). By design, this development is spatially and sectorally uneven. Spatially, investment falls off rapidly to the West. In general, the development zones in the coastal regions dwarf those in the interior. The bias towards coastal development through these zones represents a stunning reversal of Mao's policy of balancing regional growth. Sectorally, investment heavily favors real estate and social services, followed by higher end infrastructure provision such as electron, telecommunications, electricity and transportation.

Historic Background to Globalization and Science Parks in China

In general, China's emerging economic strategy of cooperative competition is designed to help build bridges with companies looking for a competitive breakthrough as a base upon which to build dominance in some area. For example, companies might cluster at a park if it became known for a software innovation. Local advantages of a science park could provide this edge, particularly in a setting where transnational companies need intercessors and interpreters. However, China's current framework of information control poses obstacles to the generation of synergistic technology transfers between foreign countries and their local counterparts. Wang (1998) has identified an absence of inter-firm connectivity to be a major impediment to the development of China's hi-tech parks into something more than zones for extraction of profit for transnational companies. Other network factors currently limiting the growth of Western-style capitalism in a Chinese context include mediating actors and institutions, rules of engagement, deeply-rooted technology transfer mechanisms and informal interaction spaces for sharing ideas and building relationships (Rosen, 1999), shortage of venture capital and over-extensive bureaucratic restrictions.

Nevertheless, the Chinese view the science park model with much optimism and fully expect the positive multipliers from Shanghai to benefit the whole economy. Part of this optimism is historic. Shanghai, at the mouth of the Yangtze, is China's traditional industrial center and trade port and has a highly trained labor pool. Since the 1842 Treaty of Nanjing, which put an end to the Opium War, the city had become an entrepot for dealing with the West.

Urban design in post-1949 People's Republic of China followed a Soviet model, which specified distinct zones for particular land uses and involved locational proximity for similar industries to reduced transportation cost and permit better integration of functions. The First Five-Year Plan intermixed industry and residents, leading to the establishment of several industrial districts for heavy manufacturing on Shanghai's periphery. Five industrial districts and seven satellite towns with specific functions, circled the central city region; and six suburbs about ten kilometers from the central district and six at a distance of forty kilometers, formed new satellite towns with populations ranging from 50–250,000 (Murphey, 1988). Several of these sites are part of the present research and indicate that the science park model dates back to the early years of the People's Republic.

Each science park was established on the basis of identifiable production foci. Caohejing originally produced electronics and scientific gauges, while Jiading was designed to concentrate on scientific research and textiles. Traditionally Minhang was a heavy engineering and machine manufacturing area and Pudong functioned as an agricultural area of small villages to the east of Shanghai (Fung *et al.*, 1992; Ning and Yan, 1995).

The ascension of Premier Deng Xiaoping in 1978 precipitated a major shift in policy both domestically and internationally, in favor of accelerated economic development and openness to the outside world. Shanghai's subsequent rejuvenation followed gradually. In 1981 Shanghai's output contributed almost 13% of GNP and its taxes supplied over 16% of national revenue. In 1983, the city's leadership passed into the hands of technocrats who were interested in even more vigorous growth. Shanghai was designated an open port in 1984 (Fung, *et al.*, 1992) and the first U.S.-China joint venture took place with the inauguration of Hewlett-Packard China in 1985. Late in 1986, the city redefined terms such as 'export' and 'technology' in order to grant special enticements to foreign enterprises (Arnold, 1993).

China was transformed in the 1980s by a new priority on economic development. Central control eased, invigorating the national economy. Following Deng's 'Southern Tour' and 'Spring Wind' speech in 1992, a tilt away from Guangdong-led growth reflected the rise to political prominence in Beijing of Shanghai-affiliated leadership such as former mayors Jiang Zemin and Zhu Rongji (Tian, 1996, She *et al.*, 1997). Shanghai's high taxation levels eased considerably, from 90% to 75% and later to the existing rate of 33%. By 1995, the Shanghai-led Chang Jiang delta equaled the Guangdong-led Pearl delta in economic strength (Tan *et al.*, 1996). The combined total of investments in the metropolitan Shanghai city-region, including two neighboring provinces, rivals that of Shenzhen-Guangdong outside Hong Kong.

The Role of Foreign Direct Investments in China's Development

Foreign direct investments (FDI) are welcomed by China if they fit the following four criteria: involve technologically advanced products or processes; generate jobs, especially at this time of State-owned enterprise (SOE) downscaling; generate foreign currency through exports, which, rather than the domestic market should be the primary focus of production; and, produce something China needs but cannot presently provide (Weidenbaum and Hughes, 1996). As part of a long-term objective to insure a 'virtuous cycle' (Qu and Green, 1997) of jobs for China's highest skilled labor, the Chinese government has set out to improve infrastructure and services to continue to attract foreign direct investment. Industries targeted for this development include the automobiles, electronic and telecommunications equipment, equipment for power plants, heavy-duty machinery and electronic equipment, petrol and precision chemistry, iron and steel and household appliances (Chesterton, Blumenauer and Binswanger, 1998).

Overall, the strategy has met with some success, as demonstrated by the steady increase in value of projects attracting foreign investments (both contracted and fulfilled) from market liberalization in 1976 through the 1990s.

FDI and Employment Creation: The Minhang Example

As China's cumbersome and hugely unprofitable SOEs were either trimmed or closed down as a result of economic restructuring, the Chinese workforce was faced with massive unemployment, a problem unknown since the communist revolution. The strategy of enticing FDI addressed this problem by creating more and better jobs until Chinese companies could catch up both in numbers (more and smaller) and techniques (modernized).

In 1982, Squibb Pharmaceutical signed a joint venture that made it the first foreign pharmaceutical company in post-1949 China. Others, such as Eli Lilly and Company which had found a foothold in pre-World War II period, came back to metropolitan Shanghai in 1994, with a branch in China-Singapore Suzhou Industrial Park (Suzhou is a historic city some 80 kilometers west of the far larger port center of Minhang) now known as SIP). The Chinese government sought to capitalize on the presence of Squibb by establishing the Shanghai Minhang Economic and Technological Development Zone (SMETDZ). Entering at roughly the same time as Squibb, were Coke, Pepsi, Johnson & Johnson and Xerox. When China proved a good market, J&J expanded its lines and facilities, from band-aids to creams, following the Chinese requirement that only foreign products made in China can be sold in China.

Although one of the smallest, Minhang's Park has one of the highest value outputs per area. The government provides land and infrastructure improvements on favorable terms as a standard location inducement, reimbursed in the long term by the subsequent increase in taxes from more firms in the area. By 1999, 141 projects in the Zone represented over US$1.75 billion in investments from eighteen countries and regions. Minhang continues to have ties with Shanghai. Many of the managers live in apartments heavily populated by foreigners near the Hongqiao airport and 10% of the workers commute from Shanghai.

FDI and Technology Transfer: The Caohejing and Pudong Examples

Caohejing High-Tech Park thrives in the heart of Shanghai, attracting major international companies like AMP (Advanced Materials Products). White shirts are a popular proclamation of office worker status, in a city with historical compradore experience wherein working for foreigners represented a giant step up the economic ladder. Shanghai's former mayor (now Premier) Jiang Ze-min established Caohejing in 1988 as the first high-tech development center among the coastal ETDZs and the first major high tech park established within the city of Shanghai. His original idea was to cast Caohejing as China's Silicon Valley, with a high quality of life and landscape amenities as enticements to the 5-sq km area only 7 km from the Hongqiao airport and close to an inner ring road (Fung *et al.*, 1992). Major industries in the park range from telecommunications, microelectronics, computer software and synthetic materials to bioengineering. In March 1997 a 20,000 sq m high tech incubator was completed. More than half (almost 300) of Caohejing's firms are Chinese; a third of the rest have American ties, followed closely by companies with Hong Kong, Japan, England and Taiwan, in that order (it is difficult to account for all Taiwanese investment, since for political reasons some is routed through Hong Kong to obscure its origin).

Chinese companies predominate in most development zones, reflecting the Chinese policy of attempting to place local enterprises in as close geographic proximity as possible to sources of foreign technology transfer. As in an earlier economic phase, industries are squeezed in among apartments in Shanghai following a policy called sticking a pin wherever there is space (He, 1993). Some Chinese firms in other parks, for example, Minhang, maintain a separate administrative and sales office in Shanghai to be closer to higher-class residences and business activity.

The overall goal of Pudong's Zhangjiang High Tech Park (ZHTP), located directly to the west of central Shanghai, is to span the gap in science and technology between China and advanced countries, developing twenty-first century initiatives in the bio-pharmaceutical industry, microelectronics and information industry and optics, mechanics and electronics. ZHTP's concentration on pharmaceutical manufacturers, developing a concentrated 'Medicine Valley' for a group of Chinese, foreign and joint venture medicine-focused research institutes and pharmaceutical plants, has led to an increasing realization of and frustration with the long lead time and high cost of the drug discovery, testing and approval cycle. From a total of seventy-nine companies in 1999 (22 are in the Innovation Base incubator), Zhangjiang's total number of enterprises tripled by the year 2000. Most of the newcomers are cutting edge Chinese firms in incubators owned by various scales from the national to the local. Governments profess a special responsibility to assist the transformation of these small and medium enterprises, transitioning from government support to market justification. One notable breakthrough in a Zhangjiang transnational firm is development of a new product tailored for China's market, under a separate brand name from that of the famous parent.

Investing in Shanghai: From the Perspective of Global Capital

The outside world that would trade with China historically coveted access to the Chang Jiang, formerly known in the West as the Yangtze River, the most important navigable route into the formerly 'sleeping dragon'. Shanghai developed at the mouth of its delta, on the western side of the Huangpu River. Across from what became a thriving Western portside Bund (from the Anglo-Indian term meaning embankment) in the early 1900s was the agricultural delta land of Pudong, or Pu-east.

Pudong and FDI

Sun Yat-sen envisioned Pudong as a development pace setter since the early 1920s (Dai, 1990). Pudong's growth spurt since 1992 is concentrated on 350-sq km, half the size of Singapore and twelve times that of the other fourteen coastal economic development zones (Tan *et al.*, 1996). Production for foreign export using foreign investment forms the central strategy, employing incentives targeted to encourage research and development and local linkages largely absent in the past (Khan, 1991). As Premier Li Peng declared in April 1990, Pudong's rapid development should be to 'boost the economy of the Chang Jiang Valley', catapulting Shanghai into the forefront of China's financial and trading centers as a vibrant modern urban area (Li, 1995).

Pudong's openness to foreign owned financial institutions should prove a major step towards providing capital for local businesses (She *et al.*, 1997). Regulations of the Shanghai Municipality for the Encouragement of Foreign Investment have made the city more attractive and accessible for foreign investors by establishing clearer ground rules (Givant, 1991). An enabling environment for FDI is created in several ways, including; allowing foreign firms to conduct local currency exchange transactions, the establishment of wholly foreign owned enterprises (wfoe, or woofies) joint ventures, contractual arrangements in which a percentage of profits are not proportional to capital invested (preferred by capital-poor Chinese) and build-operate-transfer procedures, under which MNCs construct a business that then trains Chinese managers and is ultimately turned over to Chinese nationals (Luo, 1998). The dearth of local investment capital means that foreign funds have largely financed economic regeneration of the Chang Jiang delta region through loans from the Asian Development Bank, the World Bank and some municipal and central government sources.

Despite clear advances in hosting foreign capital, there are still problem areas for profit generation and repatriation. The U.S. Commercial Service notes, for example, that while the growing senior cohort of Asia's population has attracted the attention of U.S. medical device firms (Gross, 1996), China's recently tightened price controls on healthcare particularly targeted foreign pharmaceutical products for cost limitation. Regulatory impediments and omissions in intellectual property rights also dampen outlooks for foreign life science industry efforts. A two tier of quality control system is in place for domestic and foreign companies. Chinese consumers, thus, are often willing to pay much more for what are seen as more reliable foreign drugs. Chinese interests are building bargaining power by maintaining a united front against Western business and pitting them against each other in a bidding war to conduct business in China. This practice might backfire in the long run, if Chinese bargainers seek to extract too much from the suitors and force them to leave for other locations (Wang, 1984). The classic conflict involves profit margin for producers versus protection for consumers.

A group of international planners have sought to develop synergistic interchanges between Pudong's nine distinct economic and spatial zones (Olds, 1997). Designed as China's Wall Street, Lujiazui Financial Area functions as a finance, trade and commerce center, sporting towering glass-sided hotels and banks. Its counterpart is the historic Bund of Shanghai directly across the river, with squat colonial-era buildings of the same function but a different era of greatness. Waigaoqiao Bonded

Free Trade Zone incorporates port facilities, warehouses and a base for natural resource exploration in the East China Sea. Jinqiao Export Processing Zone handles high technology, export-oriented 'clean' industries and Shanghai's version of Silicon Valley accentuating a traditional strength in textiles. By 1997, its 302 companies included 38 high tech firms, while 164 received foreign investments. The total area of 37.42 sq km absorbed 35 billion yuan of investment (Statistical Yearbook of Shanghai Pudong New Area, 1998).

The government directed the first company, the Swiss-headquartered Roche, to Zhangjiang. The company pulled in several other related businesses with which it customarily conducted business around the world. New companies are generally steered to Zhangjiang. Development, which became a focus of government attention in 1999, as connections with Shanghai via the new subway line and to the outside world though Pudong's new international airport were completed. Zhangjiang comes closest to an American suburb, with its wide, quiet streets. Zhangjiang also features several eating facilities, which help to combat a sense of isolation in the less inhabited Zone. A web page of metro events is under construction to assist integration of employees and residents with events in a wider area. The presence of an International school, along with a golf course and luxurious housing subdivision as well as plush apartments, point to high hopes for future foreign residents and well-to-do local entrepreneurs. China waits to see if its Dragon Head leads down the high tech path.

China-Singapore Suzhou Industrial Park (CCSIP) and FDI

Unlike its fellow Asian Tigers – Taiwan, South Korea and the former Crown Colony of Hong Kong (now China's Special Autonomous Republic), Singapore established itself as a Pacific Rim preeminent success story based on its ability to entice foreign companies to establish branch operations on its shores. Since its inception as a struggling city-state, Singapore has sought to survive as an export-oriented base for transnational companies. Singapore's niche in the new international division of labor was carved out by low-cost, highly educated and compliant labor in a stable, pro-investment political environment (Castells, 1992).

The CSSIP is the largest Sino-Singapore government project. As of mid-1999, the companies originated from a variety of sources: North America (27), Singapore (22), Europe (20) and Japan (9). In 2000, the proportion of ownership flipped from 35–65 favoring Singapore to place the majority share in China's hands. The two major industrial sectors in the park are electrical and electronics (31%) followed by chemical, pharmaceutical and healthcare (20%). All major infrastructures (water, electricity) within the Park are separate from those of Suzhou city, providing for greater reliability and service.

Several unique attributes distinguish SIP. One is the joint national cooperation and control between the two Chinese countries – a spry city-state whose rapid economic success sustains its political independence from larger neighbor Malaysia and the other a giant, recently emerging onto the international stage and seeking an ethnic ally for tutor to the twenty-first century. The SIP's other distinctive feature is the lot plan placing companies in similar sectors next to each other. Geographic contiguity gives co-pete an extra push in an alien land. Contiguity does not assure cooperative ventures, however, which due to human nature remain based on the relations between managers. Proximity encourages and enables easier interaction among good neighbors, as when a manager newer to the area strolls the shop floors of its neighbor's firm to observe systems at work.

An important and imposing presence in the park is Britain's GlaxoWellcome, the world's largest pharmaceutical firm. Although originally planned as a US$2 billion investment, the Asian economic slowdown caused Glaxo to halve its huge commitment. The campus remains unoccupied at present, due to an ongoing dispute with the Chinese government concerning the company's attempt at securing monopoly rights to produce certain patented products in China. For the Chinese, this conflicts with their goal of encouraging domestic companies to learn from and compete in the local market.

The lure of Shanghai's closeness makes it possible for some families to locate in the big city, with children attending one of several schools catering to foreigners, while the head of the household works in Suzhou. The recently established school in SIP runs along Singapore lines, with a more British curriculum catering to the large number of Singapore expatriates in the area. Future plans to enhance a self-contained Park community include a new downtown combining shopping and other amenities as well as educational facilities.

Each Zone location imparts a distinctive place feel; in general, the more integrated with Shanghai the more comfortable for foreign managers. Suzhou's location is far enough from the Big City to inspire a local foreigner's club. Some amenities must be purchased on trips to better-equipped stores close to Hongchiao, two hours distant even with the new highway link. The ability to conduct business in China with an English-speaking management company proves attractive to foreign companies. Housing and international schools with an English-based curriculum for expatriates are owned and managed by the development company (CSSD) The distance geographically to Shanghai, however, leaves the CSSIP feeling like a foreign island, compared to other high-tech parks in major cities.

Summary

China continues to pour funds into reinvigorating Shanghai as a means of integrating the national economy into the global system. FDI and foreign companies are sought to assist the city in regaining its1930s position as a major global city. The assigned task of the city-region's economic engine remains to pull the Chang Jiang delta and the rest of China along with it to prosperity. Emulating Singapore's experience on a larger scale, China seeks to obtain much-needed funds for development from foreign investment and exports, engendering an on going balancing act. Too many demands and too little infrastructure, foreign firms flee; too little control and China suffers all too familiar exploitation.

Realizing that they are in a learning stage, the Chinese authorities have proceeded slowly and cautiously, crossing the river by feeling for stones, in the words of then-Premier Deng Xiaoping, who unleashed the Opening and Reform movement. Now his successor Jiang Zemin's words are emblazoned in neon across a major building on Nanjing Road, transformed into a central Shanghai pedestrian mall. Innovations are the cornerstone of New China. Small Chinese companies seek ties with large multinationals to sustain them in economic hard times during the mid-level mezzanine stage of product development and marketing. Rather than a lifeline, such ties also threaten to entangle domestic firms in the maelstrom of the global monetary system.

Examples of the tug abound. Supporting promising research and development up to the profit-making production stage requires much scarce capital. So early stage companies are often housed in incubators within a tech park. To supplement funds, China wishes to encourage venture capitalist investments, funds, which largely flow from deep pocket, experienced Hong Kong investors (Saywell, 1998, Hayter and Han, 2000). Providing connecting hardware in concentrated parks is easy, providing quality and comprehensive management software in the form of good practices and enforced high standards is difficult.

China instituted several steps to ensure that, over time, developments would trend in the direction it desires, but the timetable and compliance are lagging. While requiring, for example, that foreign invested companies export a large percent of their products rather than compete in the local market with domestic producers, few follow their pledges. The requirement to nationalize the work force at all levels, including management, is more successful. Natives are thereby trained to fill quality jobs as well as assembly line positions. Jobs for China's technically educated college graduates still need to grow and here investments by foreigners fall short of planners' hopes. The new international division of labor looks much like the old, as far as non-Japanese Asia goes, with higher order positions filled at overseas headquarter locations. The competitive culture of fragmented capitalism is easier to emulate than the connective tissue of information sharing which also underlies technological advances. Some settings are better at this than others, most notably the CSSIP. Each Park evidenced forging of horizontal linkages previously observed in Shanghai (Hodder, 1990), but which were new due to contiguous location in this particular place.

The concentration within place of isolated tech parks forges its own unique connections in each development zone, even as new organizations form using job position and sector similarities. These neo-Marshallian nodes evidence outcomes observed elsewhere, as well as uniquely Chinese characteristics within the constraints of an evolving local system. Ultimately, the competition between profit-makers and distributional forces continues in many countries, from China's sporadically asserted central control to looser Western models with their own susceptibilities to economic undermining of the professedly more open political system. As this study demonstrates, different accommodations continue to be worked out across space and over time.

Note

The fieldwork conducted for this paper resulted from a Georgia State University Research Initiation Grant.

References

American Chamber of Commerce in Shanghai (1999) 1998–1999 Membership Directory. The American Chamber of Commerce in Shanghai, Shanghai.

Amin, A. and Thrift, N. (1992) 'Neo-Marshallian nodes in global networks'. *International Journal of Urban and RegionalResearch* 16, 571–587.

Anselin, L. (1997) 'Local geographic spillovers between university research and high tech innovations'. *Journal of Urban Economics* 42,422–448.

Applebaum, R. and J. Henderson (1992) *States and Development in the Asian Pacific Rim*. Newbury Park: Sage Publications.

Arnold, W. (1993) 'Japanese investment in China after Tiananmen: the case of Pudong special economic zone in Shanghai'. In G. Yu (ed.) *China inTransition*, Lantham, MD: University Press of America, Inc., 165–179.

Castells, M. (1992) 'Four Asian Tigers with a dragon head: a comparative analysis of the state, economy and society in the Asian Pacific Rim'. In R. Applebaum and J. Henderson. *States and Development in the Asian Pacific Rim*. Newbury Park: Sage Publications. 33–70.

Castells, M. and Hall, P. (1994) *Technopoles of the World: The Making of 21st Century Industrial Complexes*. London: Routledge.

Chesterton, Blumenauer and Binswanger, Industrial Services Division (1998) *Shanghai industrial park overview*. Shanghai: Unpublished document.

Dai, G. (10/22–28/90) 'Shanghai's Pudong project in full swing'. *Beijing Review* 33(43), 20–24.

Fung, K., Yan, Z. and Ning, Y. (1992) 'Shanghai: China's world city'. In Y. Yeung and X. Hu (eds) *China's Coastal Cities: Catalysts for Modernization*. Honolulu: University of Hawaii Press, 124–152.

Ge, W. (1990) 'Rules add to Pudong's appeal to investors'. *Beijing Review* 33, 16–19.

Gereffi, G., Korzeniewicz, M. and Korzeniewicz, R. (1994) 'Introduction: global commodity chains'. In Gereffi, G., M. Korzeniewicz and R. Korzeniewicz (eds) *Commodity Chains and Global Capitalism*. Westport, CN: Greenwood Press, 1–14.

Givant, N. (1991) 'Putting Pudong in Perspective'. *The China Business Review* 18, 30–32.

Gross, A. (1996) 'Asia's aging population creates opportunities for U.S. Firms'. *Medical Device and Diagnostic Industry Magazine* 12.

Halim, A., Lam, K., Chew, L. and Lee, G. (1996) 'The development of Pudong: implications and opportunities'. In T. Meng, L. Meng, J. Williams, C. Yong and Y. Shi (eds). *Business Opportunities in the Yangtze River Delta, China*. Nanyang Technological University, Singapore, 91–110.

Hayter, R. (1996) 'Research and development'. In P. Daniels and W. Lever (eds) *The Global Economy in Transition*. London: Addison Wesley Longman Ltd:164–190.

Hayter, R. and Han, S. (2000) 'Reflections on China's open policy towards foreign direct investment'. *Regional Studies* 32, 1–16.

Hodder, R. (1990) 'China's industry-horizontal linkages in Shanghai'. *Transactions of the Institute of British Geographers* 15, 487–503.

Jia, H. and Ward, R. (1998) 'Shanghai's frontier: Pudong new development area'. *The Geographical Bulletin* 40(1),11–21.

Khan, Z. (1991) *Patterns of Direct Foreign Investment in China*. Washington, D.C: The World Bank.

Kinoshita, J. (1995) 'Government focuses funds and hopes, on elite teams'. *Science* 270, 1137–1139.

Lee, Y.S. (1999) 'Labor shock and the diversity of transnational corporate strategy in export processing zones'. *Growth and Change* 30, 337–365.

Li, N. (1995) 'Pudong – full of hope'. *Beijing Review* 38, 10–14.

Luo, Y. (1998) *International Investment Strategies in the People's Republic of China*. Aldershot UK: Ashgate Publishing.

Malecki, E. and P. Oinas (eds) (1999) *Making Connections: Technological Learning Regional*

Economic Change. Aldershot, UK: Ashgate Publishing.

Malmberg, A., Solvell, O. and Zander, I. (1996) 'Spatial clustering, local accumulation of knowledge and firm competitiveness'. *Geografiska Annaler* 78 B, 85–97.

Markusen, A. (1997) 'Sticky places in slippery space: a typology of Industrial districts'. *Economic Geography*: 293–310.

Markusen, A., Lee, Y. and S. DiGiovanna (1999) 'Reflections on comparisons across countries'. In A. Markusen, Y. Lee, S. DiGiovanna (eds) *Second Tier Cities: Rapid Growth beyond the Metropolis*. Minneapolis: University of Minnesota Press. 335–358.

Murphey, R. (1988) 'Shanghai'. In M. Dogan and J. Kasarda (eds) *Mega-Cities*. Sage Publications, Newbury Park, CA, 157–183.

Ning, Y. and Yan, Z. (1995) 'The changing industrial and spatial structure in Shanghai'. *Urban Geography* 16, 577–594.

Olds, K. (1997) 'Globalizing Shanghai: the Global Intelligence Corps and the Building of Pudong', *Cities* 14, 109–123.

Organization for Economic Co-operation and Development (1987) *Science Parks and Technology Complexes in Relation to Regional Development*. OECD, Paris.

Organization for Economic Co-operation and Development (1996) *China in the 21st Century: Long-Term Global Implications*. OECD, Paris.

Park, S. (1996) 'Networks and embeddedness in the dynamic types of new industrial districts'. *Progress in Human Geography* 20(4), 476–493

Pearson, M. (1997) *China's New Business Elite: The Political Consequences of Economic Reform*. Berkeley, CA: University of California Press.

Plafker, T. (1994) 'Shanghai enlists scientists to foster economic growth'. *Science*, 265.

Radosevic, S. (1999) *International Technology Transfer and Catch-up in Economic Development*. Cheltenham, UK: Edward Elgar.

Rosen, D. (1999) *Behind the Open Door: Foreign Enterprises in the Chinese Market-place*. Washington, D.C.: Institute for International Economics.

Saywell, T. (9/10/98) 'High stakes: foreign venture capital spurs China's hi-tech start-ups'. *Far Eastern Economic Review* 161, 66–67.

Scott, A. (1999) 'Global city-regions and the new world system'. Paper presented at the Global conference on Economic Geography, Singapore.

Shanghai Committee on Foreign Economic Relations and Trade (1997) *Shanghai Foreign Economic Relations and Trade Yearbook*, Shanghai.

Shanghai Minhang United Development Co., Ltd. (1999) *Investment Guide: Shanghai Minhang Economic and Technological Development Zone 1998–1999*. Shanghai.

Shanghai *Statistical Abstract of Science and Industry (1998)* Shanghai: Shanghai Statistical Publishing House.

She, Z., Xu, G. and Linge, G. (1997) 'The head and tail of the dragon: Shanghai and its economic hinterland'. In G. Linge (ed.) *China's New Spatial Economy: Heading Towards 2020*. NY: Oxford University Press, 98–122.

State Statistical Bureau, People's Republic of China (1998) *China Statistical Yearbook, Series 17,(17)*. China Statistical Publishing House, Beijing.

Statistical Yearbook of Shanghai Pudong New Area (1998) Shanghai Statistical Publishing House, Shanghai.

Tan, C., Chong, C. and Tan, K. (1996) 'Shanghai's economic and trade zones'. In T.T. Meng, J. Williams, C. Yong and Y. Shi (eds) *Business Opportunities in the Chang Jiang River Delta, China*. Nanyang Technological University Singapore, 73–90.

Tian, G. (1996) *Shanghai's Role in the Economic Development of China: Reform of Foreign Trade and Investment*. Westport CN: Praeger Publishers.

United States Commercial Service (1999) *Best prospects/ Industry* overview: Pharmaceuticals. International Trade Administration, U.S. Department of Commerce.

Walcott, S. and Xiao, W. (2001) 'High-tech parks and development zones in metropolitan

Shanghai: From the industrial to the information age'. *Asian Geographer* forthcoming.

Wang, J.C. (1999) 'In search of innovativeness: the case of Zhong'guancun'. In E. Malecki and P. Oinas (eds) *Making Connections: Technological learning and regional economic change.* Aldershot, UK: Ashgate Publishing.

Wang, J.C. and J.X. (1998) 'An analysis of new-tech agglomeration in Beijing: a new industrial district in the making?'. *Environment and Planning A* 30, 681–701.

Wang, N. (1984) *China's Modernization and Transnational Corporations.* Lexington, MA:D.C. Heath & Co.

Wang, S., Woo, Y. and Y. Li. (1998) 'Development of technopoles in China'. *Asia Pacific Viewpoint* 39, 281–301.

Weidenbaum, M. and Hughes, S. (1996) *The Bamboo Network: How Expatriate Chinese Entrepreneurs Are Creating a New Economic Superpower in Asia.* NY: The Free Press.

Yeoh, B. (1999) 'Global/globalizing cities'. *Progress in Human Geography* 23(4), 607–616.

Yeung, H. (1997) 'Business networks and transnational corporations: a study of Hong Kong firms in the ASEAN Region'. *Economic Geography* 73, 1–25.

Young, S. and Ping, L. (1997) 'Technology transfer to China through foreign direct investment'. *Regional Studies* 31 (7), 669–679.

Chapter 8

The State and Globalization of Labor: Labor Export and Import in Taiwan's Economic Restructuring and Development

Johnathan Walker

Introduction

Taiwan has operated as an independent country and economy since the Nationalist Kuomingtang party fled the Chinese mainland and the revolution led by MaoTse-tung in 1949. The ensuing takeover of administration of Taiwan by the Nationalists led to structural changes in land reform, an economic policy of import substitution industrialization and today's status as an export giant. For many decades, the development of the island has been strongly engineered by the state via policies of investment and promotion of research and development, which ensured rapid and continuous economic growth (Li, 1995). As Taiwan's formidable export economy thrived, employment steadily shifted into the service sector. In the 1980s, employment shifts into service jobs and away from production left factories short of labor and motivated them to seek out alternative sources of labor. By and large, this took the form of international laborers posing as tourists who were then ushered into factories to fill job vacancies.

This chapter is used to review Taiwan's labor import policy (subsequently, LIP), which was spawned by and, in turn, contributed to structural changes in the country's economy. The discussion charts the policy's inception, through several stages in its implementation and into its present form and focus. Much of the information used in the discussion is obtained from newspaper reports and personal interviews of some of the important actors in the formulation and implementation of the program

Foreign Workers in Taiwan's Restructuring and Development

Structural shifts, from an overwhelmingly dominant industrial economy into services, created simultaneous employment shifts in Taiwan. The problem was exacerbated, in part, by the refusal of Taiwanese workers to accept jobs in which wages were low and health and safety conditions were deplorable (*China Post*, January 4, 1989; *China Post*, June 3, 1989). Manufacturing and construction, the two sectors most severely affected by the labor shortage, reacted by adopting a strategy of illegally hiring workers who were smuggled into Taiwan as tourists from neighboring countries (Selya, 1992). The Labor and travel agents who arranged the important keys to success coordinated the illegal process: a willing employer and a willing worker (*China News*, December 9, 1988). After several years of clandestine labor immigration to Taiwan from neighboring countries in Southeast and South Asia, the Taiwanese government recognized its inability to stop the process completely and acknowledged the need for policy to legalize and regulate the flow of laborers to meet the demands of factory and construction firms (*China Post*, August 11, 1989).

Many of the characteristics of Taiwan's labor importation mirror Sassen's (1988) analysis of the use of foreign workers in production. The use of alien laborers in Taiwan was, originally, a response to what was characterized locally as a chronic shortage of local workers, deemed unlikely to be made up in the short or long term. From the 1980s to the 1990s, Taiwan's unemployment rate was very low, reaching 1.5% in the mid 1990s (DGBAS, 1999). This quasi-full employment regime, in combination with higher levels of education for both males and females, had a significant impact on the labor market. In particular, it resulted in labor shifts from the industries that had created the Taiwan Miracle (low level manufacturing jobs), to employment that was cleaner, less physically demanding and fitting the changing composition of the society. The most seriously hit industries were construction and manufacturing, two sectors historically reliant on women and workers with low levels of education. These jobs are classified in Taiwan as the A3K Industries: jobs that are dirty, difficult and/or demanding. Taiwan's Council of Labor Affairs (CLA) Chairman Chao Shou-po strongly criticized the rejection and abandonment of these traditional jobs that meant so much to Taiwan's historical development and even suggested that the failure of local workers to follow tradition patterns of employment was unpatriotic. He noted that too many people now prefer to sit in an office '...but right now, the development of our construction and manufacturing industries is more important' (*China Post*, September 28, 1990: 12). Besides structural changes in the economy, another important explanation for labor shortages in construction and manufacturing was the unwillingness of employers in these two sectors to raise wages and benefits to attract and maintain a stable work force. Foreign workers who were allowed entrance during the first few years of LIP were targeted for these two sectors whose work conditions had ceased to attract local labor.

Prior to LIP in 1989, official statistics placed labor deficits in the construction industry at 120,000 workers (*China Post*, March 24, 1989). This high labor demand was the outcome of several important factors. First was demand generated by Taiwan's ambitious plans for infrastructure development, which included large scale, extensive projects like an additional national freeway and other major freeways to serve a population that was becoming more auto-oriented. New freeways were viewed as an economic necessity to establish better connections between production facilities and transfer and shipping points, which served the export sector, Taiwan's life blood (*China Post*, June 12, 1989). Other major infrastructure projects identified the need for urban rapid mass-transit systems that would ease traffic congestion, especially in Taipei. The demand for construction labor was increased by the two additional factors: Taipei's pre-existing urban density constrained the development of highway and transit systems either to underground locations or raised over mountainous terrain between factories and ports. The overwhelming labor demand was spurred also by the need for the construction of large-scale government housing projects that dotted locations all around the capital.

Concerns over the international competitiveness of the manufacturing sector gave impetus to a major push for the legalization and expanded use of alien workers in Taiwan. The country's Ministry of Economic Affairs (MOEA), in supporting LIP, calculated that lower labor costs would translate into lower production costs and an increased global market shares. Local manufacturers were openly supportive of the MOEA initiative. Their long-term concern was that a tight labor market that remained closed would induce labor disputes resulting in wage increases that will undermine their individual competitiveness and reduce Taiwan's international competitiveness (*China Post*, August 27, 1987).

An additional factor driving the state's involvement in labor import was recognition that capital was being drained from the local economy and invested abroad. LIP was seen as a strategy, which would provide employers with stable labor supply at fixed rates, thereby, providing capital with an option to local de-industrialization and reinvestment overseas. As former CLA Chairman Chao Shou-po observed, '...in a sense, the importation of foreign workers helps our local workers retain their jobs because I used to say that if this employer needs 100 workers in order to [run his] company, but he can only find 60 workers, [then] without the other forty workers he would not be able to keep his company running, so that means sixty workers lose their jobs' (Interview with Chao Shou-po, March 9, 1998).

Foreign workers have had a significant impact on Taiwanese production. Over the course of LIP, more than 1,000,000 foreign workers have been legally employed. Although the labor importation started slowly, by the end of 1997, more than 250,000 foreign workers were employed locally in Taiwan, accounting for nearly 3% of the overall labor force (*China News*, December 28, 1997). At the end of 1998 the number of foreign workers in Taiwan was above 270,000 laborers (Feliciano, 1999a).

The Role of the State in Labor Importation (Demand Side)

One of the motivations for LIP was to retain local capital. As was noted earlier, the threat of de-industrialization was seen as legitimate because of the magnitude of capital flight to mainland China and other destinations in Southeast Asia, including the main suppliers of labor to Taiwan, Thailand, the Philippines and Indonesia (Feliciano, 1999b; 1997c; Davies, 1997). There were concerns by the government that pronounced labor shortages would lead to even more serious capital flight (Tsay, 1994). Although LIP did not completely stave off local capital flight (Taiwanese investments were the seventh largest in the Philippines, sixth in Indonesia and third in Thailand), former CLA Chairman Chao, believes that without LIP, the de-industrialization of Taiwan would have been much more severe.

Under LIP, companies are allowed an unlimited number of imported workers to be employed in facilities in which they invested at least 200 million New Taiwan dollars (approximately US$6 million). This provision, to which I refer as the investment clause (IC), reflects the state's goal to keep manufacturing viable while the economy shifts into services. The IC induces local companies to maintain their investments in Taiwan, which already has the advantages of political and economic stability not experienced in many other countries in the region. Second, Taiwan's status as an export giant is preserved through established and new investments brought on by investor confidence in a stable work force. On the other hand, LIP has created rifts between foreign and local workers and between established foreign workers and recent arrivals. Employers have been known to exploit these differences to their own best advantage by using members from different camps to *discipline*[1] others when there is a potential for labor action against company impropriety and foreign worker contract violations.

The security offered by a readily available work force that is tied to foreign direct investment has been important to Taiwan's recent economic restructuring and the flexibility of LIP works to the advantage of capital much like similar policies employed in the 1960's by European states (Leitner, 1986). Like local capital, transnational companies have taken advantage of the IC to expand production. New production facilities have been established, especially in electronics. According to Taiwan's Industrial Development Bureau, 58% of all foreign workers employed in manufacturing at the beginning of 1999 worked in the electronics industry (*China News*, January 14, 1999). One of the largest employers is the Dutch electronics giant Philips, the largest foreign firm in Taiwan (Feliciano, 1997a). The growth of Philips in Taiwan is tied, in part, to its ability to hire foreign workers in its six factories. By 1998 Philips was employing 12,000 workers and turning over NT$150 billion in sales, most of it on product exports. In 1999 Philips announced plans to invest another NT$4 billion into upgrading and expanding capacity while also moving to cut its Taiwan workforce from 12,000 to 10,000 many of whom were foreign workers (Feliciano, 1999b). However, because of its huge investments in the country, the company has license to import more workers in the future. In addition, local electronics giants like Acer, Quanta and others all employ large numbers of foreign workers (*China News*, January 14, 1999). The LIP, therefore, bridges the gap between Taiwan's national labor composition and its production needs as its economy makes the transition from secondary to tertiary and quaternary production.

Units of the Taiwanese state were also important players in the formulation of the LIP. Taiwan's Communications Minister Kou Nan-hung spoke out about delays in the country's progress to improve the national infrastructure (e.g., the second national freeway), citing an acute labor shortage as the primary reason. Taiwan's director for public housing offered his opinion that the addition of foreign workers would reduce backlogs in demand (*China News*, December 7, 1989), while Taipei City government's Department of Rapid Transit Systems championed contractors' use of foreign workers in Taipei's new subway system (*China Post*, January 20, 1990). Officials from the Taiwan government's economic think-tank, the Council for Economic Planning and Development (CEPD), also took a stand in favor of importing labor. In addition to these government departments, the promotional arm of Taiwan's economic development structure, CETRA, collected data that confirmed that the labor shortage was not local or sectoral, but was a problem of national proportions (*China News*, July 28, 1989)

The LIP has been beneficial in maintaining economic productivity in the Taiwanese economy. In the initial phases of the policy, 40% of textile and construction firms reported worker productivity increases (Feliciano, 1996). As more foreign workers are employed in electronics industry, productivity gains are also likely in that industry.

Unfortunately, the Asian economic crisis has showed the vulnerability of all workers including foreign workers to economic downturns. As a result of the crisis, 5,300 companies closed down in Taiwan in 1998 and numerous others downsized in response to the lag effects of the crisis. These downsizing events deeply affected foreign workers in the form of forced vacations, contract terminations and involuntary repatriation (Lin, 1999). In many cases, workers who were employed on two-year contracts (with the belief that they would be eligible for a third year) had their contracts terminated. The Asian economic crisis showed the convenience with which the state or capital can dispatch foreign workers and the labor insecurity that may be associated with a program like LIP.

Economic benefits to labor exporters arrive in multiple forms. First and foremost are the earnings derived by the state from funds repatriated by overseas workers (Amery and Anderson, 1995). The benefits of remittances are widely recognized and strongly desired by government officials from labor exporting countries (Athukorala, 1990). The three countries that are major labor exporters to Taiwan, Thailand, the Philippines and Indonesia, share common problems of unemployment and underemployment, nominal levels of GNP and monumental foreign debt. All three, especially Thailand, have engaged in government-sponsored efforts to create international employment for their citizens (*China News*, January 7, 1998; Huguet, 1995; Chalamwong, 1998; Bohning, 1998; Ananta, *et al.*, 1998).

Although efforts to export labor were in place before the devastating impact of the Asian economic crisis, the Thai foreign ministry and national employment and labor offices have combined forces to find global employment for unemployed Thai workers and enhance the flow of remittances back into the depressed national economy. Thailand's Ministry of Labor have joined forces with the Foreign Ministry to contact international embassies and consulates to seek out jobs for Thai workers left unemployed by the crisis. Taiwan was targeted by this policy because it has the largest number of overseas Thai workers. Reflecting on the Labor Ministry policy, Pranee Sukkri, the Thai labor representative in Taipei commented, '...It's just routine work. It's a part of the job.' She added, '...Of course, the policy is, as we have the financial crisis, we're trying our best to get the people to come to work in [a] foreign country to earn more money for a better life, a better income and of course, the foreign currency' (Interview with Ms. Pranee Sukkri, March 6, 1998).

Remittances are crucial to the economic stability of the Philippines. In a visit to Taipei in 1997, Gabriel Singson, the Governor of the Central Bank of the Philippines, made the following observation, 'Last year we had a very big trade deficit, with our imports exceeding our exports by US$11.5 billion. But with the remittances of our OFWs (Overseas Foreign Workers), our deficit went down to just over US$ three billion' (Feliciano, 1997b). These types of announcements are now a common part of the discourse used by nearly all government officials when referring to Filipino overseas workers. Overseas workers are praised by the government as the country's new heroes and, more recently, unsung heroes. This official position is not surprising given the general consensus that remittances account for about 5% of the national GNP of the Philippines (*China News*, January 3, 1998).

Indonesia was as hard hit by the Asian financial crisis and, like Thailand, it too had practised and benefited from labor exports prior to the crisis (ILO, 1998; Nayyar, 1997). So important is this source of revenue that it has been included as projected income in the country's five-year development plan (Nayyar, 1997). Labor exports from Indonesia have grown steadily through the 1990s to long-standing international destinations in the Middle East, but also expanding rapidly to Taiwan. Increasing labor exports have translated into increased remittances to an Indonesian economy crippled by international debt and a crisis-induced radically devalued currency.

The State and the Globalization of Labor: Some Conceptual Issues

In addition to remittances, international migration theory suggests that labor migration creates a spatial vent (Samers, 1998). Following Harvey's (1982) notion of capital employing a spatial fix to extricate itself from lower rates of profit, Samers (1998) views immigration policy and especially the export of labor, as a 'spatial vent'. This spatial vent is described as the encouraged or forced relocation of labor employed by the state to overcome political friction and serve as a strategy for crisis resolution. In the states that export labor to Taiwan, the crisis balances on two important needs: the need for foreign exchange to reduce crises associated with foreign debt and trade imbalances; and the need to implement the spatial vent in a political sense by allaying potential political crises surrounding job dissatisfaction, unemployment, underemployment and chronic poverty.

Herod's (1997) recognition of the necessary theorization of labor's part in the production of space and power is also important here. The export of labor creates what could be deemed as a special economic zone for those countries evoking such a policy. However, this zone bears no likeness to actual export processing zones where taxes for investors are suspended and infrastructures are customized to export production. Rather, it provides the labor exporting state with an expanded area of accumulation. Since labor exports do not require the elaborate infrastructural support of an export-processing zone, the benefits accruing from them are collected with a minimum amount of investment by the state while the migrating worker abroad shoulders any risks.

The process of globalizing labor necessarily involves the state (Ball, 1997). At the most fundamental legal level international labor migration must be formalized through agreements by the participating states. The supplying states must, therefore, have a politically-negotiated understanding with the destinations. Taiwan's legalization of laborers originally included workers from only four states, Indonesia, Malaysia, the Philippines and Thailand, chosen because their citizens already formed an important component of the Taiwanese labor force, they enjoyed good relations with Taiwan and each had semi-official labor offices in Taiwan. They were also chosen because of their perceived empathy (or lack of enmity) toward Taiwan's precarious political existence. Workers from these four countries were not the only alien labor in Taiwan prior to LIP. India, Pakistan, Sri Lanka and Burma also had substantial numbers of workers in the country. However these states were not included in the final list for LIP because, as former CLA Chairman Chao remarked, 'the governments of these countries are quite hostile to us' (Interview with Chao Shou-po, March 9, 1998).

State Policy as Spatial Vent

Initially, contacts between countries seeking to export labor and Taiwan were generated by state representatives. Thailand and the Philippines were especially aggressive in their efforts to obtain legal work status for their citizens. In recalling the activities of the time, CLA Chairman Chao admitted that he had been lobbied hard. 'Well, they are trying to [have discussions with Taiwan] particularly officials from Thailand and also from the Philippines.' Chao further commented that 'they [Thai and Filipino officials] are very eager and they worked quite hard trying to persuade us to open our job market for their people' (Interview with Chao Shou-po, March 9, 1998).

Even though workers from four different states are employed in Taiwan under LIP, only two governments, Thailand and the Philippines, actively provide support for their citizens during their stay in Taiwan. Such support has been necessary especially in response to perceived mistreatment of workers or the believed failure of the Taiwan authorities to enforce contracts or local labor laws. On one occasion before LIP, the Thai government issued a warning to Taiwan to end mistreatment and discrimination against Thai workers employed in factories or else the Thai government would respond by suspending work permits for Taiwan nationals in Thailand (*China Post*, March 16, 1989). In another confrontation about a year later over the prolonged presence of illegal Thai workers in Taiwan and Taiwan's threat to oust them, Thai officials issued a similar warning to Taiwan investment (*China Post*, December 21, 1990).

In anticipation of LIP, the Filipino government sent an eight-member congressional delegation to meet with CLA Chairman Chao in hopes of convincing him to approve Filipino laborers in any labor importation policy (*China News*, March 25, 1989). Later, in order to generate interest in the program, the Philippine state-run television ran reports that Filipinos working in Taiwan could earn salaries of US\$ 1,000 per month for only 3–4 hours daily work (*China Post*, October 20, 1989).

Taiwan's attempts to rid the island of illegal workers before the formal labor policy was to be instituted were also met by strong reactions from Malaysian, Thai and Indonesian officials. They pressured Taiwanese investors in their countries to lobby the Taiwan government against repatriation of illegal workers (*China Post*, April 6, 1989), sending a clear message to Taipei that the international labor policy was as well a matter of economic survival as national security (*China Post*, April 6, 1989).

State officials and state-supported offices from both Thailand and the Philippines provide the structural base for the export of their nationals. Both countries maintain labor offices in Taiwan to aid in the exportation/importation process and to perform on-site promotional duties in support of retention and expansion of jobs for their nationals. The Thai Labor Office occupies a suite and employs about 10 workers to facilitate the entrance and employment of more than 100,000 Thai workers annually. The office is occupied by a Thai labor representative appointed to manage daily affairs, develop economic contacts with potential employers and to keep political contacts with Taiwan officials (Interview with Pranee Sukkri, March 6, 1998).

The Philippine Labor Center occupies a suite within the Manila Economic and Cultural Office (MECO), the Philippines' de facto embassy in Taipei. The Philippine Labor Center in Taipei employs about 15 people to carry out requests for workers and to settle disputes for the more than 100,000-strong Filipino worker community in Taiwan. Besides this institutional support in Taipei, two other labor centers are located in Taiwan's other major cities, Taichung (central Taiwan) and Kaohsiung (southern Taiwan) to service Taiwan companies' demands for Filipino workers as well as to respond to inquiries by the workers. Each office includes a labor representative, usually a labor lawyer and the Taipei office includes a local representative of the Philippine Overseas Workers Welfare Administration (OWWA) who is appointed to attend to complaints lodged by and against workers.

Although Indonesia now represents the third largest supplier of labor to Taiwan, it does not employ any state labor officials in Taipei, even though an institution of this nature does exist in Indonesia. Indonesian workers in Taiwan depend on labor brokers to intercede on their behalf when they have problems concerning working conditions or contracts. Unfortunately, the first allegiance of most labor brokers is with the employers. In 1999, Vietnam was added to the list of states approved to export labor to Taiwan (Feliciano, 1999c) after Vietnamese labor officials, seeking to secure employment in the construction and manufacturing sectors for their nationals, traveled to Taiwan and met with Taiwan labor officials (*China News*, June 19, 1999). While approval was granted, initial entry of Vietnamese labor came primarily in the form of female domestic servants, not as construction workers.

The labor offices set up by the Thai and Filipino states represent tangible extensions of state power from the home country to the global labor market. States involved in the export of labor for national benefit do so in the absence of local/national opportunities to provide full and gainful employment for their citizens – a spatial vent strategy to reduce the potential for political unrest and economic crisis. The response by labor exporting countries to the Asian economic crisis that began in 1997 showed the value of international labor migrants to national economies. As noted above, Thailand's Ministry of Labor made the unusual move of joining forces with the Foreign Ministry to create jobs for Thai workers overseas. Thailand's labor representative in Taiwan, Ms. Sukkri explained however that since Taiwan was the primary destination for Thai workers the labor department's efforts were directed at other, potential destinations. Indeed, the Thai National Labor Committee's plan contained the following labor supply targets: Taiwan (122,000 workers), Brunei (22,000), Singapore (19,000), Israel (12,000), Japan (9,200), Malaysia (8,200), Hong Kong (7,600), Middle Eastern countries (5,100), South Korea, Australia and New Zealand (2,000 workers each) as sites for expansion (*China News*, January 23, 1998).

Efforts by Philippine representatives are framed differently, but in essence achieve the same result. Philippine labor representatives were instrumental in Taiwan's approval of the Philippines as a source for legal labor imports and the promotion of Filipino labor in many different capacities. Visits from the (then) Philippine Labor Secretary Torres in 1990, an eight-member delegation in 1991 and visits by the Philippine Labor Secretary Confesor, Labor Undersecretary Brillantes and Philippine Overseas Employment Administration (POEA) Director Joson in 1992, all provided support for two main issues: amnesty for illegal Filipinos still working in Taiwan and promotion of Filipinos so that more could work in Taiwan. CLA Chairman Chao remarked in 1993 that '...a large number of ranking Philippine officials have come to Taipei to try to secure for Filipino workers access to the labor market here' (*China News*, January 13, 1993). Torres, in his visit in 1990, is reported to have indicated that promotion of Filipino labor overseas was part of a government strategy to improve national economic, social and employment problems (*China Post*, December 3, 1990). In the past few years, however, official public statements by Philippine representatives have argued that the state *does not* encourage Filipinos to work abroad. Unfortunately for these officials the weight of evidence counters these claims. The continued existence of the Philippine Overseas Employment Administration, the foreign arm of the Department of Labor and Employment is sufficient evidence that workers are still encouraged – albeit in more nuanced ways – to work overseas. In Taiwan, official institutional support is lent to a number of annual celebrations and worker tributes sponsored by the Manila Economic and Cultural Office (MECO) in Taipei, Taichung and Kaohsiung. Such celebrations have become more frequent with large gatherings organized on Christmas, Easter, Philippine Independence Day, Mother's Day and a number of other significant Philippine holidays. These events symbolize the state's interrelated involvement as an instrument of institutional protection and simultaneous promotion and public relations.

Conclusions

I have argued in this chapter that the Third World state in Asia plays a central role in the globalization of labor. Although state actions that actively promote labor export benefit migrant workers, the major beneficiaries of this process are the exporting states and global capital at the destination. This is evidenced in Taiwan where the availability of cheap migrant workers has enabled the economy to maintain its manufacturing base while making the transition to services. The organizational efficiency of globalization forces are reflected in their ability to make it possible for the Taiwanese state to exploit a globalized labor pool while making it equally possible for the exporting countries to utilize the presence of global capital to generate national income. The assistance of the state is central to these processes. This is another tribute to the organizational power of globalization – its ability to manipulate the state to make foot-loose those factors of production which yet have to become as mobile as capital.

The globalization of labor, both from the labor export and import standpoints, is key to understanding contemporary challenges to Third World countries. A proper and comprehensive understanding of the multiple modes of economic globalization is central to this challenge. The role of alien labor in economic restructuring and development provides direction for the role of labor geographies in twenty-first century economic globalization.

Note

1. The process of disciplining workers does not refer to doing them bodily harm, but (following the work of Foucault, 1995) rather taught them that any complaint about poor working conditions or work contract violations lodged with government authorities or labor brokers would be *disciplined* by swift cancellation of their work contracts and deportation.

References

Amery, H. and Anderson, W. (1995) 'International Migration and Remittances to a Lebanese Village'. *Canadian Geographer* 39 (1), 46–58.

Ananta, Aris and Kartowibowo, D. and Wiyono, C. (1998) 'The Impact of the Economic Crisis on International Migration: The Case of Thailand'. *Asian and Pacific Migration Journal* 7 (2–3), 313–338.

Athukorala, P. (1990) 'International Contract Migration and the Reintegration Of Return Migrants: The Experience of Sri Lanka'. *IMR* 24 (2), 323–346.

Ball, R. (1997) 'The role of the state in the globalisation of labour markets: the case of the Philippines'. *Environment and Planning A*, 29, 1603–1628.

Bohning, W.R. (1998) 'Conceptualizing and Simulating the Impact of the Asian Crisis on Filipinos' Employment Opportunities Abroad'. *Asian and Pacific Migration Journal* 7 (2–3), 339–368.

Chalamwong, Y. (1998) 'The Impact of the Crisis on Migration in Thailand'. *Asian and Pacific Migration Journal* 7 (2–3), 297–312.

China News, December 9, 1988, 'Broker Reveals Details About ForeignWorkers', p.11.

China News, March 25, 1989, 'Council Denies Allowing Foreign Laborers', p.12.

China News, July 28, 1989, 'Most companies want legalized alien workers', p.12.

China News, December 7, 1989, 'Foreign laborers to help construct publichousing', p.12.

China News, January 13, 1993, 'CLA threatens to end ROC-Manila agreement on import of workers', p.1.

China News, December 28, 1997, '25% of foreign workers abscond', p.2.

China News, January 3, 1998, 'Filipino remittances 5% of GNP', p.15.

China News, January 7, 1998, 'Thailand to send home alien workers', p.5.

China News, January 23, 1998, 'Thai laborers expected', p.2.

China News, January 14, 1999, 'Electronics industry has most foreigners', p.2.

China News, June 19, 1999, 'Hanoi envoys to arrive for labor talks', p.3.

China Post, August 27, 1987, 'Gov't rejects call to import alien workers', p.12.

China Post, January 4, 1989, 'Protest against illegal aliens planned by Taoyuan labor group', p.12.

China Post, March 16, 1989, 'Thailand may stop issuing work permits for locals', p.12.

China Post, March 24, 1989, 'CEPD hints at legalization of foreign labor', p.15.

China Post, April 6, 1989, 'S.E. Asian nations show concern over alien worker policy', p.6.

China Post, June 3, 1989, 'Construction labor unions object to importation of foreign laborers', p.6.

China Post, June 12, 1989, 'CEPD to allow foreign construction workers', p.6.

China Post, August 11, 1989, 'Hiring of foreign laborers to be legalized, taxed', p.6.

China Post, October 20, 1989, '70,000 Filipinos work illegally in Taiwan', p.6.

China Post, January 20, 1990, 'Legal foreign workers expected here by April', p.6.

China Post, September 28, 1990, 'Siew plans gov't help for textile companies', p.12.

China Post, December 3, 1990, 'Philippine workers suggested to remedy local labor shortage', p.12.

China Post, December 21, 1990, 'Thailand may stop giving work permits', p.16.

Council of Labor Affairs (2000) *Monthly Bulletin of Labor Statistics, Taiwan Area, Republic of China*, January, Taipei: Executive Yuan.

Davies, C. (1997) 'Taiwan aids Indonesian development', *China News*, August 21, p.10.

Directorate-General of Business Accounting and Statistics (DGBAS) (1999), *Taiwan Statistical Data Book*, Taipei: Council of Economic Planning and Development.

Feliciano, M. (1996) 'Foreign workers boost productivity, CLA report shows'. *China News*, October 4, p.5.

Feliciano, M. (1997a) 'Philips aiming for NT$1Billion in turnover'. *China News*. January 1, p.7.

Feliciano, M. (1997b) 'APNB opens Taipei office'. *China News*. July 16, p.9

Feliciano, M. (1999a) 'Philippine office gets down to business'. *China News*. March 14, p.13.

Feliciano, M. (1999b) 'Philips to invest NT$4b'. *China News*. April 1, 1999, p.7.

Feliciano, M. (1999c) 'CLA approves recruitment of workers from Vietnam'. *China News*. August 24, p.3.

Foucault, M. (1995) *Discipline and Punish: The birth of the prison*. NY: Vintage.

Harvey, D. (1982) *The Limits to Capital*. London: Blackwell.

Herod, A. (1997) 'From a Geography of Labor to a Labor Geography: Labor's spatial fix and the geography of capitalism'. *Antipode* 29 (1), 1–31.

Herod, A., O' Tuathail, G. and Roberts, S. (eds) (1998) *An unruly world?: globalization, governance and geography*. London; NY: Routledge.

Huguet, J. (1995) 'Data on International Migration in Asia: 1990–1994'. *Asian and Pacific Migration Journal* 4 (4), 519–529.

International Labor Organization (ILO) (1998) *ILO in Indonesia*. Djakarta: International Labor Organization.

Leitner, H. (1986) 'The state and the foreign worker problem. A case study of the Federal Republic of Germany, Switzerland and Austria'. *Environment and Planning C: Government and Policy* 4, 199–219.

Li, K.T. (ed.) (1995) *The Evolution of Policy Behind Taiwan's Development Success*, Singapore; River Edge, N.J.: World Scientific (second edition).

Lin, C. (1999) 'Migrants excluded from employment insurance program'. *China News*. April 11, p.13.

Nayyar, D. (1997) 'Emigration pressures and structural change: Case study of Indonesia'. *International Migration Papers* 20. Geneva: ILO, Employment and Training Department.

Samers, M. (1998) 'Maghreb Immigration, France and the Political Economy of the Spatial Vent'. In A. Herod, G. Tuathail and S. Roberts (eds) *An unruly world?: globalization, governance and geography*. London: Routledge, 196–218

Sassen, S. (1988) *The mobility of labor and capital: a study in international investment and labor flow*. Cambridge, England: Cambridge University Press.

Selya, R. (1992) 'Illegal Migration in Taiwan: A Preliminary Overview'. *IMR* 26(3), 787–805.

Tsay, C–L. (1994) 'Labor recruitment in Taiwan: a corporate strategy in industrial restructuring'. *Environment and Planning*, 26, 583–607.

Chapter 9

Trade Liberalization and Economic Development in Mexico: A Case for Globalization?

Carlos Rozo

Introduction

Mexico's foreign debt crisis of the 1980s obliged the government to restructure the country's economy and adopt the export promotion model to attract global capital. This policy required structural changes through market liberalization to create a more integrated and balanced economy that would be responsive to international competition. The centerpiece of this policy consisted of strategies to exploit Mexico's comparative advantage in labor and natural resources and to make more efficient use of its physical and financial resources. Adoption of the export-led development policy was based on orthodox notions that free trade pushes an economy towards higher levels of performance and economic output, that imported technology will improve productivity and that international competition will make local companies more efficient (Dornbusch, 1992; Baldwin and Forslid, 1996; Harrison, 1996; Feenstra and Rose, 1997). Using various indicators of liberalization and classifying countries according to a number of criteria, Sachs and Warner (1995) argue that countries that were open had grown at rates of 4.5% annually in the 1970s and 1980s while countries that were closed barely managed to grow at a rate of 0.7%.

Studies of the impact of liberalization on economic performance often use aggregate time series data for a number of countries. This methodology produces results with questionable generalizability. Rodrik and Rodriquez (1999) have argued that defenders of free trade should seek support for their position by using disaggregated data for specific countries over a specific period of time. *The Economist* (July 1999, p. 68) maintains that empirical evidence supports the position that free trade is good for economic growth, but suggests that this relationship could be established more convincingly with use of techniques which ask 'people in those countries which have successfully opened their economies during the past 20 years if their life has improved since then'.

The objective of this chapter is to use the Mexican experience to examine the relationship between economic growth and economic liberalization. The discussion is conducted in three sections. The first section makes the case that the export-led growth model works to the extent that Mexico has become one of the main exporting countries in the world and one of the largest recipients of foreign capital. The next section is used to argue that despite its ability to attract foreign capital, the export model has not resulted in higher levels of economic growth. The final section makes the case that the negative impacts of export-led development include structural polarization, which has serious implications, especially for poverty.

Positive Outcomes of the Export-Led Model

Accelerated market liberalization in Mexico in the 1980s involved the removal of customs barriers and others restrictions that had protected national industries. This policy shift obtained the results desired by the last three governments of the country During the government of Miguel De La Madrid (1983–1988), exports not related to oil grew from 6,295 to 13,854 billion USD,[1] reaching 27,168 billion USD at the end of 1994 during the government of Salinas de Gortari (a growth of 450% with an annual average of 9,397 billion USD during the first government and of 19,963 billion USD during the second government). Even more satisfactory was the growth of 525% achieved by manufacturing exports during these 12 years (although much of this occurred during the first government). The rate of growth of non-petroleum exports decreased also by 50% in the period between the De La Madrid and Salinas administrations. However, the annual average level of manufacturing exports during the Salinas government was 136% higher than the one reached during the De La Madrid administration, (growing from 7,284 to 17,212 billion USD). Nonetheless, the relation between exports and Gross National Product (GNP) only increased from 13.8% to 15.2% between 1988 and 1994.

During the first four years of the Ernesto Zedillo government, exports accelerated again, with non-petroleum exports increasing by 116.5% (an average annual increase of 49.7 billion USD) and manufacturing by 120% (45.8 billion USD). As a result of its outstanding performance, while manufacturing accounted for only 20% of exports (4.5 billion USD) in 1983, it accounted for 82% (53.1 billion USD) in 1998 When the *Maquila* industrial output of 52.9 billion USD is factored into this performance, total Mexican manufacturing exports in 1998 were 117.5 billion USD, making Mexico one of the largest exporting countries in the world (Banco de Mexico, 1999). The success of liberalization hinged on its ability to attract massive amounts of foreign investments (considered one of the successes of the Salinas regime). Between 1989 and 1994 Mexico received 97.2 billion USD in foreign capital (an annual average of 16.2 billion USD), seven times greater than the 13.6 billion USD obtained under the previous government (Nafinsa, 1995; Buffie, 1992). This flow was an exceptional achievement, not only because of its volume, but also because of the change in its composition. Before 1988, foreign investments in Mexico went directly to the production of goods and services. In 1998, foreign capital began to flow as portfolio investment, orientated towards capital and money markets through the demand of government assets or company equity (Table 9.1). During the Salinas administration an annual average of only 28% of total foreign investment entered the country as direct investment (a decrease from 100% to 13% between 1989 and 1993). By contrast, foreign portfolio investments reached their maximum level of 87% of the total in 1993 (compared to 0% in 1988).

Foreign investments continued to flow into Mexico during the first four years of the Zedillo administration, reaching 52.1 billion USD (an annual average of 13.1 billion USD). Although this flow is smaller than the average reached during the previous government, it continued to be concentrated in direct investment. After the massive outflow of capital in 1995, as a consequence of the *Tequila Effect*, the influx of portfolio capital has continuously decreased, representing only 11% of the total in 1998.

Table 9.1 Foreign Investments: 1989–1998 (million USD)

Year	Direct	Portfolio	Total
1989	3,175.5	493.3	3,668.8
1990	2,633.2	1,994.5	4,627.7
1991	4,761.5	12,742.5	17,504.0
1992	4,392.8	18,041.0	22,433.8
1993	4,388.8	28,919.3	33,308.1
1994	10,972.5	8,182.2	19,154.7
1995	9,772.5	9,714.7	57.8
1996	9,185.5	13,418.5	22,604.0
1997	12,829.6	5,037.1	17,866.6
1998	10,237.5	1,292.8	11,530.4
1999*	8,424.9	11,226.9	19,651.8

*January to September

Source: Elaborado con datos de Banca de Mexico, Incadores Economica

The indicators of export growth and capital inflows would suggest that the liberalization strategy of the last three governments has been successful. Foreign press reports and analyses by international financial organizations would support this conclusion. However, it should be noted that economic liberalization and greater integration into the world market is supposed to be a mechanism by which countries can achieve faster and higher levels of economic growth. Accelerated capital flows do not guarantee that this will occur or is occurring. To establish the impacts of foreign capital on national economic growth, it is necessary to evaluate the effects on the actual production and flow of goods and services.

Impacts of Foreign Investments on Production

The evolution of the Mexican economy over the past four decades can be characterized in terms of cyclical growth. During the first or import substitution phase (1961–1983), the national product grew at an average annual rate of 6.5% compared to only 2.2% in the ensuing fifteen years. During the second or export promotion phase (1984–1999) when the liberalization program was in operation, the national product grew by less than a third of the previous phase. Essentially, when production was orientated towards the national market and the economy was relatively protected, national production grew much faster than during the period of openness and international competition.

The slower performance of the economy during the period of liberalization is even more dramatic when viewed in terms of GNP per capita. During the second period, income capita decreased by an average annual rate of 0.17% on average yearly while it had increased at an average annual rate of 2.91% during the initial period. The magnitude of this decrease in personal income, that is in people's capacity to purchase basic goods and services, becomes more problematic when considering that population growth was higher during the first than the second period.

On the strength of the available data, there is reason to conclude that the external orientation of the Mexican economy and the open door policy towards foreign investment did not contribute to a more dynamic growth of the national product than was experienced during the previous period of protection and a closed economy. To the contrary, the growth of total and per capita GNP declined substantially. Between 1988–1990, when direct investment was higher than portfolio investment, the national product experienced growth. Since 1991, when portfolio investments increased by extraordinary amounts, the rate of growth of the national product decreased significantly, getting almost to zero in 1993 when Mexico obtained the largest inflow of short-term portfolio investment totaling 28.9 billion USD. There is a need to examine this divergence between theoretical expectations and reality.

Structural Change and Trade Liberalization

Paradoxically, when the export strategy was being fully implemented in the mid-1980s, it created a commercial deficit in 1989, which grew over time and reached 24.3 billion USD by 1994. The *Tequila effect* of 1995 temporarily reverted this negative tendency in the trade balance, but in 1998 the deficit had climbed again to 18 billion USD. The manufacturing industry (without counting the *maquillage* sector) was largely responsible this deficit. In 1998, for example, manufactures suffered a deficit of 22.6 billion USD. Only three manufacturing sectors had a positive balance in 1998: clothing and footwear (752 million USD); non-metallic mineral products (522 million USD); and the minero-metallurgy industry (62 million USD). Of these, only the clothing industry is significantly export-oriented. As a matter of fact, the two main exporting sectors, the chemicals and metal products, machinery and equipment, which together, account for 71% of all manufacturing exports, are responsible for 65% of the deficit in manufactures.

The agricultural sector has contributed to the negative trade pattern, which NAFTA, the free trade agreement with the United States of America and Canada, did not ameliorate. The president of the Federal Association of Rice Producers, Pedro Alejandro Dìaz Hartz, indicates that Mexico has become the second largest rice importer from the U.S., ahead of Canada, Saudi Arabia, Haiti and Turkey. Fifty percent of national consumption depends on these imports. José Antonio Cepeda, head of the corresponding association for potato producer notes likewise, that imports of that crop have increased by 77% in four years. The trend in agricultural imports is even more dramatic in the case of cotton. Jorge Antonio Medina, the director of the National Union of Cotton Producers indicates that Mexico is one of the main importers of this raw material while years ago cotton was one of Mexico's most important exports. In 1998, 1.4 million bales of cotton were purchased from the United States. The situation is similar in the meat industry where, according to Enrique López, Director of the

Mexican Association of Cattle Breeders, Mexico exports 5,000 tons while imports have reached 340,000 tons (Correa and Medina, 1999).

The new trade deficit may be viewed simply as a repetition of a historical pattern when placed in the context of the permanent commercial deficit the country endured between 1949–1982. However, the high rates of growth of the national product, which marked previous periods, are absent during the present deficit regime. The unique configuration of the present deficit can be attributed primarily to the role of global capital in Mexico's structural reform. During the period of import substitution global capital was directed at the internal market, domestic production was primarily for domestic consumption (as a matter of fact companies under this regime were strongly criticized for not engaging in export activities), capital goods were imported to sustain import-substitutes and the structure of production and consumption was such that there was a sustained demand for domestically produced inputs. In this way, global capital contributed substantially to the growth of national production that stimulated the internal market.

By contrast, under economic liberalization and export promotion, the inputs used by national and foreign companies for the production of goods, which are dedicated almost exclusively to exports, serve to increase both the volume and value imports. Ironically, export-promotion has created a pattern of import explosion. Imports associated with exports have grown substantially during the past five years, increasing from 37.3% to 54.2% of total imports (an increase of 45%). When intermediate inputs are added to this total, 58.6% of all imported goods in 1998 were destined for the export market. The source of the current external trade deficit is very different from that of the 1970s and 1980s because the export promotion model has created a process by which domestic inputs are substituted by imported ones. This transformation has negative consequences for the country's industrial development and the growth of its internal market. Clear evidence of this economic dysfunction is to be found in the inability of national industries to maintain the country's gross capital formation in the production of machinery and equipment. Instead, much of this is provided by global capital in the form of imports, which increased from 14% of the total production in 1988 to 26% in 1994.

The quantity of domestic inputs, measured in national value-added, which contribute to the value of exportable production, decreased constantly and systematically since export promotion was introduced at the beginning of the 1980s. The value of temporary imports, that is, materials brought into the country exclusively as intermediate goods destined for export production, grew and as a result, the internal value-added in manufacturing exports decreased. This value was reflected in the systematic decrease of the grade of national integration (GNI) from 91% in 1983 to 39% in 1994. The devaluation of December 1994, which produced the *Tequila Effect* stemmed the decline only temporarily at 46% in 1996, after which, it fell back to 40% by 1998.

These trends demonstrate that as Mexican exports have grown in value, a smaller proportion of their content has originated from domestic production, indicating that export promotion has not had the benign impact on national production that theory would suggest. As should be expected, in absolute terms, the national value-added is much higher now than it was 15 years ago. However, its expected positive feedback on national production is lower than expected. In fact, one could argue that by providing much of the intermediate and capital goods used in Mexico's manufacturing, the US enjoys most of the benefits to be gained from the former's export-led development program.

The structural transformation which has resulted from the Mexican version of export promotion is what Harry G. Johnson refers to as a model of 'ultra-pro-growth bias' in which 'more than the whole increase in national income is devoted to the purchase of imports so that the demand for home-produced goods actually falls and the country becomes absolutely less self-sufficient' (1968, p. 284). Consequently, the decrease in demand of internally produced intermediate goods that is being satisfied by imports introduces a process of 'dis-industrialization'.

It is my contention that the whole manufacturing industry is being transformed into a *maquillage* type production system that is different only in scale and impact from what is going on along the Mexican-US border. Undoubtedly, *maquillage* production has played an important part in Mexico's development, especially in employment creation. The question that needs to be asked is whether this model of industrial organization should be allowed to spread throughout the economy. I try to answer this question below by examining the relationship between economic liberalization, on the one hand and industrial and social polarization, on the other. The evidence convinces me that the '*maquilarization*' of industrial development is an imprudent path for Mexican development.

Economic Liberalization and Industrial Polarization

One of the first consequences of economic liberalization is industrial polarization between the exporting sector and the rest of the economy. This gap continues to widen each year as reflected in the high concentration of exports in only a few sectors. In 1998, the metal products, machinery and equipment sector, of which the car industry is a part, accounted for 63% of total exports, the clothing and footwear sector for 7% and the chemical sector for 7%. These three sectors, together, accounted for 78% of total exports while only one subsector (transport and communications) accounted for 37% of the total. This extremely high concentration of production, especially in the automobile industry, derives from the fact that nearly 65% of its final production is destined for the export market.

In the process of opening up the Mexican economy to global competition, trade liberalization has made Mexico almost completely dependent on US trade. The US received 89% of the entire Mexican output in 1998, compared to only 60% in 1983. This lopsided trade partnership ties Mexico's economic growth to conditions in the US market, making the former extremely vulnerable to the latter's growth cycles. Mexico's dependency on the US for trade is dangerous also, because it has the potential to create a polarization between its internal and external markets. In 1998, for example, a growth rate of 8% in the internal market could not compensate for a 10.2% drop in the exports of the 500 most important Mexican companies (Expansión, 1999).

Economic Liberalization and Social Polarization

The paradox between increased exports and economic contraction appears to occur simultaneously with deteriorating in social welfare. This can be observed in the distribution of income and its effects on the structure of poverty. The data on Table 9.2 show an apparently positive situation in which the population of poor/non-poor has not changed significantly over the past fifteen years. However, there is a certain fallacy embedded in the data. In 1999, there were 40,635,430 Mexicans living in poverty compared to 29,988,420 fifteen years earlier. Of course, it might be argued that this increase simply reflects population growth. Unfortunately, the poor population has increased at a faster rate (35%) than the total population (32%). Also, while only 15% of Mexicans lived in extreme poverty at the beginning of the liberalization, by 1999 this percentage had grown to 28%. During the same period, the percentage of population living in moderate poverty decreased from 27% to 15%. The conclusion to be drawn from this is simple. It may be true, as

Table 9.2 Distribution of Population by Wealth Groups (million)

Year	Total Population	Extreme Poor	Medium Poor	Non Poor	Total Poor
1984	71,4	10.7	19.3	41.4	30.0
1992	84.3	13.5	23.6	47.2	37.1
1999	94.5	26.5	14.1	53.9	40.6

Source: Extrapolated by author brom Banamex data, Examen de la Situacion Economica de Mexico, marzo, 19991, p.91

President Zedillo has asserted, that the export model did not create the high levels of poverty in the country, but it is also true that this model has been incapable of reducing the degree of poverty, which already existed. Even more, it has exacerbated the problem by pushing a large part of the poor from moderate to abject indigence.

The disparity between social development and economic productivity results from a model, which is incapable of creating well paying jobs in the formal sector. Between 1990 and 1998 permanent employment increased by 316,000 jobs compared to a demand of one million three hundred thousand jobs. This gap has been filled by informal employment, which has increased its contribution to GNP by 33%.

Carlos García Fernández, director of foreign investment of the Department of Commerce and Finance (SECOFI), asserts that global capital provides the largest number of jobs in the country. Using data from the Mexican Institute for Social Security, he argues that employment in the economy at large increased 24%, from 8.5 million to 10.4 million between 1993–1999. During the same period, employment by foreign investment increased by 58%, from 1.3 million to 2.1 million (Gazcón, 1999: 14). Data provided by the Ministry of Finance and Public Credit, on the other hand, show that the least number of jobs have been created in the export-oriented sectors. In the food, beverage and tobacco sector, employment increased by 3% while in the chemical and in the textile sector the increase was only 1%. The last two are important exporting sectors while the first is not. Jobs were actually lost in some export-oriented activities, for example, non-metallic minerals and basic metals (1% decline) and woods (4.3% decline).

Additional pressures are placed on employment by overall decreases in income per capita. Many workers now need to have a second job, usually in the informal sector, in order to obtain a basic income. This phenomenon is measured by the rate of real economic pressure (TPEE), which, in Mexico, has grown continuously, reaching 4% of the economically active population in 1999.

Another important factor contributing to social polarization is constant reduction in purchasing power. During the first four years of the present administration, prices of the Basic Food Basket increased by 251% while basic wages increased only by 87%. In 1997, 65% of the work force had an income equivalent to two minimum wages, compared to 61% of the workforce in 1993 (Juárez Sánchez, 1999a). The Labour Congress, a federation of labor unions, has also pointed out that the purchasing power of the minimum wage declined by 36% during this period. Meanwhile the cost of the Basic Food Basket (CBA) has increased by 482% because the cost of the 48 products included in the basket increased from 724.50 pesos in December of 1994 to 4,219.5 pesos in mid-1999. Consequently, a worker needs to earn more than three times the minimum wage (34.5 pesos daily or 1,033.5 pesos per month) to meet basic food needs.

The Center for Economic Studies of the Private Sector admits that there was an accumulated decline of 30% in general purchasing power between 1995–1997. Obviously, the World Bank's conclusion that a Mexican worker who earns a minimum wage should be in a position to buy three basic food baskets is unrealistic.

There is a similar deterioration in the Indispensable Food Basket (CBI). Ms. Juárez Sánchez, of the Universidad Obrera de México, notes that; '...[s]ince the devaluation of December 1994 until August of 1999, the prices of the CBI has increased 257.99% while minimum wages only increased 86.56% during the same period' (1999b: 14). This decline is due to the fact that during this period the price of some of the basic food products increased dramatically: electricity (529%), telephone service (418%), public transportation (254%), grapefruit (407%), papaya (549%), tortillas (367%), beans (280%), milk (280%), soup (366%) and eggs (360%) (Juárez Sánchez, 1999b: 15)

Declining salaries did not affect only basic wages but the entire income range. Average contractual salaries in the federal system as well as average wages in the IMSS system decreased by 31% between 1995–2000. A similar trend is reflected in industry: salaries in construction declined by 35% and those in manufacturing by 27%. The exporting *maquillage* industry was also affected by this negative wage trend, while salaries in the commercial sector declined by 28%.

The conditions described above result from a wage policy based on the principle of providing cheap labor in order to obtain competitive export prices, especially in manufactures. These outcomes suggest that the success of the export strategy (in terms of increased output) has been achieved on the backs of workers whose average incomes in the 1990s declined by 7.6% from 1980s levels (Correra and Medina, 1999).

Table 9.3 Index of Wages and Earnings (pesos/worker): Base Year, 1994

SECTOR	1994	1998	1999	1994-99%
Average minimum wage	13.9	10.2	9.6	-31.5
Average wage in federal sector	27.5	19.0	19.0	-31.4
Medium earnings* in manufacture	102.4	75.1	75.0	-26.8
Medium earning in maquillage sector	55.0	47.0	48.9	-11.2
Average earning is construction	42.6	27.4	27.5	-35.4
Average earnings in wholesale	67.6	52.2	48.6	-28.1
Average earnings in retail	49.6	34.2	34.1	-31.2

*includes wages and employee benefits

Source: enado de la Republica

Conclusion

The evidence presented in this chapter shows that the version of the export promotion model implemented in Mexico has fulfilled the objective of transforming the country into one of the largest exporters in the world as well as one of the main recipients of foreign investment. The drive to modernize and globalize the Mexican economy, however, has produced neither a higher level of growth for the economy, nor a higher standard of living for the bulk of the population. It could be argued that the liberalization process demanded by globalization has not fulfilled its promise because it has not also reduced poverty.[2] In addition, the export-led model has actually set back industrial growth by retarding the development of a strong local market. This has resulted from its lack of attention to mobilizing the supply side of the domestic market by producing intermediate and capital goods; and the demand side by improving purchasing power through reasonable wages and benefits. At this point, we should remember Michael Porter's comment that 'Ironically, it is vigorous internal competition which definitely presses national companies to face up to international markets just as it hardened them in order to be successful in those markets' (1990: 14). This means that the success of a nation in the international arena proceeds directly from the strength of its domestic economy.

The conventional orthodoxy that higher efficiency in resource allocation results from trade openness may be true in the export sector. However, the strategy has not created enough trickle-down to the rest of the Mexican economy to justify claims that it has benign impacts on poverty. The rising tide of exports has not lifted all boats – the poor have been left stranded on the shore. In fact, it is becoming clear that the Mexican economy is being transformed into a giant *maquillage* factory, sustained by the importation of intermediate inputs and capital goods, which substitute for national production. The major national contribution to this new dynamic is cheap labor, sustained by a minimum wage, which is incapable of providing one Indispensable Basic Food Basket; defined by the World Food Organization as the minimum consumption necessary to obtain a daily diet of calories. In this sense, Mexico clearly exemplifies ongoing processes in Latin America, generally, where labor purchasing power has declined by 27% during the decade of 1990 (OIT, 1999), leading to major social disequilibria and the further pauperization of the masses.

Notes

1. The data presented here does not considered maquila exports, those of in-bond industries, because of their special legal and geographical status.
2. For a critical view of the unfulfill promises of globalization see Rozo, 1999.

References

Baldwin, R. and Forslid, R. (1996) 'Trade liberalization endogenous growth: a q-theory approach'. *NBER Working Paper* No. 5549, April 1996.

Banco de México, *Informe Anual* 1998, abril 1999.

Buffie, R. (1992) 'On the conditions of export-led growth'. *Canadian Journal of Economics* 211–225.

Correa, G. and Medina, A. (1999) 'Los grandes perdedores del TLC: campo, salarios y emple'. *Proceso Mexico*, 29 agosto.

Dornbusch, R. (1992) 'The case for trade liberalization in developing countries'. *Journal of Economic Perspectives* Winter, 69–85.

Expansión, Informe de las 500 empresas más importantes, Junio- Julio 1999.

Feenstra, R.C. and Rose, A. K. (1997) 'Putting things in order: Patterns of trade dynamics and Growth'. *NBER Working Paper* No. 5975, March.

Gazcón, F. (1999) 'La inversión extranjera fortalece el empleo, asegura la Secofi'. *El Financiero*, 26 agosto.

Harrison, A. (1996) 'Openness and growth: A time-series, cross-country analysis for developing countries'. *NBER Working Paper* No. 5221, May.

Johnson, Harry G. (1968) 'Economic development and international trade'. In R.E. Caves and H.G. Johnson (eds) *Readings in International Economics*. NY: R.D. Irwin, 281–299.

Juárez Sánchez, L. (1999a) 'Neoliberalismo y salario'. *Trabajadores*, Universidad Obrera de México, Julio-Agosto.

Juárez Sánchez, L. (1999b) *Los trabajadores de México: entre los más pobres del mundo*. Universidad Obrera de México, mimeo, septiembre.

Nafinsa, 'La evolución de la Inversión Extranjera en México en 1994'. *El Mercado de Valores*, April 1995.

OIT (1999) *Trabajo decente y protección para todos: prioridad de las Américas*.

Porter, M. (1990) 'Dónde radica la ventaja competitiva de las naciones?'. *Harvard-Deusto Business Review* 4' trimester, 3–26.

Rodrik, D. and Rodriquez, F. (1999) 'Trade policy and economic growth: A sceptics guide to the cross-national evidence'. *NBER Working Paper* No. 7081, April.

Sachs, J. and Warner, A. (1995) 'Economic reform and the process of global integration'. *Brokings Paper on Economic Activity*, 1–118.

Chapter 10

Neoliberalism in South Africa

Richard Peet

Introduction

After a century of struggle, involving the sacrifice of thousands of lives, South Africa's black majority was liberated from apartheid and the black majority enfranchised in 1994. Subsequent elections have demonstrated overwhelming support for the African National Congress (ANC), an alliance of Black Nationalist and leftist groups standing for fundamental economic, social and political change. The leadership of the ANC has promised repeatedly that South Africa's abundant wealth will be devoted to the needs of the black majority instead of the wants of the white minority. Despite some gains, the post-Apartheid period has seen the will of a newly liberated people frustrated by internal structural limitations surviving from the past and by severe restrictions on what any country can do for its poorest people in a neo-liberal, market-driven and export-oriented world. At its root, the dilemma facing the South African people involves a lack of social control over the direction taken by the national economy. The tensions between a people persuaded that their time has finally come and an institutional structure that even following political liberation, can satisfy but a fragment of long pent-up needs, leads to a crisis of national conscience, only partly resolved by the well-publicized Truth and Reconciliation Commission. Conscience has to have real economic consequences for reconciliation to be creditable.

This chapter places the predicament of the ANC in the context of globalization with the objective of explaining how the party's policies evolved increasingly towards neoliberalism. The chapter's structure reflects the author's thinking about the topic. The initial objective was simply to review the history of ANC development policy. As it became clear that the ANC had moved from socialism towards neo-liberalism in the early 1990s, emphasis shifted towards understanding the institutional complexes directing what I still considered to be policy options. More recently I became interested in neoliberalism as a discourse, propagated by institutional complexes operating within global power relations that exercise a compelling influences on the direction of national development strategies. Most recently I have begun to think of global neoliberalism as a conspiracy, comprised of economic imaginaries shared by linked groups of theorists and practitioners with a distinct politics. My eventual aim is to uncover the origins, nature and spread of this discourse as my contribution to eradicating what I perceive to be a pernicious belief system, which promises few benefits for the poor in South Africans and other Third World countries.

Development Discourses in South Africa

The ANC made a series of formal statements on social and economic transformation as a significant active component of the anti-apartheid struggle. The Freedom Charter, one of the great documents of popular history, was adopted by the Congress of the People at a mass meeting in 1955, in Kliptown, near Johannesburg. The Charter is transformative in the twin senses of changing those who read it and changing the society it criticized. Sections 4 and 5, quoted below, deal with economic rights and land reform, two important elements of social transformation.

> The national wealth of our country, the heritage of all South Africans, shall be restored to the people;
> The mineral wealth beneath the soil, the banks and monopoly industry shall be transferred to the ownership of the people as a whole;
> All other industries and trade shall be controlled to assist the well being of the people;
> Restriction of land ownership on a racial basis shall be ended and all the land re-divided amongst those who work it to banish famine and land hunger;
> The state shall help the peasants with implements, seed, tractors and dams to save the sod and assist the tillers (Freedom Charter in Esterhuyse and Nel, 1990).

The Freedom Charter combined nationalist ideals with democratic socialist principles in a radical statement about modernist development and the potential for human liberation. 'Removing monopolistic circumstances' and similarly vague phrases necessarily employed by the ANC at the time can easily be read as the party's desire to institute state control of the commanding heights of the economy. 'Ownership of soil, banks and industries by the people' seems clearly and unequivocally socialistic. As a main signatory of the Charter the ANC was seen as a black nationalist organization with a radical, socialist politics.

During the following thirty years of turmoil, the ANC continued to use the Freedom Charter as basis for their proposals for social and political justice. In the 'Constitutional Guidelines' of 1987 ANC officials interpreted the Charter as a guide for making a just and democratic society that would sweep away the legacy of 'colonial conquest' and proceeding in accord with 'constitutional principles' (ANC, 1991: 3). Yet the document supported a more dynamic, efficient private sector to create employment but with more equitable ownership patterns. This implied a progressive redistribution of resources to the poor within responsible fiscal and monetary measures – 'responsible' interpreted still to include capital gains and transfer taxes and progressive property and land taxes. Rural development required land redistribution and state purchases of lands as part of a strategy to produce exports and food for domestic consumption. The ANC would encourage foreign investment consistent with its development goals and an investment code obliging fair labor and environment practices, cooperation with the government in achieving developmental goals and re-investment of some profits to promote continuing growth. In short, the Draft Document was for redistribution, reconciliation, development and a democratic mixed economy. The ANC national conference, held in May 1992, re-affirmed support for a 'basic needs' approach (ANC, 1992).

The period between the mid 1980s and the mid 1990s, South Africa's decade of liberation, saw intense discussion about the future course of the economy and society (for example, Sunter, 1987; Bond, 1991; Schire, 1992; Patel, 1993). During this period, experts from economic policy groups, academia, business, the World Bank and IMF, increasingly dominated the discourse

From the radical side, the middle 1980s was marked by increased neo-Marxist research on the impact of international sanctions on the South African economy and on social issues like housing and health. A series of conferences on the future of the South African economy, attended by academics, ANC, SACP and union members, was held outside the country in the late 1980s to 1990s and a number of research networks, including the following, formed around macroeconomic policy issues.

1. The Economic Trends Group (ET) formed in 1986 at the suggestion of COSATU, was composed of leftist, union-oriented academics in Johannesburg, the University of Natal and the University of Cape Town. At a meeting held in Harare, Zimbabwe among COSATU, the Economic Trends Group and the ANC's Department of Economic Planning, a Draft Resolution on Economic Policy was prepared for circulation and discussion within the ANC organization. The preamble to the Draft Resolution repeated earlier statements about white power, the oppression of black people and advocated fundamental restructuring. In response, the ANC committed itself to promoting economic growth along a new path orientated towards satisfying basic needs and empowering the disadvantaged, through a mixed economy (ANC, 1991: 3). In the early 1990s a somewhat reconstituted ET, under the auspices of the Industrial Strategy Project (ISP) and with help from the Institute for Development Studies at Sussex University and Canadian financing, conducted a detailed study whose findings were outlined in an edited book, *Manufacturing Performance in South Africa* (Joffe *et al.*, 1995). In the words of one observer 'The ISP's policy recommendations represent a distinct shift away from a national, demand-side strategy to a more global, supply-side strategy for economic reconstruction' (Padayachee, 1998: 43 7).

2. The Macro-Economic Research Group (MERG) founded in 1991 on the recommendation of a mission from the Canadian International Development Research Centre (IDRC), centered on liberal and leftist academics in the Witwatersrand University economics department. It had a wide network of contacts in the South African university system and was initially well connected with ANC members within the country, such as Trevor Manuel, later to become Minister of Finance and Maria Ramos later Director General of Finance. MERG proposed a post-Keynesian policy, which advocated a state-led social and physical infrastructure development program to be followed by sustained growth with more private investment (MERG, 1993). While the MERG proposals was recognized by many South African to be of high standards, they seem to have been ignored by the ANC – according to Padayachee (1998: 439) '...there was considerable rivalry between WRG and the ANC's Department of Economic Planning, while the participation of foreign economists in Merg was viewed with suspicion'.

The ANC's 1994 election campaign was framed around the *Reconstruction and Development Progamme* (RDP), a popular policy document written by intellectuals from various social movements and NGOS and finalized by several workshops in an open and democratic process. The South African economy was said to lie in deep structural crisis, which required fundamental restructuring. Six principles were said to guide ANC policies:

1. an integrated and sustainable program;
2. a people-driven process;
3. peace and security for all;
4. nation-building;
5. the linking of reconstruction and development;
6. the democratization of South Africa.

Of these, the key to economic policy was principle number 5. In contrast to the view that economic growth and development with redistribution were contradictory processes, the RDP document claimed to 'break decisively' by integrating the two (ANC, 1994: 6–7). Specifically, this meant a 5% economic growth rate and the creation of 300,000–500,000 non-agricultural jobs annually. The industrial strategy needed to accomplish these goals involved increased national investment especially in manufacturing, job creation and meeting basic needs. It was also thought that stable policies would create a climate conducive to foreign investment. The RDP mentioned, but did not stress, integration into the world economy and warned foreign investors that they would have to abide by the country's laws and standards, particularly with respect to labor and that the government would ensure knowledge and technical capacity transfer to allow greater worker participation in decision-making. This popular document entered the official parlance of the ANC dominated government of national unity, when most of its proposals were written into a government white paper on reconstruction and development in November 1994.

The white paper differed from the RDP document in placing greater emphasis on 'financial and monetary discipline', the 'establishment of an economic environment conducive to economic growth' and 'trade and industry policies designed to foster a greater outward orientation' (Government of the Republic of South Africa, 1994: 21). These were signs that a re-orientation of policy was already occurring. Even so, in the first free South African elections, the ANC committed itself to reconstruction and sustainable development, which 'addresses the needs of our people without compromising the interests of future generations', 'improving the quality of life through a process of empowerment which gave the poor control over their lives' and increased the poor's ability 'to mobilize sufficient development resources including from the democratic government where necessary' (ANC, 1994: 15).

Where vigorously applied, the RDP has worked well for some of the poorest, most deprived people of South Africa. For example, in the five years following its adoption, 3 million people were provided with safe drinking water from taps within 200m of their houses as part of a plan by the Ministry of Water Affairs and Forestry to supply 21 million people with basic water services. The record on housing construction, by comparison, is far less promising. The portent for the future seemed clear – this was going to be a democratic, socialistic, South Africa.

It now appears that by the 1994 elections, the ANC leadership had shifted significantly from RDP-type policies. The period 1990–1994 marks a transition during which the ANC moved from illegal to legal opposition and partial incorporation into the South African state. Statements made by ANC leaders were subject to intense and critical attention by business spokespersons, academics, official commentators and the established media. The result was an immediate disciplining of the ANC's radical positions as a result of which 'a more nuanced view won the day. When Mandela's support of nationalization earned a cool response inside South Africa and in the Western Media, a number of more qualified statements on nationalization followed' (van der Burg, 1990: 117).

A few months after his release Mandela said that the banks, mines and monopolies, but not other industries, would be nationalized and, later, that this would occur only if it boosted the economy (Mandela, 1990). Other ANC leaders (Joe Slovo, Walter Sisulu, Thabo Mbeki) now found nationalization not necessarily fundamental to ANC policy: indeed Mbeki added that nationalization had never been part of it. The ANC began to speak of alternatives, like anti-trust legislation and government-appointed directors on the boards of major companies (Ceruti, 1996: 19). Asked why the ANC had shifted its position on nationalization in an interview held in 1995, Trevor Manuel said that the collapse of the Soviet Union broke the romantic illusions of many in the ANC (Habib and Padayachee, 2000). However, the nationalization question was only the most obvious aspect of a series of changes in ANC politics (Rantete, 1994).

Increasingly, in the early 1990s, people from the business, labor and academic communities, together with foreign academics and development consultants, joined forces to produce sophisticated, well-financed, research documents. The report *South Africa: Prospects for Successful Transition* (Tucker and Scott, 1992) is a prominent case in point. When un-banning the ANC in 1990, Nationalist president F.W. de Klerk asked business leaders to articulate what the new South Africa might look like. The chairmen of NEDCOR, a holding group, whose main asset is Nedbank, one of South Africa's largest financial institutions and Old Mutual, the country's biggest life insurance company, responded by initiating a scenario exercise 'to gain greater understanding of the future business environment and ... to make the results known' (Tucker and Scott, 1992: xv). A 23-member team made up largely of academic and bank economists was assembled to run this heavily-financed project. Forty directors and senior executives of Nedcor and Old Mutual were asked to sketch two scenarios for the transitional period 1990–1995, one 'favorable' (democratic government a bill of rights, pragmatic economic policy) and one 'unfavorable' (black government African socialism, economic decline). 'Successful transition' was stable democracy based on an equally stable social fabric, with rising incomes reasonably distributed. But incomes had been falling. So they projected a 'change of gear' scenario based on assumptions of economic restructuring to a higher growth path, social investment to 'stabilize the social fabric' and a change in the political process towards liberal democracy. This was described as 'controlled revolution', or 'sweeping change with social stability' (Tucker and Scott, 1992: 8). Their slogans, repeated many times during a 400-slide, 6-hour presentation, were: redistribution through growth; and change from an inward-looking resource focus to an outward-looking manufacturing focus for the economy.

The first external briefing was made at the beginning of January, 1991, to the (then) Minister of Finance, Mr. Barend du Plessis. A week later, the team briefed four key members of the South African community – Dr Simon Brand, Dr Beyers

Naude, Mr. Mike Rosholt and Mr. Ian Steyn. In the third week of January, 1991, a six-hour presentation was made to the State President and the full cabinet. In the following days presentations were made to Nelson Mandela and members of the ANC executive committee, Dr Mangosuthu Buthelezi and members of the KwaZulu cabinet, members of the PAC executive committee, the executive committee of AZAPO and two groups of business leaders. Presentations were also made to two groups, which included senior civil servants, university rectors, embassy personnel, representatives of the media and a group of economic and other advisors to the labor union congresses and extra-parliamentary groups and to a large number of other South Africans (Tucker and Scott, 1992: xxi).

The emphasis of the report was on stability, resisting populist pressures, a shared vision of the future and achieving consensus – this in a society emerging from apartheid with inequalities as great as any society in the world (World Bank, 1997: 222–3 figures showed South Africa to be one of the most unequal societies in the world). These 'new' notions began to appear with increasing frequency in many policy discussions, eventually coming to dominate ANC discourse. What was billed as a short-term 'scenario exercise', in the guise of articulating what the new South Africa might look like 'became instead a device for implanting long-term ideas about growth and development into elite and popular consciousness'.

In the early 1990s, South Africa also came under increasing scrutiny from the IMF and the World Bank. As a prelude to a 1993, $850 million loan, the IMF published a report on the South African economy that stressed an outward-looking macro-economic strategy with growth trickling down to the poor through employment growth and increased government revenue (Lachmann and Bercuson, 1992,). A letter of intent signed with the IMF in 1993 committed the new government to 'responsible management' of the economy, interpreted as cutting state deficits, controlling inflation, wage restraint, outward orientation and the superiority of market forces over state interventions (Padayachee, 1994). According to one left critic, Patrick Bond (1997), the ANC government not only followed IMF policies, but also liberalized the economy faster and further than expected. Also, it might be noted that during the 1980s, the Afrikaner National Party had shifted from import substitution to a more market-oriented program, codified in the Normative Model Approach of 1993. While this was at first opposed by the ANC, a shift in emphasis began in 1992–3 towards a position more compatible with NEM, a 'realistic' position that encouraged foreign investment in South Africa.

Things changed rapidly when the ANC assumed leadership of the Government of National Unity after the 1994 elections. For many observers 'the main tenets of the RDP were gutted' and the 'impact of progressive policies has been limited' because the post-1990 negotiations ensured that the new government would have limited powers of moving productive assets towards a massive, state-sponsored economic restructuring program. 'It was agreed, either explicitly or implicitly, that the new government would not resort to nationalization of privately-owned assets and would not use massive state spending to offset the socio-economic inequalities inherited from the past' (*Southern African Report* November 1996: 21). The independent governmental department supervising implementation of the RDP was soon closed and its duties assumed by the office of now President Thabo Mbeki.

Growth, Employment and Redistribution

The shift in policy direction is shown by the next development report, entitled *Growth, Employment and Redistribution* (GEAR, 1996), prepared by the Department of Finance, with Trevor Manuel, as Minister and a team of academics, representatives of the Development Bank of Southern Africa, the South African Reserve Bank and the World Bank. During the GEAR discussions, the South Africa Federation (1996) had coordinated a report on behalf of the business community, advocating a neoliberal economic policy. On the other hand, the 1.8 million member COSATU's 'Keynesian' alternative, set out in *Social Equity and Job Creation* (COSATU, 1996), advocated 'an expansion of the social wage through mass state housing financed through public borrowing, a national health program, all-embracing social security and public job creation, as well as an enlarged public sector' (*Southern Africa Report*, November 1997).

The GEAR report re-iterated the RDP's link between economic growth and income redistribution, arguing that that much higher economic growth rates were necessary to achieve social objectives. Sustained growth on this higher plane (6% and 400, 000 new jobs a year) required an outward-oriented economy centered on a 'competitive platform for a powerful expansion by the tradable goods sector' within a 'stable environment for confidence' with a 'profitable surge in private investment' and 'flexibility within the collective bargaining system' (GEAR, 1996: 2).

A series of policies were recommended to promote an outward-oriented industrial economy integrated into the global environment and responsive to market pressures. The state's budget deficit was to be cut from 5.4% to 3.0% of GDP by 2000, while trade was to be liberalized. The GEAR report called for a national social agreement to create a competitive environment for investment and economic growth, for example through wage moderation. All this was to 'break current constraints and catapult the economy to the higher levels of growth, development and employment needed to provide a better life for all South African' (GEAR, 1996: 2).

In March, 1997 Minister of Finance, Manuel delivered the first ANC budget. It consolidated the ANC's support for neoliberal policies (Lehulere, 1997) and made ANC policy consistent with liberal opinion within the country, the 'Successful Transition' position and with the neo-liberal, structural adjustment policies outlined by the World Bank and the DAF.

South Africa's unions objected that the GEAR report was more favorable to big business than the working class. Critical discussion focused on three areas:

1. the proposal for cutting government expenditures as a proportion of GDP;
2. the government's commitment to 'flexible labor markets', widely interpreted as a euphemism for the suppression of unions;
3. the idea of privatization of parastatals to reduce state debt, interpreted as
4. an attack on state control of the economy in the interests of poor people.

The unions called the GEAR a self-imposed structural adjustment policy, which re-imposed social and economic conditions like those experienced under apartheid.

The ANC's reply was illustrated in Donaldson (1997). As chief director of financial planning in the South African Department of Finance, he argued that

GEAR policies were compatible with RDP goals of poverty alleviation. The unions greeted such replies with skepticism and between 1996–1998, continually threatened mass actions against the state, withdrawal of support for the ANC and the initiation of a more left party in company with the SACP.

Both Thabo Mbeki, president since Mandela's retirement in 1999 and Finance Minister Manuel have re-affirmed the government's commitment to 'sober monetary and fiscal policy'. The Ministry of Trade and Industry, under Alec Erwin, has signaled its commitment to GEAR by designating ten Spatial Development Initiatives (SDIs), to maximize foreign investment and serve as platforms for export-led growth. Despite massive opposition and with scant evidence that either growth or employment are forthcoming (growth rate dropped from 3% in 1996 to 0.1% in 1998; 160, 000 jobs were lost in the formal sector in 1998 and the unemployment stands at 37.6%) (South African Reserve Bank, 1999), the ANC, with the support of the party's elite, now stands committed to GEAR. COSATU remains fiercely opposed to the policy.

The World Bank, Development Theory and Policy Shifts in South Africa

The ANC's policy record should be placed in the context of changes in economic policy theory more generally, but especially those promulgated by the World Bank. In the post-war years, development economics was a hybrid but generally liberal enterprise, critical of conventional economics for its abstractness and claims at universality, while favoring economic structuralism, interventionary state policies and socio-economic planning. In line with this, the World Bank, headed by Robert McNamara in the 1970s, favored rural and basic needs development. A 'counterrevolution' set in as conservative backlash to the 1960s–1970s, as symbolized by the elections of Margaret Thatcher, Helmut Kohl and Ronald Reagan, all opposed to Keynesianism, structuralism and especially the more radical fringes of development theory like dependency (Toye, 1987).

By the late 1980s, a system of policy recommendations, dubbed the 'Washington consensus', dominated development discourse. It favored a neoliberal system based on classical economics, with 'prudent macroeconomic policies, outward orientation and free market capitalism' (Williamson, 1997: 18). The World Bank began its shift towards neoliberalism with the Berg report on development in sub-Saharan Africa (World Bank, 1981). The Report criticized the trade and exchange rate policies of most African countries and recommended an export-oriented agricultural strategy focused on small-holders, private competition and removal of government intervention in pricing systems. The 1983 *World Development Report* (World Bank, 1983: 29) noted that foreign trade enabled developing countries to specialize in production, exploit economies of scale and increase foreign exchange earnings. The 1984 *Report* (World Bank, 1984, ch. 3) used 'growth scenarios' to argue that developing countries would improve their positions by changing their economic policies to avoid over-valued exchange rates, reduce public spending and instituting an 'open trading and payments regime', which encouraged optimal use of investment resources, as exemplified by the East Asian countries.

By 1985, the Bank was warning that a 'retreat from liberalization' would slow economic growth (World Bank, 1985: 145). The 1987 *World Development Report* added that the ultimate objectives of development were 'faster growth of national income, alleviation of poverty and reduction of income inequalities' (World Bank, 1987: 1). The

Bank drew directly on Smith's argument that industrialization would be retarded by a low ability to trade and on Ricardo and Mill in arguing that trade gave advantages, which led to productivity increases. The Bank stressed 'efficient industrialization' as the key economic policy and devised a lending program that supported structural reforms, open markets and free trade in many Third World countries.

The Bank's recommendations focused on three main areas: trade reform, macroeconomic reform to reduce budget deficits, lower inflation, ensure competitive exchange rates and labor market reforms by decreasing wages and ending other regulations, which distorted free labor markets.

The main instrument by which these ideas were put into practice were the structural adjustment and stabilization policies imposed on countries borrowing from the IMF and the World Bank (Logan and Mengisteab, 1993). In the late 1980s and early 1990s, some commentators found the World Bank shifting slightly to a revised neo-liberal model stressing market-friendly state intervention and good governance (political pluralism, accountability and the rule of law), conditions again found typical in the East Asian 'miracle economies' (Kiely, 1998). The key statement can be found in the 1991 *World Development Report* (World Bank, 1991: 1–2)

According to the Bank, the main elements of a market approach to development were investments in people, a competitive climate for enterprise, integration with the global economy and a stable macro-economy. This involved re-thinking the role of the state, essentially in five areas: government investment in areas like education, health and nutrition, where markets alone could not be relied upon; building social, legal and physical infrastructures; mobilizing resources to finance public expenditures; providing a stable macroeconomic foundation; and protecting the environment. However the Bank continued to stress the neoliberal policies it had developed during the 1980s: less government intervention, economies open to trade and investment and macroeconomic policies involving low fiscal deficits and market-based incentives for saving and investment (World Bank, 1991: 11).

During the 1990s the various World Bank reports outlined aspects of what it termed a 'holistic approach to development': social safety nets, poverty, health, education, environment, rural areas, gender as well as more conventionally neoliberal areas like property rights, liberalization and privatization. The culmination of this line of thought was the 1999/2000 World Development Report 'Entering the Twenty-First Century' with its synthetic 'Comprehensive Development Framework' (CDF) composed of two 'complementary parts': a stable macro-economy shaped by prudent fiscal and monetary policies; and the CDF itself, stressing: structural elements like honest governments, strong property and personal rights supported by an efficient legal and judicial system; human development, as with education and health; physical infrastructure; and sectoral elements like integrated rural development strategies and urban management. The report emphasizes a kind of global-local dialectic and what it calls the institutions of governance (World Bank, 1999).

Discourse and the Academic-Institutional-Media Complex

Another way of phrasing development is to see it as a discourse formed by institutions in geographic space. Discursive formations originating in power centers, based on well-established theories, backed by mighty institutions, with billions of dollars, colonize all alternative discourses, especially those originating from the experiences of oppressed peoples. This confrontation should not be seen as a simple process of inevitable diffusion. There are anti-colonial struggles in the mind, carried out through the media of competing discourses, as well as struggles on the ground (Guha and Spivak, 1988).

Here I must seriously part company with the post-modern end of post-structuralism. The dramatic confrontations in the world today are between modernism and pre-modernism, while postmodernism is an indulgence of the world's intellectual elite. Rather than post-developmentalism's rejection of the entire developmental enterprise I suggest that progressive intellectuals should immerse themselves anew in the political economy of development using post-structural notions of power, imaginary and discourses of development but in the supportive re-construction of developmental alternatives within a political-theoretic position that might be called critical modernism. This means re-formulating discourse theory around institutional complexes and their relations. It means reviving the sense of radical commitment lost since the radical decade of the 1960s; and it means resurrecting popular developmental discourses and theoretically renewing them.

My view is that intermediate conceptions of power based in notions of class, gender, state and institution yield more exact analyses of discourses, a case in point being the power and institutional bases of development. Here the post-structural notion of 'discourse' is useful in referring to a system of ideas set down in coherent, sequential statements, by a recognized body of experts. As post-structural social theorists argue, there is a tendency for hegemonic discourses to achieve 'quasi-autonomous' powers, in the sense of being highly theorized and taken for granted as sole truth. The power of a discourse is shown by its ability to restrict serious conversation to a given range of topics and ideas or by its ability to specify the parameters of the practical, the realistic and the sensible. Yet, we need more exact specifications of the power bases and institutional systems behind this modem project than those attempted by post-structural theorists.

The ideas behind a discourse often begin as theories elaborated by academics in universities, usually working with governmental and foundational support or, increasingly, by researchers working in 'think tanks' directly financed by grants from (often conservative) corporations. There is a continual movement of ideas and personnel between these academic sources of ideas, development institutions, business organizations and the higher reaches of the governmental bureaucracies, especially the departments of finance, where real state economic power resides. Some of the ideas propagated by academic and institutional agents are picked up by the information media, especially the business sections of national newspapers like the (London) *Times* or the *New York Times*, the economic dailies like the *Financial Times*, popular economic magazines like the *Economist* and news and commentary on television and radio. Here we find significant links between business elites and the advertizing revenues, which underwrite the apparent neutrality of 'all the news that's fit to print'. At all levels, but especially at the level of popular accounts produced by the media, there are links with political parties. My thesis is that these intimately related establishments form a dominant academic-institutional-media (AIM) complex whose discursive products include policy prescriptions, press releases, popular columns and a vast panoply of well-written, illustrated books, reports and articles. The World Bank's annual *World Development Report* is the paradigmatic example of this process. In this definition, the word 'complex' should be understood as composite rather than unity. There is a struggle for discursive power within agencies and between them, which make even the most established AIMs unstable. Yet, at any time, one agency takes the lead in establishing the style for the entire complex. Thus, the World Bank has become far more important in setting development policy than its annual $7.4 billion of lending, a mere 2–3% of the capital flows to the Third World, would suggest. As one commentator puts it: 'the bank is to economic development theology what the papacy is to Catholicism, complete with yearly encyclicals' (Holland, 1998: 5).

Hegemonic discourses established by the AIM are countered, from conception to implementation, by counter-hegemonic discourses with their own bases in alternative power complexes, different in that they employ more informal media of thought, discussion and dissemination. These are usually more firmly based in popular movements and in radical academic centers, sometimes with limited financial backing from liberal funding sources and governmental institutions willing to consider developmental alternatives. Alternative AIMs are interlinked with social movements and unions. They too produce policy prescriptions, press releases, books and many scholarly articles. Counter-hegemonic formations have their greatest power when rooted in social movements supported by mass adherence. The messages coming from social movements form the discursive basis of theoretical and policy statements made by counter-hegemonic AIMs made up some organic intellectuals, but also many inorganic intellectuals who, persuaded by a variety of factors, come to support a cause they take as their own and assume a position of discursive leadership. Counter-hegemonic AIMs have their academic theoreticians, their institutional support from unions and leftist parses, with expression provided by alternative media, like small presses and even some large publishers, like Blackwell or Routledge. Counter-hegemonic formations are particularly unstable at the theoretical-discursive level. In particular, academics are forced to follow tendencies in theoretical and philosophical orientation that phase in and especially out of contact with real societal issues. They are also often readily persuaded by the grant-getting game that seldom backs radical research, unless it is hidden. They can be persuaded too into apparently 'pragmatic' policy stances, those now proposed by the World Bank, especially when given positions in governments like those now in power in South Africa

Development, thus, becomes an intensely political arena, charged with dramatic confrontations, immediately at the discursive level, more fundamentally at the level of competing social imaginations. In this I agree with much of the post-structural literature, although I want to situate discourse in more complex contexts of class and institutional power.

My argument is that dominant AIM complexes produce the documentary basis of hegemonies in Gramsci's (1970) sense of a controlling set of meanings, values and imaginaries that persuade people to consent to the *status quo* (cf. Holub, 1992: 6). I accept that hegemony as a culture is actually composed from hegemonies as discursive fragments, each produced by specialized AIMs. My speculation is that hegemonies are fabricated into hegemony by the communication media. My conclusion is that hegemony exerts its greatest power in controlling social and economic imaginaries (Peet, 2000).

These are early, simple statements that await the elaborations and corrections enabled by much more empirical research. However, the basic position is that contestations over development alternatives should be seen in terms of competing AIM complexes, each producing discourses with differential powers. These form the discursive ingredients for unstable hegemonies and counter-hegemonies that inform imaginaries or limit the range of conceivable thoughts about an issue such as development. I see this as a geography of power and discourse, characterized by centers where powerful discourses are both fabricated and opposed and sub-centers where alternatives come precariously into existence as expressions of the experiences of oppressed groups. The geographic relation of colonization I see as a two-way process: persuasion from centers of power; and co-optation of certain ideas from sub-centers and alternative critical sources by dominant institutions, as with the World Bank's Comprehensive Development Framework or its notion of sustainable development.

Conclusion: Hegemonic and Counter-Hegemonic Discourses

In the contestation over development policy in South Africa, neoliberal ideas emanating from an AIM complex centered in Washington, in concert with ideas about economic restructuring emanating from business alliances within the country, obliterated the alternative, socialistic proposals based in the anti-apartheid struggle. The contest in South Africa, as elsewhere in the Third World, was so uneven that that the victory of neoliberalism was almost inevitable and alternative policy formulations pointless. Development, we might conclude, is hopelessly compromised and should be abandoned. Indeed, in development studies today, we find two anti-developmental positions. On the one side, development (as opposed to economic growth) is attacked by neoliberalism as an unwarranted intervention into economic processes best organized by market relations. On the other side, development efforts are portrayed by post-structuralists as 'uniquely efficient colonizers on behalf of central strategies of power' (Dubois, 1991: 19). In practice, as with the case of South Africa, development remains an area of contention between competing discourses of modernity based in different social and political imaginations.

From my perspective, the conclusion reached by neoliberals and post-structuralists alike, that development (economic intervention by rational social agency on behalf of poor people), should be abandoned, needs vigorous contestation by a critical form of modernist developmentalism. In particular, the wholesale dismissal of development as a modern project of emancipation by postmodern poststructural social theorists splits the ranks of progressive intellectuals at a time when the need for new development initiatives fundamentally different from neoliberalism could not be more pressing. Hence, the present urgency in development studies is a return to the more contentious past of the battle between alternative visions.

I propose that radical theorists still committed to development should coordinate their efforts around a common set of principals. Specifically, progressive developmentalists (thinkers about development) should do two things. First, launch an investigation into the origins, development dissemination and infiltration of neoliberalism as a social, economic and political discourse founded on right wing, yet not conservative, political philosophies. My own research along these lines suggests that neoliberalism is a continuation of the anti-Marxist positions established by Frank H. Knight (1884–1972) at the University of Chicago in the 1930s, 1940s and 1950s and continued by his students, Milton Friedman and George Stigler, in concert with ideas from Friedrich von Hayek, trained by the second generation of Austrian School economists and with connections to the Chicago School, the Hoover Institution and various right wing think tanks and funding sources – Hayek was a professor at Chicago between 1950 and 1962. I particularly want to stress Von Hayek's claim that liberalism in the tradition of nineteenth century England represents a third way between conservatism and socialism (Hayek, 1984).

Second, I propose modernist, yet, critical developmental alternatives, democratic in economic form, basic needs in orientation, social-transformational in intent. Despite the recent appearance of some significant work, such as the collection of essays titled Globalization and Progressive Economic Policy (Baker, Epstein and Pollin, 1998) and Arthur MacEwan's *Neo-Liberalism or Democracy* (1999), alternative economic policy formulation remains woefully inadequate compared with the sophistication of neoliberalism. Nowhere is the need for such an alternative more evident than in post-liberation South Africa, now firmly under the political control of the ANC, yet economically controlled by outside forces, not the least of which is the developmental imaginary.

References

Adelzadeh, A. (1994) 'An Appraisal of the White Paper Discussion Document on the RDP'. *Occasional Paper Series no.1*. Johannesburg: NIEP.

Adelzadeh, A. (1996) 'From the RDP to GEAR: The Gradual Embracing of Neo-liberalism in Economic Policy'. *Occasional Paper Series no.3* Johannesburg: NIEP.

ANC (1987) *Constitutional Guidelines for a Democratic South Africa*.

ANC (1991) *Draft Resolution on ANC Economic Policy for National Conference*. ANC Department of Economic Policy.

ANC (1992) *Ready to Govern: ANC Policy Guidelines for a Democratic South Africa*. South Africa: ANC.

ANC (1994) *The Reconstruction and Development Progamme: A Policy Framework*. Johannesburg: Umanyano Publications

ANC (1997) *All Power to the People!: Draft Strategy and Tactics of the African National Congress*. Pretoria: ANC, July (draft).

Arce, M. and Daniel, G. (1999) 'The Political Economy of the Neoliberal Transition'. *Latin American Research Review* 34, 212–20.

Baker, D., G. Epstein and R. Pollin (eds) (1998) *Globalization and Progressive Economic Policy*. Cambridge, UK: Cambridge University Press.

Bauer, P.T. (1972) *Dissent on Development*. Cambridge: Harvard University Press.

Bauer, P.T. (1981) *Equality, the Third World and Economic Delusion*. London: Methuen.

Bond, P. (1991) *Commanding Heights and Community Control: New Economics for a New South Africa*. Johannesburg: Raven Press.

Bond, P. (1996) 'Neoliberalism Comes to South Africa'. *MultinationalMonitor*, May, 8–14.

Bond, P. (1997) 'Fighting Neo-Liberalism: the South African Front'. *Southern Africa Report* 12 (2), 14–20.

Bond, P. (2000) *Elite Transition: From Apartheid to Neoliberalism in South Africa*. London: Pluto Press and Pietermaritzburg: University of Natal Press.

Bond, P. with M. Khosa (eds) (1999) *An RDP Policy Audit*. Pretoria: Human Sciences Research Council Press.

Brixen, P. and Tarp, F. (1996) 'South Africa: Macroeconomic Perspectives for the Medium Term'. *World Development* 24, 989–1001.

Brohman, J. (1996) *Popular Development: Rethinking the Theory and Practice of Development*. Oxford: Blackwell.

Brown, E. (1996) 'Articulating Opposition in Latin America: The Consolidation of Neoliberalism and the Search for Radical Alternatives'. *Political Geography* 15,169–92.

Ceruti, C. (996) *How and Why the ANC's Nationalisation Policy Changed: Economic Nationalism and the Changing State-Capital Relation*. M.A.Thesis, Department of Sociology, University of the Witwatersrand, Johannesburg.

Chomsky, N. (1999) *Profit over People: Neoliberalism and Global Order*. NY: Seven Stories Press.

Colclough, C. and Manor, J. (eds) (1991) *States or Markets? Neoliberalism and the Development Policy Debate*. Oxford: Oxford University Press.

COSATU (1996) *Social Equity and Job Creation*. Johannesburg: COSATU.

Cowie, J. (1999) *Capital Moves: RCA's 70 – Year Quest for Cheep Labor*. Ithaca: Cornell University Press.

Cowie, M.P. and R.W. Shenton (1996) *Doctrines of Development*. London: Routledge.

Crush, J. (ed.) (1995) *Power of Development*. London: Routledge.

DeMartino, G. (1999). 'Global Neoliberalism, Policy Autonomy and International Competitive Dynamics'. *Journal of Economic Issues* 33, 343–9.

Donaldson, A.R. (1997) 'Social Development and Macroeconomic Policy'. *Development Southern Africa* 14, 447–462.

Dreyfus, H.L. and P. Rabinow (1983) *Michel Foucault: Beyond Structuralism and Hermeneutics*. Chicago: University of Chicago Press.

DuBois, M. (1991) 'The Governance of the Third World: A Foucauldian Perspective on Power Relations in Development'. *Alternatives* 16, 1–30.

Edwards, A. (1989) 'The Irrelevance of Development Studies'. *Third World Quarterly* 11, 116–35.

Escobar, A. (1984–5) 'Discourse and Power in Development: Michel Foucault and the Relevance of his Work to the Third World'. *Alternatives* 10, 377–400.

Escobar, A. (1988) 'Power and Visibility: Development and the Invention and Management of the Third World'. *Cultural Anthropology* 3, 428–43.

Escobar, A. (1992) 'Imagining a Post-Development Era? Critical Thought Development and Social Movements'. *Social Text* 31/32, 20–56.

Escobar, A. (1995) *Encountering Development: The Making and Unmaking of the Third World*. Princeton, NJ: Princeton University Press.

Esterhuyse, W. and P. Nel (eds) (1990) *The ANC and its Leaders*. Cape Town: Tafelberg.

Fine, B. and Z. Rustomjee (1996) *The Political Economy of South Africa: From Minerals – Energy Complex to Industrialization*. London: Hurst.

Foucault, M. (1972) *The Archaeology of Knowledge*. NY: Harper and Row.

Foucault, M. (1973) *The Order of Things*. NY: Vintage Press.

Foucault, M. (1979) *Discipline and Punish: The Birth of the Prison*. NY: Vintage Books.

Foucault, M. (1980) *Power/Knowledge: Selected Interviews and other Writings, 1972–1977*. NY: Pantheon.

Freedom Charter (1955) Appendix B in Esterhuyse and Nel pp. 157–161.

Friedman, S. (1993) *The Long Journey: South Africa's Quest for a Negotiated Settlement*. Johannesburg: Raven Press

Galbraith, J. K. (1999) 'The Crisis of Globalization'. *Dissent* 46, 3: 12–16.

Gelb, S. (1991) *South Africa's Economic Crisis*. London: Zed Press.

Giddens, A. (1990) *The Consequences of Modernity*. Cambridge: Polity.

Government of the Republic of South Africa (1994) *White Paper on Reconstruction and Development Government Gazette*. Cape Town 23 November.

Government of the Republic of South Africa (1996) *Growth, Employment and Redistribution: A Macroeconomic Strategy (GEAR)*. Department of Finance, Republic of South Africa.

Habib, A. and Padayachee, V. (2000) 'Economic Policy and Power Relations in South Africa's Transition to Democracy'. *World Developmen*, 28 (forthcoming).

Hanson, M. and Hentz, J.J. (1999) 'Neocolonialism and Neoliberalism in South Africa and Zambia'. *Political Science Quarterly* 114, 479–502.

Haque, M.S. (1999) 'The Fate of Sustainable Development under Neo-Liberal Regimes in Developing Countries'. *International Political Science Review* 20, 197–218.

Hart-Landsberg, M. and Burkett, P. (1998) 'Contradictions of Capitalist Industrialization in East Asia: A Critique of 'Flying Geese' Theories of Development'. *Economic Geography* 74 87–110.

Holland, M. (1998) 'World Bank Book (Shh)'. *The Nation*, 226, 10, 4–5.

Kapstein, E.B. (1999) *Sharing the Wealth: Workers and the World Economy*. NY: Norton.

Kapur, D. (1997) *The World Bank: Its First Half Century*. Washington D.C.: Brookings Institution.

Kiely, R. (1998) 'Neo-Liberalism Revised? A Critical Account of World Bank Concepts of Good Governance and Market-Friendly Intervention'. *Capital and Class* 64, 63–88.

Klak, T. (1998) *Neo Liberalism: the Caribbean Context*. Lanham: Rowman and Littlefield.

Klak, T. and G. Myers (1997) 'The Discursive Tactics of Neoliberal Development in Small Third World Countries'. *Geoforum* 28, 133–149.

Kim, J.T. (1999) 'Neoliberalism and the Decline of the Developmental State'. *Journal of Contemporary Asia* 29, 441–61.

Krueger, A. (1995) *The Political Economy of Trade Protection*. Chicago: University of Chicago Press.

Krueger, A. (1998) *The WTO as an International Organization*. Chicago: University of Chicago Press.

Kurtz, M.J. (1999) 'Chile's Neo-Liberal Revolution: Incremental Decisions and Structural Transformation'. *Journal of Latin American Studies* 31, 399–427.

Lal, D. (1983) *The Poverty of Development Economics*. London: IEA Hobart Paperback No. 16.

Logan, I. and Mengisteab, K. (1993) 'IMF-World Bank Adjustment and Structural Transformation in Sub-Saharan Africa'. *Economic Geography* 69 (1), 1–24.

MacEwari, A. (1999) *Neo-Liberalism or Democracy?* London: Zed Press.

MacGregor, S. (1999) 'Welfare, Neoliberalism and New Paternalism: Three Ways for Social Policy in Late Capitalist Societies'. *Capital and Class 67*, 91–118.

Mandela, N. (1990) *The Struggle is My Life* 3rd. ed. London: International Defence and Aid Fund.

Magubane, B. (1979) *The Political Economy of Race and Class in South Africa*. NY: Monthly Review Press.

Marais, H. (1997) *South Africa Limits to Change: the Political Economy of Transformation*. London: Zed Press.

Medcalf, L.J. and K.M. Dolbeare (1985) *Neopolitics: American Political Ideas in the 1980's*. NY: Random House.

Megay, Edward N. (1970) 'Anti-Pluralist Liberalism: The German Neoliberals'. *Political Science Quarterly* 85, 151–74.

Michie, J. and Padayachee, V. (eds). *The Political Economy of South Africa's Transition*. London: Dryden Press.

Murray, J.M. (ed.) (1982) *South African Capitalism and Black Political Opposition*. Cambridge, UK: Schenkman.

Niou, E.M.S. and Ordeshook, P.C. (1994) 'Less Filling, Tastes Great: the Realist-Neoliberal Debate'. *World Politics* 46, 209–34.

North, D.C. (1995) 'The New Institutional Economics and Third World Development'. In J. Harris, J. Hunter and C. Lewis (eds) *The New Institutional Economics and Third World*

Development. London: Routledge 17–26.

O'Dougherty, M. (1999) 'The Devalued State and Nation: Neoliberalism and the Moral Economy Discourse of the Brazilian Middle Class'. *Latin American Perspectives* 26, 151–74.

Overbeek, H. (1990) *Global Capitalism and National Decline: The Thatcher Decade in Perspective*. London: Unwin Hyman.

Overbeek, H. (ed.) (1993) *Restructuring Hegemony in the Global Political Economy: The Rise of Transnational Neo-Liberalism in the 1980s*. London: Routledge.

Padayachee, V. (1994) 'Debt, Development and Democracy: The IMF in Post-Apartheid South Africa'. *Review of African Political Economy* 62, 585–597.

Padayachee, V. (1998) 'Progressive Academic Economists and the Challenge of Development in South Africa's Decade of Liberation'. *Review of African Political Economy* 77, 431–450.

Patel, E. (1993) *Engine of Development?* South Africa's National Economic Forum Kenwyn: Juta.

Payer, C. (1982) *The World Bank: A Critical Appraisal*. NY: Monthly Review Press.

Peck, J. and A. Tickell (1994) 'Jungle Law Breaks Out: Neoliberalism and Global-Local Disorder'. *Area* 26, 317–326.

Peet, R. with Hartwick, E. (1999) *Theories of Development*. NY: Guilford.

Pickering, A. (ed.) (1992) *Science as Practice and Culture*. Chicago: University of Chicago Press.

Pityana, B., Ramphele, M., Mpumlwana, L. and Wilson, L. (1992) *Bounds of Possibility: The Legacy of Steve Biko and Black Consciousness*. London: Zed Press.

Pugh, C. (1995) 'International Structural Adjustment and its Sectoral and Spatial Impacts'. *Urban Studies* 32: 261–285.

Rahnema, M. with V. Bawtree (eds) (1997) *The Post-Development Reader*. London: Zed Pess.

Rand, A. (1957) *Atlas Shrugged*. NY: Random House.

Rantete, J.M. (1994) *Facing the Challenges of Transition: A Critical Analysis of the African National Congress in the 1990s*. M.A. Dissertation, Faculty of Arts, University of the Witwatersrand.

Rees, J. (1992) 'Markets – the Panacea for Environmental Regulation?'. *Geoforum* 23, 383–394.

Richards, Donald G. (1997) 'The Political Economy of Neoliberal Reform in Latin America: A Critical Appraisal'. *Capital and Class* 61, 19–43.

Rist, G. (1997) *The History of Development: From Western Origins to Global Faith*. London: Zed Press.

Robertson, R. (1992) *Globalization*. London: Sage.

Sachs, W. (ed.) (1991) *The Development Diction: A Guide to Knowledge as Power*. London: Zed Press.

Schrire, R. (ed.) (1992) *Wealth or Poverty? Critical Choices for South Africa*. Cape Town: Oxford University Press.

Simon, D. (1995) 'Debt Democracy and Development: Sub-Saharan Africa in the 1990s'. In D. Simon, W. Van Spengen, C. Dixon and A. Narman (eds) *Structurally Adjusted Africa*. London: Pluto Press 17–44.

Simon, D. (1997) 'Urbanization, Globalization and Economic Crisis in Africa'. In Rakodi, C. (ed.) *The Urban Challenge in Africa*. London: United Nations University Press, 74–110.

Soros, G. (1998) *The Crisis of Global Capitalism: Open Society Endangered*. NY: Public Affairs.

Stein, H. (1992) 'Deindustrialisation, Adjustment, the World Bank and the IMF in Africa'. *World Development* 20, 83–95.

Streeten, P. (1987) 'Structural Adjustment: A Survey of the Issues and Options'. *World Development* 15, 1469–1482.

South African Reserve Bank (1999) *Quarterly Bulletin* no 211 (March) Pretoria: South African Reserve Bank.

Sunter, C. (1987) *The World and South Africa in the 1990s*. Tafelburg: Human and Rousseau.

Tapscott, C. (1995) 'Changing Discourses of Development in South Africa?'. In G. Crush (ed.) *Power of Development*. London: Routledge, 176–9 1.

Toye, J. (1987) *Dilemmas of Development: Reflections on the Counter – Revolution in*

Development Theory and Policy. Oxford: Basil Blackwell.

Tsongas, P. (1981) *The Road from Here: Liberalism and Realities in the 1980s*. NY: Knopf.

Tucker, B. and Scoff, B. (eds) (1992) *South Africa: Prospects for Successful Transition*. Kenwyn: Juta.

Turok, I. (1995) 'Restructuring or Reconciliation? South Africa's Reconstruction and Development Programme'. *International Journal of Urban and Regional Research* 19, 305–318.

Veltmeyer, H. *et al.* (1998) 'Neoliberalism and Class Conflict in Latin America'. *Journal of Interamerican Studies and World Affairs* 40,127–30.

von Hayek, F. (1956) *The Road to Serfdom*. Chicago: University of Chicago Press.

von Hayek, F. (1984) *The Essence of Hayek*. Sanford: Hoover Institution Press.

Wade, R. (1992) 'East Asia's Economic Success: Conflicting Perspectives, Partial Insights, Shaky Evidence'. *World Politics* 44, 270–320.

Waters, M. (1995) *Globalization*. London: Routledge.

Watts, M. (1994) 'Development H: The Privatisation of Everything'. *Progress in Human Geography* 18, 371–384.

Weyland, K. (1999) 'Neoliberal Populism in Latin America and Eastern Europe'. *Comparative Politics* 31, 379–401.

Williams, G. (1994) 'Why Structural Adjustment is Necessary and Why It Doesn't Work'. *Review of African Political Economy* 60, 214–225.

Williamson, J. (1997) 'The Washington Consensus Revisited'. In Louis Emmerij (ed.) *Economic and Social Development into the XXI Century*. Washington D.C: Inter-American Development Bank.

Williamson, J. (ed.) (1990) *Latin American Adjustment: How Much has Happened?* Washington: Institute for International Economics.

World Bank (1981) *Accelerated Development in Sub-Saharan Africa: An Agenda for Action*. Washington D.C: World Bank.

World Bank (1983) *World Development Report*. NY: Oxford University Press.

World Bank (1987) *World Development Report*. NY: Oxford University Press.

World Bank (1991) *World Development Report*. NY: Oxford University Press.

World Bank (1996) *South Africa – Industrial Competitiveness and Job Creation*. Project ID ZAPA 48606.

World Bank (1997) *World Development Report 1978–1997*. CD ROM edition. Washington D.C: World Bank.

World Bank (1999–2000) *World Development Report*. NY: Oxford University Press.

Chapter 11

From Anarchy to Renaissance in Africa in the New Millennium: New Regionalisms as Responses to Globalizations

Timothy M. Shaw

More than anything, Africa's people need to regain their self-confidence. Only then can Africa engage as an equal with the rest of the world, devising its own economic programmes and development policies. Only then can they make deals to end wars and build political institutions: institutions they can actually believe in. 'The Trouble with Africa.' *Economist* 12 May 2000.

Regionalism has been brought back into the academic debate as well as the policy one after some decades of neglect. This renewed trend, often labeled the new regionalism, is characterized by its multidimensionality, complexity, flexibility, fluidity and non-conformity. It is therefore appropriate to speak of regionalism in the plural rather than the singular form Hettne and Soderbaum (1998: 4) Guest editorial to special issue on the new regionalism

Globalization offers great opportunities for human advance but only with stronger governance Globalization is creating new threats to human security in rich countries and poor...National and global governance have to be reinvented with human development and equity at their core. UNDP (1999: 1, 3 and 7) Human Development Report 1999.

Introduction

Allegedly, Africa is the most marginal of the continents in an era of globalizations (Hoogvelt, 1997). Paradoxically, however, the new international dynamics may reveal more about new forms of regionalism(s) in Africa than in more integrated regions even if the Asian crises of the late-1990s impacted this continent less directly than others (Boas, Marchand and Shaw, 1999a; Hettne and Soderbaum, 1998; Shaw 1998). Given its position in the periphery of the new world order, it may also be the least affected by any particular contemporary instabilities in the global financial architecture. Yet, it has been profoundly and negatively impacted by recent interrelated ideological, institutional and structural changes, which reflect the several dimensions of globalizations (Germain, 2000; Held *et al.*, 1999; Sassen, 1998; Scholte, 2000; UNDP, 1999). This is especially the case with the rise of neo-liberalism since the early-1980s. The end of bipolarity and the emergence of a range of new security issues have reinforced changes brought on by neoliberalism since the early-1990s (Shaw and MacLean, 1999; Shaw and Schnabel, 1999).

The balance in Africa between regional cooperation and regional conflicts, between confidence and uncertainty, is a fragile one. Any prospect of an African renaissance has receded as fighting flared from Sierra Leone to the Horn, Congo to Angola in the first few months of the twenty-first century. To be sure, Africans are resilient and productive even in apparent anarchy marked only by the accumulation of wealth from resource plunder (Shaw, 2000b). Certainly, not all of the continent's problems are internal; some can be traced to inappropriate adjustment conditionalities as the *Economist* (12 May 2000) blithely indicated as it escalated its rhetoric from At Risk in Africa (22 April 2000) to Hopeless Africa.

Whether African countries face risk or hopelessness is underlain by inconsistent and weak state control over the institutions of government. The African ruler finds himself trapped, desiring power and control while the outside world makes demands about democracy, human rights and good governance, which weaken his position and could exacerbate instability and chaos. As this process unfolds, states are increasingly becoming shell which, on the outside have all the trappings of a modern state; but which, on the inside, have been hollowed out.

This chapter seeks to use the notion of new regionalisms to project a new reality on the continent as the new millennium proceeds. These new regionalisms include: developmental economies, ecologies, corridors and triangles; civil societies and medias; war economies and peace-building responses. Given the complex nature of these developments, is the continent anticipating either renaissance and/or anarchy in the new century (Ottaway, 1999). How compatible are the features of new regionalisms over time (Shaw and Nyango'ro, 2000). Despite the current focus on matters of post-bipolarity, -industrialization and local to global governance (Stiles, 2000), is the continent in the vanguard of new forms of realism in both theory and practice at century's end (Shaw, 1998). What lessons can be learnt from this peripheral continent for comparative studies of new regionalisms (Boas, Marchand and Shaw, 1999a). I assert that meso-level regional analysis, if appropriately informed, can throw better light on the diversities of political economy and culture on the continent than more established approaches. Such insights entail profound applied, policy and analytic implications as suggested in the final section of the chapter (Grugel and Hout, 1999; Payne 1998 and 1999, van Walraven, 1999). As Hettne and Soderbaum (1998: 4) suggest in their opening citation above, regionalism has been brought back in.

The backdrop to the new regionalism perspective is constituted of regional or meso-level dynamics between global and local or macro- and micro-level connections (Stiles, 2000). These dynamics, which involve cross-border exchange, may be crucial in explaining the descent of a few failed or collapsed African regimes into shadow states. Cases like Sierra Leone and Somalia suggest that the erstwhile franchise state now gets licensed not only by the IFIs but also by private debt bond and security agencies. If such examples proliferate then just as we were concerned about the prospects of Lebanonization in the 1980s, we may come to define a distinctive typology of shadow regimes in the new millennium, characterized by a multiplication of mafias and other forms of transnational criminal networks. The analytic and policy challenges of conceptualizing as well as containing such shadow states are profound (Shaw and Nyango'ro, 1999).

The discussion in this chapter takes it to be axiomatic that any local to global social relationship (Shaw, 2000a; Stiles, 2000) inevitably includes a trio of heterogeneous actors:

1. states (and interstate global and regional institutions);
2. economic structures (e.g. multinational corporations (MNCs) and informal sectors) (Shaw and van der Westhuizen 1999); and
3. civil societies (from international non-governmental organizations (INGOs) to grass-roots movements) (Van Rooy, 1999).

Most of these transitions have been less dramatic than the *Economist* suggests. Yet, the central characteristics of the continent have been transformed over the last two decades.

Happily, the brother of the initiator of the notion of an African renaissance, Moeletsi Mbeki (1998), has suggested that such a renaissance at the turn of the century is not meant to be primarily a state-led one, unlike earlier epochs of African nationalisms. Rather, the dynamics of such momentum would come from economic and social changes, for example, the development of indigenous private enterprises and civil societies, professional associations and black empowerment in culture, economics, finance and technology (c.f Vale and Maseko, 1998). To be sure, the balance among the trio of state, economy and civil society varies between regions and over time, but none of them can be excluded or overlooked in any ongoing relationship in either Africa or elsewhere (Shaw and Nyang'oro, 2000). This is especially so at the intermediate, meso-level, which is increasingly characterized by a range of heterogeneous actors, coalitions and relations, which are both cooperative and conflictual formal and informal, legal and illegal.

I turn first to an overview of the genesis and current state of new regionalisms as both analysis and praxis with a focus on trilateral relations among states-interstate organizations, companies and civil societies in a post-neoliberal era in which new skepticism about the gains and sustainability of globalizations and markets is being voiced (Boas, Marchand and Shaw, 1999a). Second, I identify a range of novel forms of regional interactions and institutions beyond established, intergovernmental regional organizations (Shaw, 1999a). Third, reflective of renewed conflict and related realist analysis, I examine new as well as old forms of confrontation and alliance: beyond peace building to sustainable human security? The fourth section treats the recent, critical perspective on the real international political economy of lingering conflicts in cases like Angola and Sierra Leone – i.e. production and accumulation for the minority in the midst of destruction for the majority, characterized by regional and global connections, especially the world of diamonds (Shaw, 2000b). In the fifth section, I focus on the other side of new (and old) regionalisms, civil societies at the regional level (MacLean and Shaw, 1996; Shaw and MacLean, 1999). These include not only ubiquitous non-governmental organizations (NGOs) but also ethnicities, genders, professions, regions, religions, sports (Boas, Marchand and Shaw, 1999b). In the final and sixth section, I attempt to highlight some salient lessons, which might be learned from African cases and debates for both older disciplines and discourses as well as future policy interventions.

New Regionalisms and Trilateral Relationships in a Post-Neoliberal Context

The old regional studies focused on formal, interstate economic and strategic relations (Hettne, Inotai and Sunkel, 1999, Hettne and Soderbaum, 1998). By contrast, new regionalisms attempt to capture the diversities of definition and interaction, such as Europe defined by MNCs or mafias. This approach includes in its treatment, non-state and informal interactions at the national and global levels. This makes it possible to treat the interconnections between more and less statist relations as well as to transcend the official, by recognizing how the latter relates to the unofficial in myriad ways: the multiple conceptions of regions as well as diversity of issue areas, from ecologies and ethnicities to civil societies and private armies (Boas, Marchand and Shaw, 1999a).

The new unlike the old regional studies also incorporates all three major types of actors in its purview, not just states but also companies and communities. Recognition of the trilateral character of all social relations, especially since the end of the Cold War and the concomitant hegemony of neo-liberal values, is an essential attribute (and advantage!) of new regionalisms. *State* here includes official governmental organizations from local to global (e.g. IFI and UN systems); *economies* include informal (and illegal?) sectors as well as the more familiar world of MNCs; and *societies* incorporate not only indigenous and international NGOs but also charities, cooperatives, grass-roots groups, medias and new social movements (Aulakh and Schechter, 2000; Lindberg and Sverrisson, 1997; Van Rooy, 1999).

The old regional studies gradually extended its purview to include the South, at least in terms of formal, interstate economic institutions. By contrast, the literature of the new regionalism is largely rooted in non- or semi-state cases from the South – e.g. maquiladoras and export-processing zones (EPZs), growth triangles in Asia, corridors in Southern Africa (Gelb and Manning, 1998) (see next section below), diasporas from the South in the North, track-two diplomacy and confidence-building measures (CBMs)/peace-keeping operations (PKOs) and increasingly links with IPE, development and human security perspectives (Boas, Marchand and Shaw, 1999b and c). Not only are the old and new regionalisms different in terms of theoretical geneses and affinities, they are not always compatible in practice. In Southeast Asia, for example, the connection between, say, EPZs and ASEAN, is not clear (Chen and Kwan, 1997).

Cox's (1999) article on varieties of civil societies as well as of regionalisms is insightful in terms of advancing typologies of regional capitalisms and social relations compatible with the new regionalism perspective. He treats diversities of civil societies over time as well as between salient regions: North Atlantic, Asian, East European as well as African. He insists that the definition of such social movements needs to be flexible, given continuing social changes. He insists also, that civil society has become the comprehensive term for various ways in which people express collective wills independently of (and often in opposition to) established economic and political power (Cox, 1999: 10). He proceeds to distinguish between top-down and bottom-up impetuses for distinct (divergent?) NGOs:

> In a bottom-up sense, civil society is the realm in which those who are disadvantaged by globalization of the new world economy can mount their protests and seek alternatives... By

contrast, in a top-down sense, states and corporate interests influence the development of this current version of civil society towards making it an agency for stabilizing the social and political status quo.

Building on these notions, this chapter highlights four areas derived from sub-Saharan African cases which illuminate the emerging discourse about new regionalisms and may be contrasted with some disquieting forms of more or less (in)formal conflicts elsewhere as treated in entries 3 and 4 below. Together these cover the spectrum of formal/informal, West/East/Southern Africa, issue areas, range of involved actors and analytic perspectives. In many ways, these make us go back to Samir Amin's (1972) seminal essay on the distinctive types of post-colonial regional political economies on the continent: Africas of the peasant economy, mining economy and labor reserves. Today we would presumably identify the several Africas of emerging markets, transitions/reconstruction, peacekeeping operations and anarchies.

Beyond Regional Organizations: Corridors, Ecologies, Triangles and New Forms of Meso-Level Governance

The prevailing perspective about regionalism in Africa is that it is a disappointment because formal sector regional trade has failed to grow faster than at the global level (McCarthy, 1996; Teunissen, 1996)). However, its informal sector exchange continues to boom, partly in response to formal level constraints. Moreover, official statistics only record official trade within established inter-governmental groupings such as the Common Market of Eastern and Southern Africa (COMESA), Economic Community of West African States (ECOWAS) and Southern African Development Community (SADC) (Gibb, 1998; Nel and McGowan, 1999; Vale, Swatuk and Oden, 2000). Yet palpably, ECOWAS is characterized by a vast network of informal flows, which may yet be augmented by large-scale official schemes, such as the proposed West African Gas Pipeline agreed in mid-1999 with Chevron and Shell to transport natural gas from their Nigerian wells to Ghana through Benin and Togo.

This section seeks to identify some contemporary regional responses to the constraints and opportunities of globalizations, as both praxis as well as ideology (Germain, 2000; Gills, 1997; Murphy, 2000; Scholte, 2000). In particular, it seeks to highlight some current indigenous reactions to exponential globalizations as well as to privilege some of the continent's own distinctive, yet, under-appreciated contributions to comparative analysis and praxis. These have developed out of a significant tradition of innovative forms of regionalisms, partly in response to colonial and/or settler resistance (Clapham, 1998). Such non- or semi-state strategies were themselves developed in reaction to the settler regimes own unholy alliance, which came to control a shrinking proportion of the territory and population of the remaining white-ruled states.

In short, regional groupings, state and non-state alike, do not necessarily have to include all the territory or population, communities or resources of participating countries. As we will see in the next section, complex and dynamic strategic partnerships among several state and non-state actors around the current Congo conflicts split some countries and communities in Central Africa. Guerilla struggles led to the first corridor in Africa in the mid-1980s, the *Beira Corridor* connecting Zimbabwe to global trade through the middle waist of Mozambique. This has since been replicated and upgraded in current plans for some nine corridors within SADC, including three (the most advanced in terms of infrastructural and organizational development) around the perimeters of post-apartheid South Africa, particularly its now post-mineral/-industrial heartland, Gauteng (Gelb and Manning, 1998: vi), with divisions of labor among several levels of states, companies and civil societies (Shaw, 1999).

Maputo Corridor between Gauteng and Maputo port is designed to advance development in the relatively impoverished Mpumalanga Province of South Africa as well as of Southern Mozambique. It is a regional project in which the private sector plays a leading role, but in which city and provincial authorities and the two national regimes are also positively engaged.

Trans-Kalahari Corridor between Lobatse in Botswana and Windhoek in Namibia, linking Gauteng with the Atlantic coast at Walvis Bay, cutting some 500 kms off the trip and completing the Maputo-Walvis Bay Indian Ocean-Atlantic Oceans link. Again, largely a corporate initiative, albeit with national state involvement by Botswana and Namibia.

Lubombo Corridor linking Durban with Maputo via Northern Kwazulu-Natal and Swaziland. This is more of a South African Spatial Development Initiative (SDI) than a short-term corporate venture. It involves more community participation because of high population densities in the region (Gelb and Manning, 1998).

Lesotho Highlands Water Project, already well under way towards completion, involves the damming and flow reversal of the Orange/Senqi River into the Vaal Dam so that water and HEP are delivered to Gauteng. It is largely a South African private sector corporate investment with Rand Water support. It is opposed by many ecological and developmental NGOs and local Basotho communities, although supported by the Lesotho state, which stands to collect R 6.5 million rent each month as well as gain access to some water and electricity (NB ongoing World Commission on Dams is the first such global commission to be located in the South – Cape Town – with South Africa's first Minister for Water Affairs, Dr Kader Asmal, as Chair).

Cahobra Bassa Dam transmission line rehabilitation: a 1 440 km long power line rebuilding, largely by the South African private sector, not only to bring HEP to Gauteng but also to enable the regional grid to be connected, from the powerful Congo River to Cape Town.

In all these five, current corridor-type projects, especially the first (and others which are much longer-term such as Lobito, Malange and Namibe) forms of multi-stakeholder or trilateral governance have yet to be agreed, let alone effected (Taylor, 2000). Thus, there is a palpable democratic deficit not only in SADC (African Development Bank, 1993), which has only embryonic links outside its state members to the local and global corporate and civil society worlds, but also in these sub-regional projects. SADC like the ECA may now seek to develop dialogue with civil society as well as the private sector along with its extra-regional partners; but its credibility in such links is problematic and it has yet to sustain such accountable relationships over time. Whether SADC will really deal as partners if not equals with the Southern African Development Council NGO Coordinating Committee or ECA's embryonic Centre for Civil Society, remains to be seen, with important implications for the future of regionalism (Barnard, 1998; MacLean and Shaw, 1996).

The primary beneficiaries of corridor or triangle arrangements tend to be larger South African companies, both state (e.g. Eskom, SAA and Transnet) and private (e.g. Anglo American, SA Breweries) and local to national official jurisdictions rather than local communities or NGOs. The degree to which these sub-regional arrangements reinforce or dilute somewhat moribund established interstate institutions such as SADC is quite problematic given the still state-centric character of the latter. Surprisingly, to date, there has been no analytic attention given to such issues of compatibility, although there is a discourse about old/new, inner/outer, upper/lower case SADC (Dunn and Shaw, 2001; Vale, Swatuk and Oden, 2001).

In addition to such corridor projects, Southern Africa in particular, but sub-Saharan Africa in general, has been characterized by its own emerging pattern of hubs-and-spokes: airlines (e.g. Kenya Airways and SAA, but also Air Afrique and Ethiopian Airlines), cable TV and internet servers plus websites (e.g. MNet and iAfrica), distribution or logistics companies (e.g. Avis and Unitrans), financial centers (e.g. Johannesburg Stock Exchange) (Kenny and Moss, 1998), franchises (e.g. Spur, Steers, Nandos), think-tanks and universities, private- and state-funded business and economics program. These tend to be replicated in the NGO world also, with Gauteng again being dominant (c.f Barnard, 1998), as well as in other sectors of civil society such as medias (e.g. SABC and Weekly Mail and Guardian as well as Mnet). Export Processing Zones (EPZs), the icons of flexible globalization, likewise tend to be concentrated around already established economic cores like Gauteng and Cape Town, which are also centers in the middle of corridors. Their attractiveness is now reinforced in terms of offering not only cheap labor and infrastructure but also security through gated communities and compounds (UNDP, 1994).

New as Well as Old Forms of Conflict and Alliance: Beyond Peace-Building to Sustainable Human Security

Africa has not benefited from any post-Cold War peace dividend. Indeed, internal and regional conflicts have proliferated and escalated in the 1990s, with profound implications for regional and continental security and stability, especially when redefined in terms of human security (Shaw, 1999b; Shaw and MacLean, 1999; Shaw and Schnabel, 1999). Although almost all African conflicts are internal in origin, they invariably become regional in scale as they progress. Moreover, the declared Revolution in Military Affairs (RMA) has at best been perverse on the continent: a return to basic strategies and technologies such as machetes, landmines and AK47s (Boutwell and Klare, 1999; Tomlin, 1998). Further, such struggles never involve only national armies; they always include non-state actors, both conflictual and economic, short-term crisis-oriented and longer-term developmental. Many are long-running as they involve competition over scarce resources, control of which enables factions to continue fighting (e.g. diamonds in Angola and Sierra Leone) (Reno, 1998). In short, these are not really complex political emergencies (Cliffe, 1999): complex definitely, but typically economic and ecological as well as political and rarely crisis length (Ali and Matthews, 1999). The apparent inability of states to eliminate or contain such conflicts has led to the privatization of security in the form of private armies, whether of the more organized corporate Executive Outcomes style (Howe, 1998; Shearer, 1998) or the more chaotic child soldier variety.

As indicated in the next section, the sustainability of such conflicts is apparent around Angola, Liberia/Sierra Leone and the Horn, with the first and last spilling over into the Great Lakes and Congo. Moreover, as such conflicts have sucked in a growing range of actors, so revisionist notions of neo-realism become attractive again, albeit in a post-Westphalian and bipolar context (Shaw and Dunn, 2001; Vale, Swatuk and Oden, 2001). The salience of a focus on meso-level patterns of conflict and response is apparent in Lionel Cliffe's (1999: 89) analysis of continuing conflicts in the Horn:

> cross-border or inter-regional dimensions a pattern of mutual intervention. Each government sought to deal with its own internal conflicts by some degree of support for insurgencies in neighboring states regional stability (is affected by) the role of regional bodies in combining economic cooperation, peace making and security roles.

Regional responses on the continent to persistent conflict have stretched from a redesigned OAU facility to attempts by inter-state organizations such as ECOWAS, Inter-Governmental Authority on Development (IGAD) and SADC to establish confidence-building and peacekeeping structures. Some of these may be little more than thinly disguised forms of regional hegemony appropriate to the 1990s. The ECOMOG reaction, for example, is largely a Nigerian creation to force peace in Liberia then Sierra Leone (van Walraven, 1999). While the controversial Organ for Politics, Defence and Security may be less clearly a South African initiative, its stillborn character is a reflection of simmering competition between Mugabe's Zimbabwean regime and the post-apartheid state in South Africa (Gibb, 1998; Vale, Swatuk and Oden, 2000). The continuing standoff is in stark contrast to the relatively successful and cooperative anti-apartheid and -destabilization Inter-State Defence and Security Committee of the Front Line States (FLS). Meanwhile, IGAD continues to evolve away from its initial ecological and functional emphasis towards a broader mandate to advance human security as well as human development; protracted track-two diplomacy over the long-standing inter-related tensions in Southern Sudan and the Horn (*Current History*, 1999).

Both IGAD and SADC are being impacted by the interrelated crises at yea's or decade's (even century's?) dawn: the strategic or leadership one around Congo and the economic or political one around land in Zimbabwe. Clearly, despite all the assertions, none of the competing coalitions can easily capture the extensive, anarchic territory of the Congo. Consequently, the armies of Angola, Namibia and Zimbabwe on the one hand and of Rwanda and Uganda on the other, face a protracted stalemate in which neither side can appear to be weak! Similarly, the discredited Mugabe regime in Zimbabwe can neither afford to lose the 2002 presidential elections after its narrow victory in the 2000 general elections, nor can it afford to sustain its war in Congo. So, events in early-twenty-first-century, constitute something of a regional conjuncture in addition to broader global trends. What is the potential impact on old/new regionalisms in South(ern) Africa? Will economic rationalities and civil society commonsense win out, with positive longer-term effects, or will the discredited state cling to power for a variety of parochial reasons?

The diversity of actors, interests and relations in such new regionalisms not only complicates notions of human development and security; it also opens up new possibilities for pressure. Sanctions and incentives are no longer the exclusive preserve of states. They may be imposed on and by non-state actors; e.g. corporate and cultural boycotts and affirmative actions. Anti-apartheid sanctions came to be imposed by a wide range of actors, to crucial effect (Crawford and Klotz, 1999).

In addition to recognizing the multiple forms of state-non-state relations in emerging forms of regionalisms (conflictual and cooperative alike) – we need to begin to appreciate the *diversity of regionalisms* in Africa as elsewhere. This may include distinctions among primary issue area (e.g. economic, ecological, strategic); degree or sustainability of integration; and diversity of state and non-state partners. Just as NGOs have begun to recognize divisions of labor amongst themselves in terms of roles in PKOs (Weiss, 1999) – e.g. health by MSF, housing by CARE, reconstruction by OXFAM or World Vision, so we need to identify crucial catalysts in different regions (e.g. Makerere in the East African Community in the 1960s or South African Airways and MNet in today's SADC) (Grugel and Hout, 1999). One, quite distinctive form of new regionalism in Africa, is the emergence of the minerals/mafias syndrome in which scarce resources are exchanged for protection as well as regime enrichment (Shaw, 2000b). Alas, the simplistic, stereotypical assertion of Kaplan (1994: 46) misses the point, as anarchy is not entirely unstructured or unpredictable, just unfair and unstable. West Africa is becoming *the* symbol of worldwide demographic, environmental and social stress, in which criminal anarchy emerges as the real strategic danger.

Towards a Real Political Economy of Conflict: Local, Regional and Global Connections

Orthodox peacekeeping and peace-building strategies, from preemptive CBMs to humanitarian interventions (MacFarlane, 1999), have not always been efficacious in Africa or elsewhere. They have tended to be subverted particularly when regional contexts facilitate cross-border trade, which keeps the guns and other supplies flowing through profitable global networks (from local informal to global formal, with myriad middlemen and goods-facilitators/money-launderers). The ubiquity of small as well as weak states on the continent means that Africa has more borders than any other region. The emergence of seemingly sustainable war economies serves to complicate any easy response, leading to a veritable military and NGO industry of lessons learned. Yet, if anything is to be learned, it is that conflict is positive and profitable for some, even as it is disastrous and debilitating for the majority (Smillie, Gberie and Hazelton, 2000). The case of Sierra Leone is symptomatic (Cilliers and Mason, 1999), even as related illustrations from Angola and Somalia (Reno, 1998; Spears, 1999) lend nuance and support for the thesis. For, not only does this emblematic case throw established wisdoms into disarray, its salience suggests that any success stories thus far about peace operations may be the exceptions (van Walraven, 1999).

The recent shadow states or warlord regimes in Freetown (or Abuja, Kinshasa, Luanda or even Mogadishu) are but the latest iteration of the tendency or inclination of ubiquitous transnational as well as local informal sectors to subvert any notion of state authority or delivery, let alone efficiency or legitimacy (Reno, 1998). To be sure, the hold on power of such rapacious regimes is tenuous, especially in small rather than larger states (c.f pressures on Freetown by contrast to those on Luanda). Such cowboy or pirate economies are not new. Rather, informal markets in precious stones, let alone energy and skills, are as old as the slave trade. As in previous centuries, the ultimate markets for Africa's cornucopias are not on the continent itself. Rather diamonds get processed through complex and dynamic networks of trust from informal sector mine to formal sector trader/distributor/advertiser/seller in the EU, Japan and US.

Cox (1999: 14–15) places such covert forms of organization in the context of a dialectic of perverse forms of (un)civil society of profound importance to Africa; when the latter is weak the covert and extreme tend to thrive:

> The covert world comprises intelligence services, organized crime, terrorist groups, the arms trade, money-laundering banks and secret societies. The covert world penetrates the visible authorities in government and corporations The political space between constituted authority and the people is the terrain on which civil society can be built. A weak and stunted civil society allows free rein to exclusionary politics and covert powers. An expansive participant civil society makes political authority more accountable and reduces the scope for exclusionary politics and covert activity.

Thus, dramatic levels of income/profit/rent from diamond or oil sales in Sierra Leone and Angola, respectively, serve to perpetuate the rationale and means for protracted struggles characteristic of war economies, replete with child soldiers. Clearly, these are not familiar anti-colonial nationalist movements or liberation struggles. Rather, these bandits corrupt what remains of the state for their own enrichment. In so doing, they postpone any notion of peace agreements or reconstruction plans. Conditions in Freetown, Luanda and Mogadishu are not so much anarchy (Kaplan, 1994) as a distinctive form of African capitalism, exacerbated by ethnic, generational or racial tensions, complicated transitions, forms of globalizations, regional opportunities and impossible SAP conditionalities (Cox, 1999: 24–25; Crawford, 2000). While continuing conflicts in Central and West Africa and the Horn may serve to defeat extant PKO reactions, they may also constitute the wave of the future.

The problematic incidence and impact of such cowboy constitutes a profound challenge for the continent's remaining intellectuals and think-tanks (van Walraven, 1999: 109–123). What is the realistic human security response? What form of governance would transcend such an unfortunate legacy? (UNDP, 1999: 97–114). Certainly, any informed PKO reaction would need to reassure citizens that the international community would protect lives and properties. In short, getting towards an agreed process of peace building and reconstruction is part of a protracted and inseparable undertaking. According to Klaas van Walraven (1999: 109–124), Nigeria's advocacy of ECOMOG was always problematic and doomed. The partisan and partial character of the regional force made it less than appropriate from day one. Nevertheless, it is still vital for global and regional interests to try to work together in such complicated contexts, lest parochialism reinforces trends towards more globalizations and away from cosmopolitan forms of governance appropriate for a new and complex century.

Alternative Regionalisms: Civil Societies at the Meso-Level

In contrast to the preceding pessimistic war economy scenario, more optimistic analyses of new regionalisms in Africa as elsewhere need increasingly to recognize the present and prospective impacts of civil societies on patterns of regional cooperation and conflict. Such transnational links are not necessarily compatible with formal inter-state regional structures. They may embrace different spatial areas and be concerned about more than economic and strategic issues. While regional organizations in Africa are beginning to encourage dialogue with business associations and NGOs (even trade unions and women's groups), they are not yet ready to share power. Such consultations tend to have a formal or ritual quality to them. Effective governance has yet to begin to trickle down to sub-state levels. Hence the democratic deficit in all African regional institutions to date, which may simplify decision-making somewhat but undermines any accountability, identity, legitimacy, transparency or support. Conversely, we need to recognize the limited degree of autonomy, which some NGOs and MNCs possess in their relations with certain states. Non-state actors are rarely completely separate from regimes. Just as the UN or World Bank may co-opt certain NGOs in terms of subcontracting, so regional organizations may create or cajole regional NGOs for their own purposes (Lindberg and Sverrisson, 1997; Kleinberg and Clark, 2000; Murphy, 2000; van Rooy, 1999).

Non-state definitions of regions may reflect a variety of relations: from continuing bases like ecology (e.g. shared geographic zones from savannah/forest to valleys/mountains) and ethnicity (history, language, myths etc) to modern cultural events (e.g. regional book fairs, fashion competitions); NGOs (e.g. after Mwengo and Ravdo, the proposed Southern African Development Council NGO Coordinating Committee (Barnard, 1998); professional associations; regional gatherings of kinspersons; religious congregations both orthodox and informal, sports competitions (regional leagues/media coverage/cups). Such regional communities may include tertiary education/training, such as the historic roles of, say Makerere University for East Africa and UNISA for Southern and now regional graduate programs at the Southern African Regional Institute for Policy Studies (SARIPS) or via African Economic Research Consortium (AERC) (Quadir, MacLean and Shaw, 1999). Both African and global companies define their own regions on the continent in terms of corporate structures including headquarters and branch plants, distribution lines, franchise licenses, production chains, sub-contracting (Shaw and van der Westhuizen, 1999).

Increasingly, regions, especially corridors and triangles, as indicated above, will be defined by contemporary *infrastructures*, such as electricity (and related dams and water distribution), gas/oil pipeline and telecommunications grids (including cable television and related services, the internet, especially servers), transport routes and community and corporate networks (Vale, Swatuk and Oden, 2001). If such new regional designs continue to be effected, then in the second or third decade of the new century, we may find new meso-level structures emerging, such as the Great Lakes, Nile Valley and Rift Valley communities, somewhat parallel to the embryonic Horn and Sahel groupings. These would not necessarily be mutually exclusive, especially if participation was reflective of trilateral realities; that is, companies, civil societies and the state.

African regions do not end at the shores of the continent: African countries, communities and companies are involved, for instance in sub-global groupings like Atlantic and Indian Ocean Rims, Cairns group on agriculture in the WTO, the Conventions on International Trade in Endangered Species (CITES) the Commonwealth, *la francophonie* and Non-Aligned Movement.

Lessons Learned for Other Disciplines and for Future Interventions

I conclude with a few more speculative reflections on some of the possible range of implications of such new regionalist analysis for established disciplines and debates, including discourses not only about globalizations but also about interdisciplinary studies and policy directions/options. As already indicated, the stark, almost stereotypical, dichotomy between coming anarchy and African renaissance has been moderated somewhat at the start of the new century by the presence or dominance of each of these trends in different regions (Shaw and Nyango'ro, 2000). This shift is partly symbolized by the apparent promise of a generation of New Africans who were insurgency leaders: Issayas of Eritrea, Kagame of Rwanda, Meles of Ethiopia and Museveni of Uganda (Clapham, 1998). Yet, their transition into international statesmen has not been unproblematic. Continued border skirmishes and other signs of instability in the Great Lakes and the Horn suggest that the inherently problematic process of reconstruction of infrastructures and institutions is more protracted than anticipated.

The elusiveness of anything approaching a security community (Adler and Barnett, 1998) on the continent at the turn of the century has encouraged my own rediscovery of new realism. New, because the conflicting states are quite distinctive and realist as their relationships are far from being only inter-governmental and strategic (Shaw, 1998; 2000b). Moreover, some authoritarian regimes continue defiant (e.g. Moi in Kenya and Mugabe in Zimbabwe) and some shadow regimes remain resilient (e.g. Angola, Congo, Liberia, Sierra Leone and Somalia) (Reno, 1998). Such contemporary divergences are indicative of the imperative of a creative rethink of analytic regions in Africa which would parallel that proposed by Samir Amin almost three decades ago: that is, a variety of areas in terms of types of conflict and peace-building responses, themselves reflective of variations in state-economy-civil society strengths and relations (Shaw, 2000b). Such new regional perspectives on the continent hold promise for a range of overlapping disciplines/debates, particularly several social sciences, in addition to those over globalizations. This type of introspection would be relevant in several disciplines.

Political science, which needs to reexamine assumptions about bilateral state-economy-society relations. These dynamic exist at all levels: local, national, regional and global. However, their content and balance have changed dramatically since the post-independence and -bipolar eras (Baylis and Smith, 1997; Clemens, 1998).

International relations/foreign policy, which are no longer the monopoly of state and interstate agencies but include the other pair of (non-state) actors in the trilateral structure – i.e. economies/companies and civil societies/NGOs – and also embrace an increasingly extensive and heterogeneous range of issues (Dunn and Shaw, 2000; Shaw and Nyang'oro, 2000). The new regionalisms draws attention to other broader issues, for example, landmines, ozone, trade, peace-building, new forms of rent extracted from diamonds and oil production, AIDS, ecology, all of which lead to broad mixed actor global coalitions (Keck and Sikkink, 1998; Lipschutz with Mayer, 1996; Tomlin, 1998).

Security studies, which have to begin to transcend state-centric and bipolar assumptions and emphases in both theory and practice in favor of a catholic range of actors and strategic issues from ecology to viruses, migrations to small-arms at regional as other levels, from confidence-building to reconstruction which involves civil societies at all stages (e.g. track-two). Any rehabilitation of a neo-realist perspective would have to incorporate a range of non-state actors/interests and -traditional issues/relations (Nel and McGowan, 1999).

International political economy (Stubbs and Underhill, 2000), which has to begin to treat destruction and reconstruction as well as production and new technologies as the new economy (globalization). This process has distinct forms in the South, for example, a mix of high-tech islands and profitable informal sectors (example, drugs, minerals even mercenaries) in a sea of poverty (Castells, 1989), which generates its own security challenges (Shaw and Nyango'ro, 2000). Moreover, informal and illegal sectors continue to grow, particularly at the regional level, from basic needs to money laundering, with multiple forms of market-responsiveness in between. As indicated above, new IPE of protracted conflicts is beginning to emerge to treat the role of diamond and other resources in civil wars in Angola, Congo and Sierra Leone (Clapham, 1998; *Current History*, 1999; Reno, 1998; Richards, 1999; Shaw, 2000b; Smillie *et al.*, 2000).

The new regionalisms also pose challenges to a range of more applied perspectives with profound policy implications. These would include the following.

1. *Development studies/policies*, which are no longer concerned just with sustainable development or structural adjustments but also, increasingly, with more flexible varieties of regionalisms along with the causes and consequences of increasingly protracted conflicts. This has led to a growing focus on, say, human development/security (Dickson, 1997; Hoogvelt, 1997; Payne, 1998; UNDP, 1994; 1999).

2. *Comparative transitions*, from insurgencies to regimes with profound regional implications for forms of cooperation (example, Museveni-Kagame alliance) and conflict (example, patterns of alliance among non-state as well as state interests around the interrelated Horn/Great Lakes/Congo conflict) (Shaw, 1998)

3. *Civil societies/varieties of NGOs*, especially at fluid new regionalist or meso-levels: both augmenting/containing old regional arrangements concentrated in the economic and strategic issue areas while also advancing new regionalist developments (Boas, Marchand and Shaw, 1999a; Holden, 2000; MacLean and Shaw, 1996).

4. *Studies of new forms of governance* appropriate to the new regionalist level/orientation, in which all tri-lateral actor types are represented, whether at local or regional, corridor or company/civil society level. This would include also, civil-military relations extending to NGOs and private security forces along with

governance at all stages of the peace-building nexus (Held *et al.*, 1999; Keck and Sikkink, 1998; Lipshutz,1996; Shaw, 2000a and b; Stiles, 2000; Van Rooy, 1999).

5. *Alternative futures*, both existential and analytic. What new regionalisms in Africa and elsewhere can be expected in the twenty-first century – more anarchy and or emerging markets, more realism, more idealism (Ottaway,1999; Shaw and Nyang'oro, 2000)

Note

This and related papers benefit immeasurably from continuing collaboration with colleagues associated with an informal transnational network around studies of new regionalisms based on the Global Development Section in the ISA and Research Commission #40 in IPSA, notably Morten Boas, Sandra MacLean, Marianne Marchand, Fahim Quadir and Fred Soderbaum. It is also informed by two weeks of debates at two research workshops at Dalhousie University in mid-August 1999 and 2000 on aspects of regionalisms, globalizations and governance in the South, cosponsored by the Ford Foundation, SSHRC and UNU, as well as the third conference of the CSGR at Warwick University in September 1999 and a symposium on globalization and the South at the University of Georgia in April 2000.

References

Adler, Emmanuel and Michael Barnett (eds) *Security Communities.* Cambridge, UK: CUP.

African Development Bank (1993) *Economic Integration in Southern Africa.* Abidjan: Ivory Coast, Three volumes.

Amin, Samir (1972) 'Underdevelopment and Dependence in Black Africa: origins and contemporary forms'. *Journal of Modern African Studies* 10(4), December: 503–524

Aulakh, Preet S. and Michael G. Schechter (eds) (2000) *Rethinking Globalization(s): from corporate transnationalism to local interventions.* London: Macmillan.

Barnard, D. (1998) *PRODDER: the South African Development Directory, 1998/9.* Braamfontein: HSRC.

Barnard, D. (ed) (1997) *PRODDER: the Southern African Development Directory, 1997/8.* Braamfontein: HSRC.

Baylis, J. and Smith, S. (eds) (1997) *The Globalization of World Politics: an introduction to international relations.* Oxford: OUP

Boas, M., Marchand, M. and Shaw, T. (eds) (1999a) Special Issue: New Regionalisms in the New Millennium. *Third World Quarterly* 20(5), October: 987–1070

Boas, M., Marchand, M. and Shaw, T. (1999b) 'The Weave-world – regionalisms in the South in the new millennium'. *Third World Quarterly* 20(5), October: 1061–1070

Boutwell, Jeffrey and Michael T. Klare (eds) (1999) *Light Weapons and Civil Conflict Controlling the Tools of Violence.* Lanham: Rowman and Littlefield for AAAS and Carnegie Commission.

Braathen, Einer *et al.* (eds) (2000) *Ethnicity Kills? The politics of war, peace and ethnicity in Sub-Saharan Africa.* London: Macmillan.

Bryans, Michael *et al.* (1999) 'Mean Times: humanitarian action in complex emergencies – stark choices, cruel dilemmas'. *Coming to Terms.* Toronto: University of Toronto, 1(3), January

Castells, Manuel (1989) *The Informational City.* Oxford: Blackwell.

Chabal, P. and Daloz, J. (1999) *Africa Works: disorder as political instrument.* Oxford: James Currey for IAI.

Chen, E. and Kwan, C. (eds) (1997) *Asia's Borderless Economy: the emergence of sub-regional zones*. St Leonards, NSW: Allen and Unwin.

Cilliers, J. (1999) 'Regional African Peacekeeping Capacity: mythical construct or essential tool?'. *African Security Review* 8(4), 20–33.

Cilliers, J. and Mason, P. (eds) (1999) *Peace, Profit or Plunder? The privatisation of security in war-torn African societies*. Halfway House: ISS.

Clapham, C. (1996) *Africa and the International System: the politics of state survival*. Cambridge, UK: Cambridge University Press.

Clapham, C. (ed) (1998) *African Guerillas*. Oxford: James Currey.

Clemens, Walter C. (1998) *Dynamics of International Relations: conflict and mutual gain in an era of global interdependence*. Lanham: Rowman and Littlefield.

Cliffe, L. (ed) (1999) Special Issue: Complex Political Emergencies. *Third World Quarterly* 20(1), March,1–256

Court, Julius (1999) 'Development Research: directions for a new century'. *UNU Work in Progress* 16 (1), Winter, 1–20.

Cox, Robert W. (1999) 'Civil Society at the Turn of the Millennium: prospects for an alternative world order'. *Review of International Studies* 25(1), January, 3–28.

Crawford, Darryl (2000) 'Chinese Capitalism: cultures, the Southeast Asian region and economic globalization'. *Third World Quarterly* 21(1), February, 69–86.

Crawford, N. and Audie, K. (eds) (1999) *How Sanctions Work: lessons from South Africa*. London: Macmillan.

Dicklitch, S. (1998) *The Elusive Promise of NGOs in Africa: lessons from Uganda*. London: Macmillan.

Dickson, A.K (1997) *Development and International Relations: a critical introduction* Cambridge, UK: Polity.

Duffield, M. (1999) 'Globalization and War Economies: promoting order or the return of history?'. *Fletcher Forum of World Affairs* 23(2), Fall, 21–36

Dunn, K. and Shaw, T. (eds) (2001) *Africa's Challenge to International RelationsTheory*. London: Macmillan.

Gelb, S. and Manning, C. (1998) 'Spatial Development Initiatives: unlocking economic potential'. *Development Southern Africa* 15(5), Summer, 717–942.

Germain, R. (ed) (2000) *Globalization and its Critics: perspectives from political economy*. London: Macmillan.

Gibb, R. (1998) 'Southern Africa in Transition: Prospects and Possibilities Facing Regional Integration'. *Journal of Modern African Studies* 36(2) June, 287–306.

Giddens, A. (1998) *The Third Way: the renewal of social democracy*. Cambridge: Polity.

Gills, B. (ed) (1997) Special Issue: Globalization and the Politics of Resistance. *New Political Economy* 2(1), March, 5–200.

Gourevitch, Philip (1999) *We wish to inform you that tomorrow we will be killed with our families: stories from Rwanda*. NY: Picador.

Grugel, J. and Hout, W. (eds) (1999) *Regionalism Across the North-South Divide: state strategies and globalization*. London: Routledge.

Held, D., McGrew, A., Goldblatt, D. and Perraton, J. (1999) *Global Transformations: politics, economics and culture*. Cambridge, UK: Polity.

Helmich, H. and Smillie, I. (eds) (1999) *Stakeholders: government-NGO partnerships for international development*. London: Earthscan.

Hettne, B. and Soderbaum, F. (eds) (1998) Special Issue: the New Regionalism. *Politeia* 17(3), 1–142.

Hettne, B., Inotai, A. and Sunkel, O. (eds) (1999) *Globalism and the New Regionalism*. London: Macmillan for UNU/WIDER.

Holden, B. (ed) (2000) *Global Democracy: key debates*. London: Routledge.

Hoogvelt, A. (1997) *Globalisation and the Postcolonial World: the new political economy of development*. London: Macmillan.

Howe, H. (1998) 'Private Security Forces and African Stability: the case of Executive Outcomes'. *Journal of Modern African Studies* 36(2), June, 307–331.

Hulme, D. and Edwards, M. (eds) (1997) *NGOs, States and Donors: too close for comfort?* London: Macmillan for SCF.

Kaplan, R. (1994) 'The Coming Anarchy'. *Atlantic Monthly* 273(2), February, 44–75.

Kasfir, N. (ed) (1998) 'Special Issue on Civil Society and Democracy in Africa: critical perspectives'. *Commonwealth and Comparative Politics* 36(2), July, 1–149.

Keck, M., Sikkink, K. (1998) *Activists beyond Borders:advocacy networks in international politics*. Ithaca, NY: Cornell University Press.

Kennedy, P. (1999) 'Sub-Saharan Africa's Current Plight and the Threat or Promise of Globalisation?'. *Global Society* 13(4), October, 441–466.

Kenny, C. and Moss, T. (1998) 'Stock Markets in Africa: emerging lions or white elephants?'. *World Development* 26(5), May, 829–843.

Kingma, K. (ed) (2000) *The Impact of Demobilization in Sub-Saharan Africa*. London: Macmillan for BICC.

Kleinberg, R. and Clark, J. (eds) (2000) *Economic Liberalization, Democratization and Civil Society in the Developing World*. London: Macmillan.

Lindberg, S. and Sverrisson, A. (eds) (1997) *Social Movements in Development: the challenge of globalization and democratization*. London: Macmillan.

Lipschutz, R. and Mayer, J. (1996) *Global Civil Society and Global Environmental Governance*. Albany, NT: SUNY Press.

MacFarlane, S. Neil (1999) 'Doing Good, Doing Wrong'. *International Journal* LIV(4), Autumn, 537–561

MacLean, S. and Shaw, T. (1996) 'Civil Society and Political Economy in Contemporary Africa: what prospects for sustainable democracy?'. *Journal of Contemporary African Studies* 14(2), 247–264.

Marchand, M., Boas, M. and Shaw, T. (1999) 'The Political Economy of New Regionalisms'. *Third World Quarterly* 20(5), October, 897–910.

Mbeki, Moeletsi (1998) 'The African Renaissance'. *South African Yearbook of International Affairs 1998/9*. Johannesburg: South African Institute of International Affairs, 209–217.

McCarthy, C. (1996) 'Regional Integration: part of the solution or part of the problem?'. In S. Ellis (ed) *Africa Now: people, policies and institutions*. London: James Currey, 211–231.

Murphy, C. (ed) (2000) *Egalitarian Social Movements in Response to Globalization*. London: Macmillan.

Nel, P. and McGowan, P. (eds) (1999) *Power, Wealth and Global Order: an international relations textbook for Africa*. Cape Town: UCT Press for FGD.

Ottaway, M. (1999) 'Africa'. *Foreign Policy* 114, Spring, 13–25.

Payne, A. (1998) 'The New Political Economy of Area Studies'. *Millennium* 27(2), 253–273.

Payne, A. (1999) 'Reframing the Global Politics of Development'. *Journal of International Relations and Development* 2(4), December, 369–379.

Quadir, F., MacLean, S. and Shaw, T. (1999) *Pluralisms and the Changing Global Political Economy: ethnicities in crises of governance in Asia and Africa*. Halifax: Ford Project, Dalhousie University.

Reno, W. (1998) *Warlord Politics and African States*. Boulder, CO: Lynne Rienner.

Richards, P. (1999) *Fighting for the Rain Forest: war, youth and resources in Sierra Leone*. Oxford: James Currey for IAI.

Schechter, M. (ed) (1999) *The Revival of Civil Society: global and comparative perspectives*. London: Macmillan.

Scholte, J. (2000) *Globalization: a critical introduction*. London: Macmillan.

Schuurman, F. (2000) 'Paradigms Lost, Paradigms Regained? Development studies in the twenty-first century'. *Third World Quarterly* 21(1), February, 7–20.

Shaw, T. (1998) 'African Renaissance/African Alliance: towards new regionalisms and new realism in the Great Lakes at the start of the twenty-first century'. *Politeia* 17(3), 60–74.

Shaw, T. (1999) 'Globalisations and Conflicts in Africa: prospects for human security and development in the new millennium'. *ACCORD Conflict Trends* 3, 20–22.

Shaw, T. (2000a) 'Overview: global/local – states, companies and civil societies'. In K.Stiles (ed) *Global Institutions and Local Empowerment*, 1–8.

Shaw, T. (2000b) 'Conflicts in Africa at the Turn of the Century: more of the same?'. In Albert Legault (ed) *Conflicts in the World, 1999–2000*. Quebec: IQHEI, Laval University.

Shaw, T,. MacLean, S. (1999) 'The Emergence of Regional Civil Society: contributions to a new human security agenda'. In Ho-Won Jeong (ed) *The New Agenda for Peace Research*. Aldershot: Ashgate, 289–308.

Shaw, T. and Nyango'ro, J. (1999) 'Conclusion: African Foreign Policies and the Next Millennium: alternative perspectives, practices and possibilities'. In S. Wright (ed) *African Foreign Policies*. Boulder, CO: Westview Press, 237–248.

Shaw, T. and Nyango'ro, J. (2000) 'African Renaissance in the New Millennium? From Anarchy to Emerging Markets?'. In R. Stubbs and G. Underhill (eds) *Political Economy and the Changing Global Order*, 275–284.

Shaw, T. and Schnabel, A. (1999) 'Human (In)Security in Africa: prospects for good governance in the twenty-first century'. *UNU Work in Progress* 15(3), Summer, 16–18.

Shaw, T. van der Westhuizen, J. (1999) 'Towards a Political Economy of Trade in Africa: states, companies and civil societies'. In B. Hocking and S. McGuire (eds) *Trade Politics*. London: Routledge, 246–260.

Shearer, D. (1999) 'Outsourcing War'. *Foreign Policy* 112, Fall: 68–81.

Smillie, I., Lansan, G. and Hazelton, R. (2000) *The Heart of the Matter: Sierra Leone, diamonds and human security*. Ottawa: Partnership Africa Canada.

Spears, I. (1999) 'Angola's Elusive Peace: the collapse of the Lusaka Accord'. *International Journal* LIV(4), Autumn, 562–581.

Special Issue on Africa's Wars (1999) *Current History* 98(628), May, 195–241.

Stiles, K. (ed) (2000) *Global Institutions and Local Empowerment: competing theoretical perspectives*. London: Macmillan.

Stubbs, R. and Underhill, G. (eds) (2000) *Political Economy and the Changing Global Order*. Toronto: OUP. Second edition.

Taylor, Ian (2000) *Public-Private Partnerships: lessons form the Maputo Development Corridor toll road*. DPRU, University of Cape Town.

Teunissen, Jan Joost (ed) (1996) *Regionalism and the Global Economy: the rise of Africa*. The Hague: FONDAD.

Tomlin, Brian *et al.* (eds) (1998) *To Walk without Fear: the global movement to ban landmines*. Toronto: OUP.

UNDP (1994) *Human Development Report 1994*. NY: OUP.

UNDP (1999) *Human Development Report 1999*. NY: OUP.

Uvin, P. (1998) *Aiding Violence: the development enterprise in Rwanda*. West Hartford: Kumarian.

Vale, P. and Maseko, S. (1998) 'South Africa and the African Renaissance'. *International Affairs* 74(2), April, 271–287.

Vale, P., Swatuk, L. and Oden, B. (eds) (2001) *Theory, Change and Southern Africa's Future*. London: Macmillan.

Van Rooy, A. (1999) 'Civil Society and Global Change'. *Canadian Development Report 1999*. Ottawa: North-South Institute.

Van Walraven, K. (1999) *The Pretence of Peace-keeping: ECOMOG, West Africa and Liberia (1990–1998)*. The Hague: NIIR, November.

Weiss, T. (1999) *Military-Civilian Interactions: intervention in humanitarian crises*. Lanham: Rowman and Littlefield.

Wright, S. (ed) (1999) *African Foreign Policies*. Boulder, CO: Westview Press.

Chapter 12

State, Donor and NGO Configurations in Malian Development 1960–1999: The Enactment and Contestation of Global Rationalized Myths in an Organizational Field

Kent Glenzer

Introduction

Mali is undertaking one of the more earnest decentralization programs in Africa. This process has three strategic goals: liberalization and privatization of the economy, democratization and decentralization of decision-making to the grassroots level. Progress towards these goals has earned the Malian state plaudits from the international community. USAID has called Mali the IMF's star pupil in the region (USAID, 1995: 4) and the UNDP and World Bank both champion Mali's new development vision (Ministère des affaires étrangères et des maliens de l'extérieur, 1997; Mission Résidente de la Banque Mondiale au Mali, 1996). The government depends on civil society organizations to deliver many basic social services to achieve its development objectives (Poulton and Youssouf, 1998).

This chapter uses world polity theory (Thomas *et al.*, 1987; Boli and Thomas, 1999) to analyze changes in the *organizational field* comprising state, donor and nongovernmental organizations (NGOs) over the past forty years. The discussion is used to explore the theme that evolving configurations regarding the proper roles, practices and interrelationships of civil society, state and donors are rooted, partly in contestation amongst these organizational actors over global, institutionalized myths. The discussion is also used to problematize the changing geometries in the organizational field of development agencies in Mali, to offer explanations for this phenomenon, offer an alternative interpretation of these changes and raise some questions about the future success of the state's decentralization program.

Theoretical Approaches to State, Donor and non Governmental Organizations (NGO) Relations

Current interpretations of state-donor configurations can be broken into three schools: rational actor, open system and postmodern/discursive. The three are not mutually exclusive and two or even all three can be combined in the same study. Rational actor approaches tend to emphasize goal setting, resource allocation, planning and implementation/evaluation functions within a single organizational actor. Case studies of particular organizations are common and tend to focus on how NGO, donor, or state decision-makers can efficiently accomplish set goals; re-align organizational processes and structures to deliver these goals; marshal resources, identify accurate measures or indicators of success; and continuously monitor performance (see Edwards and Hume, 1996; Bratton, 1994; Fatton, 1995; Chazan, 1992).

The open system approach places emphasis on the environment in which a single organization (donor, state, or NGO) operates. It also emphasizes dialogue between individual organizations and their operating contexts. Lawrence and Lorsch's (1967) contingency theory, based on the assumption that a single, best way does not exist to operate organizations and that effective donor, state, or NGO performance must be based on adaptation to the nature of the environment in which it operates, constitutes the most dominant position in open systems approaches. These approaches stress the importance of resource control by donors (Hulme and Edwards, 1997), embeddedness of civil society organizations in local social structures (Ndegwa, 1996), conflicts over power and resources (Bayart, 1986; Chabal and Daloz, 1999) and or the ideological apparatus of neoliberal policy (Dicklitch, 1998).

The discursive/postmodernist approach suggests that civil society is a contested social field constituted by donors, the state, NGOs and African citizens, seeking to denaturalize both the concept and dominant assumptions about donor, state and NGO interrelationships. This approach also analyzes the discursive and epistemic frames within which civil society policies are conceived, implemented and assessed (Crush, 1995; Escobar, 1995; Ferguson, 1994). It takes the position that the authority to define problems, salient development categories and, therefore, policies and programs, cannot be considered to be value-free, logical outcomes of objective social science (Appfel *et al.*, 1990; Sachs, 1992; Cowen and Shenton, 1996; Trust, 1997). Related to the discursive, postmodern approach is a handful of ethnographic investigations, which seek to understand how concrete social relations and structures are implicated in daily struggles over the forms and functions which civil society may take (Long, 1992; Peters, 1994; Haugerud, 1995; Crewe and Harrison, 1998; Gupta, 1998; Koenig *et al.*, 1998; Arce and Long, 1993; 2000; Moore, 2000).

Although all three approaches offer valuable insights into the inter-relationships between actors in the development arena, each has limitations. Rational actor paradigms tend to overemphasize the extent to which each category of actors can control its own destiny; open systems approaches tend to focus only on material factors and implicitly retain rational actor assumptions while widening the arena of calculation, while discursive approaches tend to ignore organizational theory altogether. The neo-institutional approach helps to overcome many of these difficulties.

The New Institutionalism in Organizational Analysis

The new institutionalism in organizational analysis (Powell and DiMaggio, 1991) is rooted in social constructionism (Berger and Luckmann, 1967; Geertz, 1973), which posits that sets of beliefs, norms and cultural rules are formed in social interaction and serve as guides for behavior in a variety of social settings. Neo-institutional research demonstrates a loose coupling between what organizations say they do and what they actually do. Organizational signposts such as their strategies, visions, mission statements and management practices are seen to be much more mimetic than rationalistic (Meyer and Rowan, 1977) and are bound by cultural norms (Haveman and Rao, 1997), responses to government policy (Dobbin and Dowd, 1997), simple imitation in order to secure legitimacy and symbolic capital (Goodrick *et al.*, 1997) and population dynamics in a given organizational field (Barnett and Carroll, 1987; Carroll, 1984; DiMaggio, 1991; Hannan and Freeman, 1977; see also Scott, 1998). By institutions, neo-institutionalists mean cognitive, normative and regulative structures and activities that provide stability and meaning to social behavior (Scott, 1995). As in Bourdieu's (1977) or Giddens' (1979) models, neo-institutional organizational scholars hold that individuals in organizations construct and constantly negotiate everyday social reality within a wider context of constitutive cultural systems and symbolic frameworks which are constructed as objective, external to the actor and which provide orientation and guidance (see also Zucker, 1977).

The critical unit of analysis for neo-institutional scholars is not the single organization but rather the *organizational field*, defined as those organizations that constitute a recognized area of institutional life: key suppliers, resource and produce consumers, regulatory agencies and others (DiMaggio and Powell, 1983; Scott, 1994). The concept of the organizational field is particularly apropos for analyzing changing relationships, normative expectations and ideological struggles between donors, the African state and NGOs and offers a methodological opening for bridging individual organizational actions with broader social, economic, political and ideological processes.

Research has demonstrated that much organizational behavior within an organizational field is governed by deeply held and unquestioned institutionalized rules. Such institutionalized rules are what Meyer and Rowan (1977) call *rationalized myths* because they are widely held beliefs whose effects inhere, not in the fact that individuals believe them, but that they know everyone else does and take them, for all practical purposes, to be true (Meyer, 1977). These myths are rationalized in that they are accompanied by and take the form of rules, which specify proper organizational behavior, roles and forms (Meyer and Rowan, 1977; Scott, 1998).

World Polity Theory More so than other neo-institutional researchers, world polity theorists have made the global evolution of state structures and international civil society a direct object of study. Using global data sets, they have documented global convergence (or homogenization) over the past century in areas as diverse as state bureaucracies, constitutions, educational systems, justice systems, labor and human rights precepts.[1] In addition, they have provided the strongest empirical account of the proliferation of international civil society and the authority it exercises on social, economic and cultural policies in a large number of states and international organizations.

World polity researchers posit that this convergence is problematic and like neo-institutional organizational sociologists in many other domains, have sought institutional explanations (Thomas *et al.*, 1987; Boli and Thomas, 1999).[2] Their hypothesis is that these processes are rooted in widely-shared assumptions or norms (rationalized myths), which undergird the cultural project of modernization. Rather than responding rationally to specific, unique, local environments, world polity theory holds that states, donors and civil society organizations enact legitimized myths (lodged at the global level),[3] which are framed by five attributes: individualism (individuals as both target and motor of progress, possessing alienable legal, civil and increasingly social and economic rights);[4] progress (the goal and *raison d'être* of both states and individuals); justice and equality (the global modernist project makes axiomatic the absolute equality of sovereign units and individuals); universalism (myths about the nature of the individual, progress, rationality justice and equality are presumed to be time and space independent); and rationalization (underpinned by Weberian rationalizations regarding individualism, progress, justice and universalism) (see also, Boli, 1999; Robertson, 1992).

Civil Society, the State and International Development Organizations (1960–1999)

Since a detailed history of post-independence Mali is beyond the scope of this chapter,[5] I focus on changing constructions of the proper duties, responsibilities, roles and actions of key organizational actors as revealed in their own discourse. Mali gained independence in 1960 and adopted a socialist approach to development. Increasingly in debt in the early years of independence, the state took ever-more repressive steps to channel resources into centralized state-building.[6] In 1968, a cadre of army officers organized a successful, bloodless coup. The new regime, under General Moussa Traoré, continued to pursue centralized, planned development while trying to make parastatals more efficient. In the 1980s, Mali's debt and balance of payments problems worsened and the government grudgingly signed a series of structural adjustment accords. By 1990, the Traoré government was under attack from international donors and protests by student and labor groups gained momentum. A second coup in 1991 was followed by a short period of transition and multi-party elections, which led to the presidency of Alpha Oumar Konaré. Konaré implemented policies consistent with the prescriptions of the international financial institutions (IFIs) regarding democratization, economic liberalization, government restructuring, privatization and decentralization.

Relationships with donors changed several times during the period. Between 1960–1968, France was Mali's largest single financial backer. Significant support was also received from the Soviet bloc and China, with smaller contributions from USAID and the West. Much of this aid went towards infrastructure, agriculture, import-substituting industries, mineral exploration and education (Hyden, 1995).

Official Development Assistance (ODA) shifted in the period from 1968–1980 when, in the wake of the 1968–74 Sahel drought and famine, emergency assistance formed the most important part of overall aid. The decade of the 1980s saw dramatic shifts in ODA, both due to IFI structural adjustment programs (beginning in 1982) and a movement towards longer-term development programming. The share of ODA going to agricultural and environmental programs increased as integrated rural development became the standard approach to assistance and ODA was increasingly tied to conditionalities. After the coup and democratic elections in the early 1990s, a new aid regime was born, which gave prominence to respect for human rights, market and democratic liberalism, government downsizing and decentralization. This regime also accorded a central role in national development to indigenous civil society organizations.

The composition and foci of international non-governmental organizations (INGOs) and Malian civil society organizations has altered radically over the past 40 years. Under the early socialist government, village cooperatives were mandated and organized by the state and INGOs were almost entirely absent. This changed as a result of the 1968–74 and 1983–4 droughts. Between 1970 and 1980, INGOs arrived at the approximate rate of 2 each year; increasing to 3–6 per year between 1980–1983. Twenty-six new INGOs arrived in 1984 alone, 15 more in 1985;[7] and by 1999 there were about 114 active INGOs in Mali.

The growth in the number of local NGOs was even more explosive. In 1978, only one local NGO existed; by 1983 there were 6 and by 1986 there were 50.[8] The number of local NGOs registered with the government rose to more than 600 by the late 1990s along with more than 4000 local associations of various types and sizes and 40 political parties (Touré, Deme and Poulton, 1999). While the programming approaches amongst this vast array of organizations vary, some general trends exist. In the 1970s, the vast majority of INGO programs were emergency-related, often focusing on food distribution, emergency medical assistance and agricultural inputs. In the 1980s, INGOs diversified their programs, by adopting integrated rural development as a common paradigm and expanding into areas like primary health care, reproductive health, small enterprise development, food security, environmental preservation and gender issues. These same foci were present in the 1990s, with the addition of new programming areas like income-generation, urban development and sustainable development.

Construction of an Organizational Field: State, Donor and Civil Society (1960–1999)

During the period 1960–1968, the Malian state operated under one development plan (Ministère du Plan, no date). The state adopted a broad cultural modernization focus for national development, targeting 8% GDP per capita economic growth as the fundamental measure of development. The explicit aim was to establish a planned socialist economy, which would ensure economic independence and rising living standards (Ministère du Plan, no date: 6). Within this framework, the plan identified l'encadrement rural as critical, with the state's role and responsibility being to develop the national conscience, train cadres and mobilize the popular masses (Ministère du Plan, no date: 9),[9] through an interlocking series of cooperative structures, from the village to counties, to regions, to the nation. During this period, there was little mention either of international donors, or of INGOs, in state discourse. Rather, the state defined its role as one of creating viable rural organizations to harness to the yoke of modernist, planned development from the top.

Despite its socialist rhetoric during the period, the state received significant ODA. It joined the IMF in 1963 and by 1965 had received $17 million in loans and external aid accounted for 56% of all government expenditures (Ministère de la Coopération, 1965; Jones, 1969). Although eight United Nations agencies operated in Mali during this period, there were significant divergences between donor and state interpretations of the country's problems. France criticized the first national development plan for aiming more at creating a development mystique than a serious examination of local development potential (Ministère de la Coopération, 1965: 69). The Food and Agriculture Organization (FAO), in 1962, also criticized the state's focus on building a 'national consciousness', arguing that a more important priority was soil conservation and environmental protection (FAO, 1962: 73).

There were also areas of agreement between the state and donors. Donors generally approved of the state's focus on directed transformation of rural organization (i.e., *encadrement*) via the cooperative system, agreed that a major obstacle to development was the psychology of the peasant and supported government strategies to wrest rural villagers from their harmful, traditions. During this period, there was no mention of independent civil society organizations in either state or donor documentations.

Sparked by the 1968 coup d'état, the 1968–74 the Sahel drought and famine, as well as changing ideas about development in general, the period from 1968–1979 was marked by major transformations in normalized roles and responsibilities on the part of all actors. The state published two separate development plans: a three-year economic recovery program for 1970–1972 and a five-year development plan for 1974–1978. These documents revealed that the state was redefining development from a social-cultural to an economic project (Direction Generale du Plan et de la Statistique, 1970: 9). New language also arose regarding the role of civil society (although the phrase civil society would not appear until the 1990s). While there was still no mention of NGOs , the plans replaced *encadrement* with professional rural organizations. One important result being the establishment of new relationships between the state cotton production parastatal, *Comité Malien pour le Développement de Textile* (CMDT) and farmer groups, in which the former relied on *associations villageoises* (AVs) to facilitate cotton production. CMDT ranked AVs on criteria such as the number of literate members, economic activities and capacity for making productive investments and for managing, marketing and credit activities. Groups with high scores assumed more responsibility for their own extension and marketing and received fixed rebates on cotton sales (Bingen, 1994).

Despite the state's reorientation towards an economic rather than a cultural agenda, the period was marked by continuing conflict with donors and INGOs. The state was criticized for placing so-called national economic independence from foreign domination above the provision of basic needs for the masses (Anonymous, 1975: 4). Although explicit accusations of government mismanagement and corruption were rare, both donors and INGOs staked out their own territories for development assistance, often ignoring state priorities. In contrast to the 1960s, donors now considered the state to be part of the problem. With the cooperative system in shambles, AVs deemed too small and hard-to-manage and no Malian NGOs in existence, donors considered INGO programs to be the preferred option for circumventing the state.

While muted in the 1970s, antagonism between state, donors and civil society exploded in the early 1980s. The indexical referent of the state's domination was the international development apparatus, which the state perceived to be agents of foreign domination (Anonymous, 1981: 3). Although the state wished to withstand pressure from the IFIs and USAID to undertake structural adjustment, the 1981–85 plan revealed key conciliation to donor requirements, especially in its repudiation of free, socialized education and health care and the need to reduce public employment.

Partly in response to growing international demands for a more prominent role in development for INGOs and partly in an effort to maintain some control over development planning, the state abandoned the cooperative network, which had been in operation for two decades and identified *les tons villageois* as the new form of rural organization. Thousands of these organizations were proposed as the new trustees of rural development. They were designed to serve multiple social and economic ends, for example, collectively negotiating production and commercialization, mobilizing communities for efficient resource use and managing land.

International donors used the fact that ODA provided as much as 80% of the state's operating budget to continue pressuring it to abandon its sociocultural aspirations more completely. The state was persuaded to enter into formal economic restructuring programs throughout the 1980s and the single party was encouraged to open the political system up to greater local representation and democracy. When the state retreated from both aspects of liberalization (Poulton and Youssouf, 1998), the World Bank reacted by withdrawing funding in 1987. Despite these tensions, overall ODA to Mali increased during the period (Ministry of Planning, 1981) and the conflict became more technical than ideological.

A collaborative planning effort in 1982 involving USAID, the UN's World Food Programme, INGOs, state technicians and outside experts from the regional inter-governmental organization *Comité Inter-état pour la Lutte contre la Sécheresse au Sahel* (CILSS) resulted in a 10-year food security strategy for Mali (Ministère de l'Agriculture, 1982). This comprehensive document still did not identify a role for INGOs or local NGOs but, rather, supported the government's focus on *tons*. The strategy reiterated long-standing arguments to use the *tons* to change the attitudes of rural farmers towards economic production (Ministère de l'Agriculture, 1982). Further inter-organizational collaboration occurred in the creation of another 10-year strategy for the country, the *Programme Substantiel d'Action Pour le Développement Acceleré du Mali, 1981–1990* (Ministère du plan, 1981) and in the formulation of the 1987 10-year National Strategy for the War on Desertification (Ministère des ressources naturelles et de l'élevage, 1987).

These examples of significant state-INGO cooperation during the NGO decade of the1980s (Fowler, 1988) belied underlying mistrust between the two (Postma, 1994). The NGO community reacted to perceived state antagonism in 1982, by forming an umbrella organization under the leadership of Euro-Action-Accord and the coalition of Swiss NGOs. Originally the organization comprised of eight members and its ostensible writ was as an informal, temporary, information-sharing body, which would meet monthly to address common problems (Touré *et al.*, 1999). That same year, an evaluation commissioned by France was highly critical of INGOs, claiming mismanagement, inefficiency, petty turf battles and corruption (Touré *et al.*, 1999). The report galvanized the state's criticism of INGOs, culminating in a regime of strong control of INGO operations.

INGOs took the French report very seriously and attempted to address its criticisms by formalizing the group of eight into an oversight organization. In 1983, twenty-two INGOs formed the *Comité de Coordination des Actions d'Urgence des Organisations non-Gouvernementales* (CCAU-ONG), whose charter called for the following remedies:

10   Unite efforts to support government actions in the war against the immediate affects of the drought;
20   Collect information from NGOs, authorities and all other sources;
30   Research the best ways to facilitate the intervention of NGOs in particularly affected zones;
40   Harmonize and promote joint action;
50   Periodically report on member activities to government authorities;
60   Promote collaborative reflection with the Government regarding the best methods of intervention;
70   Disband the organization in 1984 unless circumstances require its continuation.

The last objective was dropped in 1984 when the government of Mali gave the group formal recognition. In 1985, the group dropped the word *urgence* from its name, becoming simply CCA-ONG, a permanent coordinating body that continues to exist.

CCA-ONG quickly gained donor support and grew into an organization of both international and local NGO members. At first, the group focused largely on improving state perceptions of NGOs, by trying to demonstrate that they were competent, professional, guarantors of participative development programming. With this battle won, CCA-ONG turned its attention to improving relations between international and local NGOs, a shift in focus heavily influenced by international trends.

In 1987, the first global conference of NGOs held in London, concluded that southern NGOs were dominated by INGOs and called for a new relationship in which the former were accorded equality and a leading role in development programming in their home countries. INGOs, themselves, were judged by donors to be flexible, cost-effective, efficient and more closely in touch with rural priorities than the state (Korten, 1990). They were deemed also to be more supportive of grassroots initiatives and with objectives that are consistent with the new paradigm of Adjustment with a Human Face (UNICEF, 1987; see also, Boulding, 1990).

INGOs were now positioned in Mali as important ombudsmen of *both* state and donor development policies and practices. The only concession they had to make, following the London meeting, was to accept greater participation in their activities by local NGOs. The CCA-ONG began taking public positions on major economic, social and political matters and, increasingly, INGOs were offered a seat at the table (or at least in the room) when the state and donors met to determine priorities. Accordingly, international bilateral and multilateral donors increased the percentage of ODA that they accorded to INGOs and, in the late 1980s, local NGOs also begin receiving such assistance.

Following the coup on 26 March 1991, the state adopted a program of standard recommendations from the international community: state enterprises were shut down or privatized, multi-party democratic pluralism was adopted and government downsizing and decentralization were pursued.[10] Unlike many African countries in which decentralization amounts to little more than deconcentration of administrative power, the Malian government was serious about the transfer of power in 1998 to 682 locally elected rural *Communes* and 19 urban *Communes*, which were to have authority over land-use and investment policies in their areas (Poulton and Youssouf, 1998). State budgeting and fiscal policies were reorganized to ensure that locally-elected bodies had adequate funds to engage in development programs.

By this time, it was impossible to differentiate between state, donor and NGO analyses of the development challenges facing the country. In fact, the State's 5-year development plan for 1998–2002 was created in collaboration with and co-authored by, UNDP. For the first time, the state completely planned and implemented policies in line with World Bank priorities, a fact that was highlighted in the Bank's 1997–8 annual report. For the first time, the role of so-called civil society organizations was explicit in both state and donor discourse of development. As USAID summarized it, the government's;

> ...commitments to human resource development and private sector-led growth, coupled with the decentralization policy being put in place, are intended to create conditions for a responsive and responsible participation of civil society (i.e., everything above the family and below the lowest level of government) in deciding the course and direction of development (USAID, 1995: 16).

The plans and strategies of the Malian state, donors and both local and international NGOs from the late 1990s constructed all of these major actors as partners in development. Donor language described their new role as catalysts, facilitators and brokers of new ideas rather than as financial sponsors. This new language (also adopted by the state and INGOs in reference to their *own* roles) referred to *other* organizational actors, as well as Malian citizens, as clients and customers in the development process. For the first time, now-standard phrases as civil society and good governance appeared in Malian development discourse. In contrast to earlier constructions of the poor as at worst as incompetent and at best as under-educated, they were described in the 1990s as rational, intelligent, interest-seeking and the focus of development. The state and the international community had a new role as the nearly invisible, guiding hands in the modernization project (AMADE, no date, no page numbers).

Initially constructed as a counterweight to donor and state development thinking in the 1980s, civil society organizations in the late 1990s, civil society became the fundamental pivot upon which success in decentralization and national development turned. INGOs became trainers, advisors and technical consultants to local NGOs within the discursive constructions of institutional or organizational development. International organizations rapidly nationalized their staffs, either completely turning over operations to Malian management or retaining but one or two expatriate staff to oversee operations at the most senior levels. All actors (i.e., NGOs, state and donors) agreed that their overarching goal was to promote sustainable human development (Nations Unies, 1998).

This trend should not obscure the fact that struggles over resources, ideas, policies and programs continued between the main actors. Independent evaluations conducted by several donor and UN agencies in the mid-to-late 1990s pointed out that the rhetoric of participation and partnership was not representative of the actual processes by which donors, the state and civil society organizations actually crafted and implemented their programs (Service d'Examen des Opérations IOV, 1994; Brigaldino, 1997). The rapidly proliferating micro-level NGOs created under the decentralization strategy to deliver basic social and human services, commenced a low-intensity warfare over territory and access to external resources.

The Enactment of and Contestation Over Global Rationalized Myths in an Organizational Field: The Malian Case (1960–1999)

Mainstream development literature has a difficult time accounting for many central themes in the evolution of state, donor and civil society relationships in Mali since 1960. What, for example, can explain the reversal of donor policies in Mali between the 1960s and late 1970s? What can help us account for a similar reversal in the construction of civil society's role in Malian development, from none in the 1960s, to buffer and ombudsman of both the state and donors in the 1980s, to integral partner of both in the late 1990s? To what can we attribute the changing normalizations in this organizational field?

While admittedly international politics, economic globalization and international relations are important here, I argue that the changing geometry of the organizational field comprising the Malian state, donors and civil society organizations was at least, in part, a result of these organizations enacting the five rationalized myths posited by world polity theory; foregrounding and emphasizing different myths at different times; and disagreeing about critical components of the definitions of these myths.

The configurations and re-configurations of state, donor and civil society organizations over the past forty years in Mali, when viewed in this light, can be seen as an ongoing cultural project of social deliberation in an organizational field, in the midst of ambiguity. I argue that high levels of conflict between the Malian state, donors and civil society, particularly between 1980–1991, were actually rooted in and permitted by wide agreement on assumptions about the sacralization of the individual; progress; justice and equality; universalism and rationalization. Conflict and contestation regarding these myths resulted in problems concerning which should be pre-eminent, how to negotiate the inherent contradictions contained within this system of cognitive frames (e.g., the well known conflict between individual equality and individual freedom) and how to allocate the division of labor within the national development project.

From this perspective, three distinct cultural phases are apparent in Malian development: 1960 to about 1980, 1981–1990 and 1991 to the present. In each, relationships between and definitions of the proper role of state, donors and civil society have coalesced into distinct configurations.

The Impresario State: 1960–1980

This phase was characterized by both the state and donors foregrounding the myth of progress. Both concurred on the statistical measures of progress, the importance of building a local industrial sector and on the importance of investments in infrastructure and mineral exploration. Both donors and the Malian state agreed that the cognitive unit of analysis for measuring development was the nation state as a whole rather than sub-units within the state (e.g., regions). This similarity in state/donor foregrounding of myths of rationality, led to a situation in which Malian development became balkanized into discrete sectoral domains (infrastructure, industry, natural resources). It was assumed that each one of these sectors could be developed through planned, organized efforts from the top. This helps to explain the absence of attention to civil society during this period.[11] This analysis of the organizational field in 1960s Mali also helps to explain why civil society was included in the development project, not as equal partner, but in the form of state-created, state-run and state-supported production cooperatives. These particular organizational forms mesh well with the underlying organizational field with a cultural frame emphasizing progress, equality and rationalization rather than individualism, freedom, or justice.

All for None and None for All: 1981–1990

Many analysts see the 1980s as an era during which economic approaches to development crystallized and gained hegemony in the form of IMF/World Bank economic restructuring programs. While I do not refute the validity of this argument, it fails to explain the high levels and particular forms of conflict and tension that existed among donors, the state and civil society in Mali during this decade. Instead, I suggest that the specific form and configurations acquired by the state-donor-civil society triangle can once again be better accounted for through the lens of contestation over widely accepted rationalized myths in an organizational field.

The Malian state, maintaining a critical center that promoted state-driven national development, switched focus from cooperatives to *tons villageois*, an embryonic mechanism for legitimate civil society participation in development. The state assumed that these voluntary, local organizations could both satisfy conditions of national progress as well as respond to increasing demands by INGOs (which established operations in Mali in large numbers between 1974–1985) for more participative, community-based development. During this decade, INGOs in Mali also appropriated global discourse surrounding environmental protection, population control and women-in-development. For INGOs, such appropriation represented a strong emphasis on rationalized myths of the sovereign and sacrosanct individual as well as appealing to the myth of universalism or universal truths.

Tensions between donors and the Malian state over the size of government, role of parastatals and the nature of development itself were not only the result of fundamental cleavages in political philosophy, but also rather a debate over different applications of norms of justice and equality. For the Malian state, justice and equality still implied that the state must control the distribution of the fruits of development; for donors, they implied not a guarantee of distributional benefit for each Malian but, rather, a guarantee that opportunities were equally distributed, whether individual Malians benefited or not.

Throughout the decade, the state resisted both INGO and UN attempts to raise universalism and individualism to the pinnacle of decision-making. It claimed consistently that Malian development was unique and belonged to Malians. Ironically, this form of particularism (evidenced by the proliferation of 10-year strategies created by the government in collaboration with INGOs, inter-governmental organizations and local UN and donor agencies) is possible only with broad agreement regarding the definition of development, the general nature of problems needing solution, as well as the proper roles and actions of development actors. Viewed in this light, particularism can be seen, not only as resistance (which it certainly is) but also as enactment of rationalized myths, which sanction and promote particularism. With the state invoking global cultural norms of equality and progress while actively fighting INGOs over the meaning of universalism in a local context, donors basing their programs on assumptions of progress and rationalism and INGOs and the UN increasingly invoking scripts associated with individualism and universalism, the stage was set for the great paradigmatic shift in Mali to Adjustment with a Human Face.

Through the lens of the enactment of institutionalized myths, Adjustment with a Human Face represented an epistemological compromise between economic efficiency/performance and social progress via the fulfillment of basic needs. Such agreement, which was gradually coming together throughout the early 1980s, resulted in a large arena of agreement within which: tensions between state, donors and civil society could be managed by all actors; and increased involvement of INGOs, the overwhelming champions of individualism and universalism, became necessary for both political and practical reasons and local NGOs could establish themselves.

Civil Society as Development Linchpin: 1991 to the Present

New configurations of the state-donor-civil society relationship in Mali could taken different forms in the 1990s. With the Traoré regime in crisis and various governments supporting opposition groups, students, workers' unions and capital-based associations joined together and overthrew the twenty-three year-old military regime. After a brief transitional period, a new president and government were elected, bringing with them different priorities, which led to a very real and concrete set of transformations, evidenced, for example, by such events as the proliferation of political parties, which actually win elective office at all levels, media outlets, growth in the private sector and elimination of an entire level of the political bureaucracy and reconfigurations of all others. Within these larger processes, there occurred a signal convergence on the part of the state, donors, the UN and NGOs (both local and international) regarding the leadership role to be played by civil society in the twenty-first century development process (Toé, 1997).

From a world polity perspective, this convergence can be explained by a rather curious agreement by all actors regarding fundamental human rights – an epistemo-logical consensus that development be focused on the individual, that the individual be free to choose his or her own development trajectory in line with various UN charters defining political, civil and socio-economic rights. In this cultural complex, macro-economic progress was positioned as a means and not an end; democratic pluralism as an end and not a means (in contradistinction to 1980s economism which posited just the reverse). Definitions of national problems such as environmental degradation, health and food security were both measured by and referenced to individual success. The new consensus on individualism as the starting point for development was reflected in proliferation of target groups considered – young men/women, children, the elderly, the handicapped, small/medium/large entrepreneurs, farmers, in a seemingly endless parade of social categories. Global rationalized myths about justice and equality were the necessary bedfellow of this sacralization of the individual and their combination with individualism formed the epistemological, moral and ethical boundaries to the late 1990s organizational field of development agencies in Mali.

Consequently, civil society organizations became considered by all as, perhaps, the most important ingredient to the success of the cultural project of national development. Local civil society organizations fit well with the important subsidiary myth of rationality: local NGOs were constructed as more knowledgeable about Malian culture than INGOs; they were more accountable for their performance as they live or perish by satisfying the needs of their fellow citizens; being Malian, they inherently had a better understanding of local development problems and solutions than expatriate technical experts.

Within this complex, the new role of INGOs was to undertake organizational development, which involved helping local NGOs in financial management, administrative efficiency, strategic planning and training in proposal writing to obtain funds from international donors. This new dynamic between local NGOs and INGOs helps to explain the shift in the constructed role of donors from that of funders to facilitators of new ideas. Both the state and donors became nearly invisible orchestrators of nation-building rather than active and implicated participants. The underlying principle of this new approach is that if all development is individual and the individual is ultimately free, then both the state and donors can do nothing but apply a light, guiding hand to the processes.

The Malian state, in close collaboration with nearly all major donors, made civil society organization performance the linchpin of its decentralization strategy. Village and inter-village organizations were encouraged to provide many social services that were previously the responsibility of the government. Concomitantly, concrete measures were taken both to devolve decision-making and economic resources to local levels. If civil society organizations failed to perform their assigned roles, most observers agreed that the state's decentralization and democratization process would also fail. It is to this issue that the chapter now turns.

The Future of State-Donor-Civil Society Configurations in Mali

This chapter has presented an alternative lens on the evolution of the constructed, proper roles of the state, donors and civil society in Mali since 1960. I have used the analytical unit of the organizational field, comprising the three and tried to demonstrate how configurations in this field are constituted in important ways by enactment of and contestation over rationalized myths held as sacred in the world polity. This analysis runs counter to political, economic, or other rational-actor approaches to understanding relationships between the three actors. It suggests that, increasingly over the last forty years, the constitution of this organizational field in Mali owes much to cognitive, normative and regulative frames rooted in normalized and increasingly shared cultural norms regarding development, modernity and progress. Indeed, it is the increasingly shared nature of these rationalized myths that make local-level contestation over specific definitions and specific emphases by different actors in the organizational field possible. While I make no claim as to the wider applicability of such an analysis, the global nature of the rationalized myths discussed in this chapter suggest that it would be worthwhile to study how these configurations have shifted in other countries.

I conclude with some observations regarding the future of the state-donor-civil society organizational geometry in Mali, particularly given the pre-eminent role currently accorded to local NGOs in the state's decentralization process. As stated above, most observers agree that the success of the decentralization process is to be marked by the ability of local NGOs to provide adequate social welfare services to local communities and that the success of NGOs in this endeavor is critical to state stability. Could there be problems in the horizon as these complex state/non-state relationships unfold?

First, at the grassroots levels, many newly-formed NGOs and village-based membership organizations are firmly aligned with long-standing local elites who represent a reactionary bloc and there is already evidence that they are neither democratic nor pluralistic and not always concerned with programs designed to serve their constituents. Research from other parts of the developing world (Dicklitch, 1998; Gupta, 1998; van Ufford, 1993; Uvin, 1998) demonstrates that local associations and NGOs are necessarily rooted in long-standing norms and patterns of social organization, cultural politics and power and historical processes outside and often in opposition to state development. Donors and INGOs often elide these dynamics. Concomitantly, Uvin (1998), Ferguson (1990) and others have convincingly revealed the inherent anti-politics of the development enterprise. This bias creates blind spots about socio-cultural power politics and can serve to exacerbate inequality in developing countries rather than engender equitable human development. In essence, the penetration of rationalized myths regarding both the importance of formal organization as well as the role construction that this entails for the state, donors and civil society organizational field means that among the variety of interests that men [sic] have, those interests that have been successfully collected to create corporate actors are the interests that dominate society (Coleman, 1974: 49). Such a dynamic means, of course, that non-organized persons or social groups may be left behind.

Second, as UNDP's Mamadou Amadou (1993) pointed out specifically for the Malian case, the localization of responsibility for *autodéveloppement* at the grassroots level and the central role given to local civil society in this project, risks a *new* hierarchy. Particularly in remote, resource-poor communities, individuals and organizations with a uniquely local view will fail to address larger, structural factors. Amadou refers to this as actions localisées de survie en oasis. Ironically, it is likely to create a situation in which the real empowerment of local communities leads to an increasing marginalization of those same communities vis-à-vis national and global development policies.

Third, the socio-cultural politics of local civil society organizations aside, it seems highly unlikely that they can acquire the requisite managerial skills quickly enough to satisfy their new role in development. The prevailing rationalized myths (individualism, universalism, justice, etc.), will mean an ever-proliferating identification of weaknesses, problems and shortcomings in local development processes, creating ever-higher expectations by citizens for additional programs.[12] The state or donors do not have the resources to meet such an explosion in perceived needs (increasingly constructed as *rights*).

Finally and perhaps most critically, the logic of the state decentralization process demands a gradual phasing out of both INGO and UN organizations as the developmental vision of More Mali, Less Aid (USAID, 1995) is operationalized. Both sets of actors have been very successful at consistently carving out new roles for themselves as discursive frames have changed over the past forty years. As configurations in the state-donor-civil society triangle shifted in Mali, organizational theory would suggest that it will be very difficult for them to shut down: this is going to be particularly true as the current trend towards nationalization of these organizational bureaucracies deepens and Malians come to have complete management responsibility over them. The trend will be not to decrease the size and role of these organizations, but to increase them, creating ever-more conflict within the civil society sector itself over resources, definitions of problems, identification of priorities and control of local and national development processes. If past is at all prelude, the likely outcome of this process will be a new set of normalized roles in the organizational field to treat such conflict.

Lest the above comment be seen as too pessimistic, civil society, donor and state conflict in Mali is already readily apparent. Postma (1994) found that although funding for local NGOs and associations in Mali was increasing, program support mechanisms do not necessarily facilitate NGO partnership formation or local institutional development. UNDP/NGO desks officials stressed that Réseau Afrique 2000 and Partnership in Development (PID) programs seek to facilitate the emergence and development of local NGOs. However, they are uncertain how NGOs, which receive only small grants, can develop institutionally and they describe national NGOs as difficult to supervise (Postma, 1994). Donors like USAID and the Canadian International Development Agency (CIDA) routinely demand that a Canadian or American NGO supervise local organizations and ensure the correct use of funds, creating tension between local and international NGOs.

My research in Mali (summers of 1999 and 2000), which consisted of a series of interviews with state, donor and international and local NGO leaders, confirmed such tensions. While state, World Bank, bilateral donor, UN and INGO rhetoric increasingly identifies local civil society as the new trustees (Cowen and Shenton, 1996) of development, local NGO leaders routinely told me that the rhetoric of partnership, collaboration and cooperation masked subtle power and decision-making hierarchies. They claim that local NGOs are subordinated, subjected to double standards regarding program performance and largely assumed to be last among equals. Such dynamics suggest that the Malian state's decentralization process, founded as it is upon a successful, client-centered civil society sector, will face tough times in the near to mid-term.

Notes

1. To be clear: world polity theory makes no claims about the internal struggles in a particular nation-state that are hidden behind outward isomorphism/convergence. As will be seen below, local-level contestation over global institutional myths is one of the predictions of world polity scholars. But outward form and content of such social structures are considered, in world polity research, to be critical data at a symbolic level which not only indexes legitimacy but also, through such symbolic capital, reaps resources for modern organizations.
2. Realist or neo-realist arguments (of which neoliberalism and neo-classical economics are examples) logically must posit that, since individuals and organizations respond in a rational, calculated manner to the opportunities and constraints in their environment, operating environments must largely have been identical around the globe over the past five or more decades.

3. It perhaps bears repeating that 'institutions' refer to 'cognitive, normative and regulative structures and activities that provide stability and meaning to social behavior' (Scott, 1995: 33). All five myths presented here include all three aspects although the ensuing analysis, for this paper's purposes, does not seek to pull these apart.

4. See Mauss (1985) and Jackson & Karp (1990) for anthropological accounts of how the construction of 'the person' has changed over the course of human history as well as how modern development programs construct a notion of the person that is culturally rooted.

5. More general histories of changes in Malian politics (Imperato, 1989; Vengroff and Koné 1993), civil society (Coulibaly, 1987; CCA-ONG, 1999), economics (Zulu & Nsouli, 1985; USAID, 1985; Mission Résidente de la Banque Mondiale 1996) and social services (Nations Unies, 1998) were consulted.

6. A concise summary of the Keita government's approach to national development can be found in R. James Bingen, 'Agricultural Development Policy and Grassroots Democracy in Mali', *African Rural and Urban Studies* 1, 1 (1994): 57-72.

7. Wider, global trends of course were also at play. Donor financing of Northern and Southern NGOs, globally, rose from US$1.04 billion to US$2.13 Billion between 1980–88 (Therkildsen and Semboja 1995: 17).

8. Again, wider global trends were influential. According to one source, there were 350 NGOs in the North in 1900, 1700 in 1980 and 2,542 registered in OECD countries (Robinson, 1991), although one must remain suspect about the earlier figures. Fowler (1995) notes that funds available to such NGOs doubled between 1985–95 to US$5.5 billion, or 14% of ODA, comprising 35% of NGO funding.

9. The French word encadrement is an important signifier. As opposed to other, possible synonyms, encadrer brings with it implicit senses of controlling, directing and supervising farmer actions, of enclosing the object of state efforts within an imposed frame.

10. Keeping in mind larger processes, it's of note that in 1989, 39 of 45 Sub-Saharan countries had authoritarian rule; by 1995, 31 of 45 had implemented democratic presidential or parliamentary elections (United Nations, 1996).

11. While most analysts of civil society's role in Malian development (particularly the role of INGOs) largely assume that INGOs were simply 'young' and not ready to implement programming, this belies the fact that organizations such as CARE, Save the Children, the Red Cross and Oxfam had been operating in other African countries since the 1950s.

12. This has been observed in Kenya, Tanzania and Uganda. Therkildsen and Semboja note that in these three countries which embarked on decentralization processes earlier than Mali, 'demand appears to be growing. Past achievements have not satisfied people's present demands'. Moreover, 'increased social differentiation over the past decades has amplified the demand for more and better services, especially among the better-off' (Therkildsen and Semboja 1995: 4).

References

Amadou, Mamadou (1993) *No Title*. In Centre Djoliba. *Décentralisation, organisations locales et ONG au Mali*. Mémoire du séminaire de Bamako 29–31 mars 1993. Pp. 30–34. Bamako: Association Djoliba Homme et Développement avec l'appui de la Fondation pour le progrès de l'Homme.

AMADE. Asociation Malienne Pour le Developpement: *Service Juridiques en Milieu Rural. Promotional Brochure*, no date.

Anonymous (1975) Mali: Plan Quinquennal 1974–1978 de Développement. In *Les Plans de Developpement des Pays d'Afrique Noire, 3rd édition*, numéro spécial du bulletin de l'Afrique noire, ediafric la documentation africaine, Paris.

Anonymous (1981) *Plan Quinquennal 1981/1985*. Bamako: Editions Imprimeries du Mali.

Appfel Marglin, F. and Marglin, S. (1990) *Dominating Knowledge: Development, Culture and Resistance*. NY: OUP.

Arce, A. and Long, N. (1993) 'Bridging two worlds: an ethnography of bureaucrat-peasant relations in western Mexico'. In M. Hobart (ed.) *An Anthropological Critique of Development: The Growth of Ignorance*. London and NY: Routledge.

Arce, A. and Lojng, N. (2000) 'Reconfiguring Modernity and Development From an Anthropological Perspective'. In A. Arce and N. Long (eds) *Anthropology, Development and Modernities: Exploring Discourses, Counter-tendencies and Violence*. London and NY: Routledge, 1–31.

Barnett, W. and Carroll, G. (1987) 'Competition and Mutualism among Early Telephone Companies'. *Administrative Science Quarterly* 32, 400–421.

Bayart, J.F. (1986) 'Civil Society in Africa'. In P. Chabal (ed.) *Political domination in Africa: Reflections on the limits of power*. Cambridge, UK: Cambridge University Press.

Berger, L. and Thomas, L. (1967) *The Social Construction of Reality*. NY: Doubleday.

Bingen, R. (1994) 'Agricultural Development Policy and Grassroots Democracy in Mali'. *African Rural and Urban Studies* 1(1), 57–72.

Boli, J. and Thomas, G. (eds) (1999) *Constructing World Culture: International Nongovernmental Organizations Since 1875*. Stanford, CA: Stanford University Press.

Boli, J. and Thomas, G. (1999) 'INGOs and the Organization of World Culture'. In J. Boli and G. Thomas (eds) *Constructing World Culture: International Nongovernmental Organizations Since 1875*. Stanford, CA: Stanford University Press, 13–49.

Boulding, E. (1990) 'Building a Global Civic Culture'. *Development* 2, 37–40.

Bourdieu, P. (1997) *Outline of a Theory of Practice*. Richard Nice (Trans.). NY: Cambridge University Press.

Bratton, M. (1994) 'Civil Society and Political Transitions in Africa'. In J. Harbeson, D. Rothchild and N. Chazan (eds), *Civil Society and the State in Africa*. Boulder and London: Lynne Rienner, 51–82.

Brigaldino, G. (1997) 'Managing European Aid Resources in Mali'. In C. Jerker, G. Somolekae and N. van de Walle (eds), *Foreign Aid in Africa: Learning from country experiences*. Uppsala, Sweden: Nordiska Afrikainstitute, 128–146.

Carroll, G. (1984) 'Organizational Ecology'. *Annual Review of Sociology* 10, 71–93.

Chabal, P. and Daloz, J. (1999) *Africa Works: Disorder as Political Instrument*. Oxford, UK and Bloomington, Indiana: James Currey and Indiana University Press, 1999.

Chazan, N. (1992) 'Africa's Democratic Challenge: Strengthening Civil Society and the State'. *World Policy Journal* 9, Spring, 279–307.

Coleman, J. (1974) *Power and the Structure of Society*. NY: Norton.

Couloubaly, P. (1987) 'Crises Economique et Contre-Pouvoirs au Mali'. *Africa Development* XII (2), 57–87.

Cowen, M., Shenton, R. (1996) *Doctrines of Development*. London and NY: Routledge.

Crewe, E. and Harrison, E. (1998) *Whose Development? An Ethnography of Aid*. London: Zed Press.

Crush, J. (1995) 'Introduction: Imagining development'. In J. Crush (ed.) *Power of Development*, London: Routledge, 1–23.

Dicklitch, S. (1998) *The Elusive Promise of NGOs in Africa: Lessons from Uganda*. NY: St Martin's Press.

DiMaggio, P. (1991) 'Constructing an Organizational Field as a Professional Project: U.S. Art Museums, 1920–1940'. In W. Powell and P. J. DiMaggio (eds) *The New Institutionalism in Organizational Analysis*. Chicago: University of Chicago Press, 267–92.

DiMaggio, P., Powell, W. (1983) 'The Iron Cage Revisited: Institutional Isomorphism and Collective Rationality in Organizational Fields'. *American Sociological Review* 48, 147–160.

Direction Générale du Plan et de la Statistique (1970) *Programme Triennal de Redressement économique et Financier, 1970–1972*. Bamako: République du Mali.

Dobbin, F., Dowd, T. (1997) 'How Policy Shapes Competition: Early Railroad Foundings in Massachusetts'. *Administrative Science Quarterly* 42, 510–529.

Edward, M. and Hulme, D. (1996) *Beyond the Magic Bullet: NGO Performance and Accountability in the Post-cold War World*. West Hartford, Connecticut: Kumarian Press.

Escobar, A. (1995) *Encountering Development*. Princeton, NJ: Princeton University Press.

FAO (1962) *Enquîte de la FAO Sur L'Afrique, Rapport National: République du Mali: Problèmes et Perspectives du Développement Rural*. Rome: FAO.

Fatton, R. Jr. (1995) 'Africa in the Age of Democratization: The Civic Limitations of Civil Society'. *African Studies Review* 38 (2), September, 67–99.

Ferguson, J. (1994) *The Anti-Politics Machine: Development, Depoliticization and Bureaucratic Power in Lesotho*. Minneapolis, MN: University of Minnesota Press.

Fowler, A. (1988) *Non-Governmental Organizations in Africa: Achieving Comparative Advantage in Micro-Development*. Discussion Paper 249. Institute of Development Studies, University of Sussex.

Fowler, A. (1995) 'NGOs and the Globalization of Social Welfare'. In J. Semboja and Ole Therkildsen. *Service Provision under Stress in East Africa: The State, NGOs & People's Organizations in Kenya, Tanzania & Uganda*. Denmark: Centre for Development Research (in association with London: James Currey), 51–69.

Geertz, C. (1973) *The Interpretation of Cultures*. NY: Basic Books.

Giddens, A. (1979) *Central Problems in Social Theory*. Berkeley: University of California Press.

Goodrick, E., Meindl, J. and Flood, A. (1997) 'Business as Usual: The Adoption of Managerial Ideology by U.S. Hospitals Research'. *The Sociology of Health Care* (14), 27–50.

Gupta, A. (1998) *Postcolonial Developments: Agriculture in the Making of Modern India*. Durham and London: Duke University Press.

Hannan, M. and Freeman, J. (1977) 'The Population Ecology of Organizations'. *American Journal of Sociology* 82, 929–64.

Haugerud, A. (1995) *The culture of politics in modern Kenya*. Cambridge: Cambridge University Press.

Havemann, H. and Rao, H. (1997) 'Structuring a Theory of Moral Sentiments: Institutional and Organizational Coevolution in the Early Thrift Industry'. *American Journal of Sociology* 102, 6, 1606–51.

Hulme, D. and Edwards, M. (1997) *NGOs, states and donors: too close for comfort?*. NY: St. Martin's Press in association with Save the Children.

Hyden, G. (1995) 'Bringing Volunteerism Back In Eastern Africa: Comparative Perspective'. In J. Semboja and Ole Therkildsen (eds) *Service Provision under Stress in East Africa: The State, NGOs & People's Organizations in Kenya, Tanzania & Uganda*. Denmark: Centre for Development Research (in association with London: James Currey Ltd.), 35–50.

Imperato, P. (1989) *Mali: A Search for Direction*. Boulder, CO: Westview Press.

Jackson, M. and Karp, I. (1990) *Personhood and Agency: the experience of self and other in African cultures*. Uppsala and Washington, DC: Smithsonian Institution Press.

Jones, W. (1969) 'Economics of the coup'. *Africa Report* 14, 3–4, 23–26, 51–53.

Koenig, D., Diarra, T., Sow, M., Diarra, O., Fofana, M., Koné, F., Konaté, S. and Maiga, F. (1998) *Innovation and Individuality in African Development: Changing Production Strategies in Rural Mali*. Ann Arbor: University of Michigan Press.

Korten, D. (1990) *Getting to the 21st Century: Voluntary Action and the Global Agenda*. West Hartford CN: Kumerian Press.

Lawrence, P. and Lorsch, J. (1967) *Organization and Environment: Managing Differentiation and Integration*. Boston: Harvard University.

Long, N. (1992) 'Introduction'. In N. Long and A. Long (eds) *Battlefields of Knowledge: The Interlocking of Theory and Practice in Social Research and Development*. London and NY: Routledge.

Mauss, M. (1983) 'A Category of the Human Mind'. In M. Carrithers (ed.) *The Category of the Person*. NY: Cambridge University Press, 1–25.

Meyer, J. (1977) 'The Effects of Education as an Institution'. *American Journal of Sociology* 83, 55–77.

Meyer, J. and Rowan, B. (1977) 'Institutionalized Organizations: Formal Structure as Myth and Ceremony'. *American Journal of Sociology* 83, 340–63.

Ministère de l'Agriculture (1982) *...laboration de la Stratégie Alimentaire. Commission d'élaboration de la stratégie alimentaire*. Bamako: CILSS/Club du Sahel, OCDE.

Ministère de la Coopération, France (1965). *Republique du Mali: ...conomie et Plan de Développment*. Prepared by M.R. Julienne, Paris: Ministère de la Coopération, 2nd edition.

Ministère des affaires étrangères et des maliens de l'extérieur (1997) *Note de stratégie nationale: Cadre d'intervention du système des Nations-Unies au Mali, Période; 1997–2001*. Bamako: Ministère des affaires étrangères et des maliens de l'extérieur.

Ministère des ressources naturelles et de l'élevage (1987) *Programme National de Lutte Contre la Désertification, Tome I: Diagnostic de la situation actuelle et concept de Lutte*. Bamako: République du Mali.

Ministère du Plan (1981) *Programme Substantiel d'Action Pour le Développement Acceleré du Mali, 1981–1990*. Bamako: République du Mali.

Ministère du Plan et de L'...conomie Rurale (no date) *Rapport du Ministre du Plan et de l'économie Rurale à l'Assemblée Nationale sur le Plan Quinquennal de Développement ...conomique et Social de la République du Mali, 1961–1965*. Bamako: République du Mali.

Ministry of Planning (1981) *International Conference of Donors For the Economic Recovery and Development of the Republic of Mali, Volume I: Summary Report*. Bamako: Republic of Mali.

Mission Résidente de la Banque Mondiale au Mali (1996) *La Coopération Mali-Banque Mondiale*. Cité du Niger, Bamako: Imprim Color.

Moore, D. (2000) 'The crucible of cultural politics: reworking development in Zimbabwe's eastern highlands'. *American Ethnologist*, 26(3), 654–689.

Nations Unies (1998) Conseil d'administration du Programme des Nations Unies pour le Développement et du Fonds des Nations Unies pour la population, PNUD: Cadres de Coopération avec les pays et questions connexes: premier cadre de coopération avec le Mali (1998–2002). Bamako: PNUD, 17 février 1998, DP/CCF/MLI/1.

Ndegwa, S. (1996) *The Two Faces of Civil Society: NGOs and Politics in Africa*. West Hartford, CN: Kumerian Press.

Peters, P. (1994) *Dividing the Commons: Politics, Policy and Culture in Botswana*. Charlottesville, VA: University Press of Virginia.

Postma, W. (1994) 'NGO Partnership and Institutional Development: Making it Real, Making it Intentional'. *Canadian Journal of African Studies* 28 (3), 447–471.

Poulton, R., Youssouf, I. (1998) *A Peace of Timbuktu: Democratic Governance, Development and African Peacemaking*. NY and Geneva: United Nations.

Powell, W. and DiMaggio, P. (1991) *The New Institutionalism in Organizational Analysis*. Chicago: University of Chicago Press.

Robertson, R. (1992) *Globalization: Social Theory and Global Culture*. London: Sage Publications.

Robinson, A. (1991) 'Development NGOs in Europe and North America: A Statistical Profile'. *Charity Trends: Annual Report of the Charities Aid Foundation*. Tonbridge: Charities Aid Foundation, 154–165.

Sachs, W. (1992) *The Development Dictionary*. NY: St. Martin's Press.

Scott, W. (1994) 'Conceptualizing Organizational Fields: Linking Organizations and Societal Systems'. In U. Derlien, Uta Gerhardt and F. Scharpf (eds) *Systemrationalitat und Partial Interesse [System Rationality and Partial Interests]*. Baden-Baden, Germany: Nomos Verlagsgesellschaft, 203–221.

Scott, W. (1995) *Institutions and Organizations*. Thousand Oaks, CA: Sage.

Scott, W. (1998) *Organizations: Rational, Natural and Open Systems*. 4th Edition. Upper Saddle River, NJ: Prentice Hall.

Service d'Examen des Opérations, IOV (1994) *Mali: Evaluation de la coopération bilatérale entre le Mali et les Pays-Bas, 1975–1992*. Den Haag: Ministerie van Buitenlandse Zaken, Inspectie Ontwikkelingssamenwerting te Velde (IOV).

Therkildsen, O. and Semboja, J. (1995). 'A New Look at Service Provision in East Africa'. In J. Semboja and Ole Therkildsen (eds) *Service Provision under Stress in East Africa: The State, NGOs & People's Organizations in Kenya, Tanzania & Uganda*. Denmark: Centre for Development Research (in association with London: James Currey Ltd.), 1–34.

Thomas, G., Meyer, J., Ramirez, F. and Boli, J. (1987) (eds) *Institutional Structure: Constituting State, Society and the Individual*. Newbury Park, CA: Sage.

Toé, R. (1997) *La Décentralisation au Mali: Ancrage Historique et Dynamique socio-culturelle*. Mission de Décentralisation et des Reformes Institutionnelles: Bamako.

Touré, M., Deme, Y. and Poulton, R. (1999) *Rôle des ONG dans le développement économique et social du Mali*. Unpublished monograph.

Trust, G. (1997) *The History of Development: from Western Origins to Global Faith*. London and NY: Zed Press.

UNICEF (1987) *Adjustment with a Human Face*. NY: UNICEF.

United Nations (1996) 'Democratization'. *African Recovery* 10 (2), 24.

USAID/Mali (1985) *Mali: economic policy reform program*. Washington, DC: USAID.

USAID/Mali (1995) *USAID/Mali: Strategic Plan*. Bamako: USAID.

Uvin, P. (1998) *Aiding Violence: The Development Enterprise in Rwanda*. West Hartford, Connecticut: Kumerian Press.

Van Ufford, P. and Quarles, P. (1993). 'Knowledge and ignorance in the practices of development policy'. In M. Hobart (ed.) *An Anthropological Critique of Development: The Growth of Ignorance*. London and NY: Routledge, 135–160.

Vengroff, R. and Koné, M. (1993) 'Mali: democracy and political change'. In J. Wiseman (ed.) *Democracy and Political Change in sub-Saharan Africa*. London and NY: Routledge, 45–73.

Zucker, L. (1977) 'The Role of Institutionalizaiton in Cultural Persistence'. *American Sociological Review* 42, 726–43.

Zulu, J. and Nsouli, S. (1985) *Adjustment Programs in Africa: The Recent Experience*. Washington, DC: IMF.

Chapter 13

Peripheral Vision: Globalization, Sustainable Development and the Political Ecology of Cotton Production in Mali

William Moseley

Introduction

The textile industry was one of the first manufacturing activities to become organized globally, with mechanized production in Europe using cotton from the various colonies. Cotton and textile production are still organized globally, albeit with a different spatial distribution. One cog in the global textile loom is Mali, currently the leading cotton producer in Sub-Saharan Africa.

Mali is extremely marginal in the world economic system, ranking among the poorest in the world with a 1998 per capita income of $US 250. The country has recently been racked by droughts whose origins are contested and range from natural causes, demographic change, to cotton cultivation. Due to its situation on the periphery of the world economic system, its involvement in one of the oldest global industries and the disputed nature of its environmental problems, Mali offers a good case to study the economics and ecology of commodity production within current discourses regarding the market, the environment and the ideological dimensions of globalization.

This chapter uses Mali to explain the evolving dynamic between cotton production for the world market, environmental degradation and global development paradigms, in terms of two inter-related questions. How has cotton production policy in Mali changed over time and how does this evolution implicate globalization discourse? What have been the environmental impacts of cotton production and how is this problematized and solutions evoked within globalization discourse? A major sub-text of this analysis is that the economy-environment nexus in Mali is the result of intersecting processes operating at different spatial scales: the global cotton market, national level policy and local production decisions; all underlain by environmental impacts. The political ecology approach adopted here is important for unbundling the multi-scale, political, economic and environmental dynamics of cotton production (Greenberg and Park, 1994; Peet and Watts, 1996; Bryant, 1997).

Conceptualizing the Problem

In its most general sense, globalization refers to the increasing interconnectedness between national economies and the integration of people around the globe into a world society. Scholars differ on whether or not globalization represents a distinctly new phase of international capital (Fagan, 1995; Korton, 1995; Bryan and Farell, 1996) or simply a new term for a long-standing world economy (Hirst and Thompson, 1996; Glyn and Sutcliffe, 1992; Gordon, 1988).

Proponents of the strong version of globalization assert that a truly global economy has emerged since the 1970s, in which national economies are increasingly irrelevant and the market is increasingly unencumbered by government regulations (Fagan, 1995; Bryan and Farell, 1996). Some have referred to this process as the crisis of nationally regulated capitalism (Brecher and Costello, 1994) marked by capital mobility and manifested in the Third World by *a new* phase of cooperation between global capital and the state, in which the latter (with the encouragement of the international financial institutions, IFIs) assists the former to subdue the last vestiges of the unruly frontier (Sandbrook, 1997; Loxley and Seddon, 1994; Roy, 1997; Bracking, 1999). Strong globalizationists also point to the emergence of a global culture (Hannerz, 1990; Smith, 1990; Tenbruck, 1990) and the dispersion of common ideas (Smart, 1993; Johnston *et al.*, 1995; Klak and Myers, 1997), facilitated by increasingly sophisticated communication networks which are used effectively by the private sector, government and multilateral and bilateral organizations to promote a particular world view.[1]

Supporters of the weak globalization thesis argue that an international economy is not unprecedented and that the scale and scope of globalization has been exaggerated (Hirst and Thompson, 1996). Much of the globalization discourse lacks historical depth as the last several hundred years have been marked by periods of protectionism as well as periods of mobile capital and free trade.[2] Far from being global, the world economy is concentrated in Europe, Japan and North America (Hirst and Thompson, 1996; Grant and Agnew, 1996; Cook and Kirkpatrick, 1997). The nation state is still relevant and wields sufficient power to shape national economies (Hirst and Thompson, 1996). Weak globalizationists also argue that the power of local culture, to filter outside influences and impact global ideologies, has been underestimated (Pieterse, 1995; Marden, 1997).

Much of the globalization discourse is directed at the spread of neo-liberal economics and multiparty democracy. However, the neoliberal agenda also involves socially constructed conceptions of the natural environment, environmental degradation and sustainable development (WCED, 1987), which may be as hegemonic as their counterparts in economics and politics (Logan, 1999; Gupta, 1998; Frank, 1997). Environmental paradigms, causal explanations and narratives have a tangible impact when they are translated to policy and program design, or used to interpret history. For example, Fairhead and Leach (1996) have demonstrated how preconceptions about environmental degradation in Africa significantly influence interpretations of environmental change in Guinea. Glenzer (1999) has discussed the influence of international paradigms of human-environment relationships on interpretations of drought and ecological crisis in the Malian Sahel. Concerns about environmental degradation have led some analysts to argue for the adoption of universal environmental norms (Sarre, 1995; Miller, 1995), which are dependent on causal explanations that may not be relevant in all ecological contexts.

Sustainable development has been particularly influential in environmental and development studies since the late 1980s and has made it possible for some scholars to assert that economic growth is a prerequisite for sustainable natural resource use (e.g. Beckerman, 1992; Pearce and Atkinson, 1993; Barret, 1996; see also, World Bank, 1992). The converse position, also articulated by the Brundtland Commission (WCED, 1987) and subsequently re-articulated at other international fora (e.g., UNCED, 1993) and by multilateral institutions (e.g., World Bank, 1996), suggests that the poor and hungry destroy or consume environmental resources so that they may meet their short-term survival needs.

The promulgation by bilateral and multilateral donors of the dual package of economic growth and environmental stewardship under the name of sustainable development has been criticized by a number of scholars. Logan (1999: 2) asserts that '[s]ustainable development is archetypal of the twin processes of globalization and colonization of environmental ideas and practices in Africa'. Many argue that economic growth is antithetical to environmental conservation (e.g., Hueting, 1995; Cheru, 1992; Goodland, 1991; Daly, 1991) and that export production, rather than poverty, may largely be responsible for environmental degradation in many developing countries (Cheru, 1992; Marshall, 1999; Gupta, 1998).

Mali's high rates of poverty and significant levels of natural resource degradation (World Bank, 1996)[3] have encouraged conceptualizations of sustainable development that problematize the former as cause of the latter (see, e.g., FEWS, 1997; Davies, 1996; Leisinger and Schmitt, 1995). This point is underscored by Bingen (1998), who argues that cotton production and the wealth it generates represent the only element of success in Malian agriculture. This argument was also enunciated earlier by the World Bank, which associates most of Mali's environmental problems with increasing populations rather than with cotton production (World Bank, 1988).[4]

Cotton Production: From the Global to the Local

How, if at all, has the promotion of cotton production in Mali changed over time and what are the implications of this evolution for globalization theory? This question is handled in three related sub-sections: the institutional context, the chronology of cotton production and the relationship between the state, global capital and cotton production.

The Institutional Context

The first tangible effort by the French to encourage commercial cotton production in Mali (then the French Soudan) was in 1904 in the middle Niger valley. Concerned about steady supplies of cotton to their factories, especially after the American civil war interrupted the world cotton market in the 1860s, the French looked to the Soudan as a logical choice for commercial cotton production since it had a vibrant, indigenous cotton farming and weaving tradition. From the start, the colonial administration worked closely with the Association Cotonnière Coloniale (a non-profit enterprise founded by French industrialists) and French and Lebanese private traders to encourage the production of cotton for the export market. The French were committed to the use of price incentives to encourage cotton farming for the external market (rather than forced labor). Colonial efforts to export sizeable quantities of cotton largely failed until the 1950s because the indigenous cotton market offered a higher price to farmers than the world market (Roberts, 1995; Roberts, 1996).

Cotton production for the external market expanded in the 1950s when the French began to focus on the promotion of rain-fed cotton (as opposed to irrigated varieties) in the southern third of the country. The French parastatal Compagnie FranÁaise pour le Développement des Fibres Textiles (CFDT), or the French Company for the Development of Textile Fibers, was responsible for facilitating cotton production in southern Mali (Roberts, 1996; Bingen, 1998)[5] from 1950–1974. The problem of competition from the indigenous market was resolved through a policy of 'flooding' the local cotton market (Roberts, 1996).

In 1974, the Malian Government and the CFDT agreed to create the Compagnie Malienne pour le Développement des Textiles (CMDT), or Malian Company for Textile Development, with 60% Malian government and 40% CFDT capital (Serafini and Sy, 1992; Bingen, 1998).[6] Bingen (1998: 269–270) suggests that this was a mutually beneficial move as it gave the Malian government a means to attract new foreign capital (mainly from the World Bank) and allowed the CFDT to invest its capital more directly in profit-related production and marketing activities. The CMDT has benefited from a continued relationship with the CFDT. As part of the CFDT cotton and development group, CMDT has access to over 50 years of French investment in cotton research throughout West and Central Africa (Eisa, 1994). CMDT also has close links to the CFDT marketing unit, COPACO (Compagnie Cotonnière). COPACO accounts for 15% of world trade in cotton and ranks among the world's nine largest international cotton merchants (Malian cotton accounts for 3% of global trade) (Bingen, 1998). CMDT's relationship with COPACO allows it greater leverage in world markets. The CFDT has also benefited from its partnership with the Malian government, for example, being able to work through the Ministry of Agriculture to seek foreign public grants and loans (at concessionary rates) to purchase agricultural inputs The creation of the CMDT could be seen as an expansion of the state's role in the management of the national economy. However, in nationalizing CFDT, the state chose to ally itself with, rather than shun international capital, rather akin to previous collaboration between industrialists and the French government.

In the mid 1980s, the Malian government accepted the World Bank's recommendation to change the legal statute of the CMDT from a government agency to a parastatal commercial and industrial enterprise (société à caractère industriel et commercial). This legal change clarified CMDT's status as a subsidiary of CFDT. The Malian government later accepted the World Bank's recommendation to privatize the CMDT (Bingen, 1998). The CMDT's national company status allows it to have a monopoly on the country's cotton processing and marketing (it has held this monopoly since 1988).

While the World Bank was successful in encouraging privatization of the CMDT, it has been less successful in breaking up the CMDT's monopoly, or liberalizing cotton processing and marketing. To protect its position, the CFDT vehemently opposes World Bank liberalization efforts that would oblige Mali and other countries to dismantle their exclusive relationship with it (Bingen, 1998).

I would argue that the privatization of the CMDT does not represent a fundamental departure from the long-standing collaboration between the government and private capital in the cotton sector. Ownership of the company remained the same (60% Malian government and 40% CFDT) as did its ties to the world cotton market.

Chronology of Cotton Production

In the early 1960s Modibo Keita's (Mali's first president) collectivization program imposed obligatory cotton production on some of the cotton-growing regions of Northern Mali (Imperato and Imperato, 1982). Many villagers got into cotton production because they needed the money to pay the government head tax as well as other expenses (Imperato and Imperato, 1982). By 1992, Mali ranked fourth on the continent in total cotton production and its average yield (1,300 kilogram/hectare) was the highest in the world for rain-fed cotton. In 1990, cotton accounted for 7% of Mali's GDP, 50% of its exports and 59% of its agricultural exports (Serafini and Sy, 1992).

Despite low earnings, many farmers stayed in cotton production because it was the only means by which they could obtain credit to purchase inputs. Furthermore, if field crops were rotated with cotton year after year, a farmer was able to capitalize on the residual effect of fertilizers, a concrete benefit often used by extension agents, who point out that a successful cotton farmer is also a successful millet farmer. There was also an organized marketing structure for cotton that was not available for any other crop. Through the early 1990s, therefore, government policies, especially price support and guaranteed purchase (which assured bank loans), were in place to encourage continued cotton cultivation.

Although low profit margins, uncertainty over the government's ability to maintain the price support program and soil degradation caused some farmers to turn away from cotton production (Biladeau, 1992), the economics of cotton production in Mali was positive for much of the 1990s. The country was Sub-Saharan Africa's leading cotton producer in 1998 and cotton was its leading export (ahead of cattle and gold) (Economist Intelligence Unit, 1998; CIA, 1999; Tefft *et al.*, 1998; Bingen, 1998).

Many analysts believe that the major explanation for the continued success of cotton production in Mali, especially in the late 1990s, was an increase of 84% in the nominal producer price and 26% in the real producer price, between 1990–93 and 1997–98 (Tefft *et al.*, 1998). This increase was driven primarily by a 100% devaluation of the CFA in 1994 coupled with a period of relatively high world cotton prices.[7] Although the devaluation also increased the price of imported inputs,[8] farmers responded to it by replacing mineral fertilizers with manure and compost (Tefft *et al.*, 1998).

According to Tefft *et al.* (1998), the price incentives for increased cotton production were mixed, depending on a farmer's wealth. Well equipped, wealthier producers, tended to increase their net revenues from cotton, while semi-equipped and non-equipped producers saw their real net returns decline.[9] The same study showed that the profitability of grain production was greater than that of cotton.[10] The ambiguous price signals for all but the wealthiest farmers suggest that government incentives for cotton cultivation still play an important role in production. Cotton is now the only remaining commodity for which there is a fixed floor price and guaranteed purchase offered by the CMDT.[11] In part because of this assured price and purchase, cotton continues to be one of the few crops for which banks are willing to extend agricultural credit.

The State, Global Capital and Cotton Production

Mali's cotton sector has gradually become incorporated into the world market over the past 100 years. This process has not occurred naturally at the behest of an unfettered market. From the beginning, the state (first the French colonial administration and then the Malian government) has worked closely with private capital to encourage cotton production for export. In the absence of consistent and sufficient price incentives from the world market, the state has collaborated with private capital to provide additional inducements to farmers (e.g., buffered producer prices, access to agricultural credit). This active state involvement in promoting cotton is quite common in a number of Francophone African countries (Tefft *et al.*, 1998).[12]

The volatility of the world cotton market means that it is a very unfriendly place for small-scale producers with limited capital. The Malian state and the CFDT realizing that this volatility would drive most producers out of the market, buffer producer prices to ensure continued production. The CMDT remains in business because it is able to generate a significant *average* profit for the Malian state and the CFDT, by withstanding years of low world prices with the help of a cotton stabilization fund.[13] This type of cooperation between global capital and the state is not a new phase in Mali's export cotton industry, but rather the only form of organization this sector has ever known.

No dramatic shift occurred in the organization of Malian cotton production in the 1970s or 1980s, a time when proponents of the strong globalization thesis suggest that the world economy began to undergo fundamental change. While the cotton company in Mali changed its form over time, becoming nationalized in 1974 and privatized in the mid 1980s, these changes are more indicative of strategic adaptation to a changing political environments than of a fundamental shift in long standing collaboration between the state and capital.[14] Furthermore, farmer response to an upswing in cotton producer prices in the 1990s does not suggest a significant departure from tradition, since the state and the CMDT continued to support cotton production during this period with non-market inducements.

If a major shift occurred in the Malian cotton sector, it was during the colonial era when the French worked for 50 years (approximately 1900–1950) to subvert the local cotton market and reorient production towards the outside market. Since then, Malian cotton has been an integral part of the global economy.

It has been argued that the international financial institutions (IFIs) play a key role in the globalization process in Africa by opening up economies to the world market through structural adjustment. In the case of Malian cotton, the government and private sector have selectively and opportunistically adopted IFI policy. The Malian state and the CFDT agreed to privatization in the mid 1980s when it was in their financial interest to do so, but have successfully resisted liberalization when it portended to have negative impacts on the cotton sector. The irony of the Malian case is that true liberalization would undermine cotton export by dismantling policies that have encouraged farmers to keep producing for a volatile export market.[15]

Cotton Production and Environmental Change

Prior to introduction of cash cropping of long fiber cotton, Northern Mali had an ecologically well-adapted system of short fiber cotton production, Gossypium herbaceum var. africanum (Prentice, 1972), to supply the local textile industry. Two broad practices were prevalent. In the first, farmers would clear an area of large grass (usually Andropogon gayanus) and small trees, then broadcast cotton and sesame seeds over the partially cleared field. The farmer would then scrape the soil surface (without turning over the soil) with a hand held hoe, simultaneously uprooting all weeds and grasses and covering the previously broadcast seeds with a layer of dirt and vegetative manner, a process somewhat akin to the no till strategies that are increasingly employed in modern agriculture for soil conservation purposes (Richards, 1991). The second tradition involved nonlinearly spaced mounds on which cotton seeds would sown, with sweet potatoes, cowpeas, yams or chickpeas planted around the sides.

When long fiber cotton was introduced by the French, fields were tilled in linear furrows with an oxen drawn (moldboard) plow.[16] Export-oriented cotton farming increasingly relied on manufactured inputs and government agricultural extension agents actively discouraged any form of intercropping in the new cotton production system. The ecological effects associated with long fiber cotton include the following.

1. Soil erosion and declines in soil fertility because the cotton plant does not provide adequate ground cover for most of the rainy season. Erosion is exacerbated by the abandonment of traditional soil conservation strategies (mainly rock lines and grass strips) that occurred with the introduction of the plow (Moseley, 1993).
2. Cotton pests, including (*Diparopsis castanea, Pectinophone gossypiella, Cryptophlebia leucotreta* and *Eria spp.*), cotton stainers (*Dysdercus spp.*) and beetles (*nkobo* in Bamanan) or sucking bugs (*Empoasca facialis, Helopeltis spp.* and *Aphis gossypii*) are also an increasingly difficult problem.
3. Soil organic matter is run down as chemical fertilizers allow cultivation to occur after organic matter has been seriously depleted.

Many of these changes have been experienced in the whole of southern Mali where cotton is grown. The fact that cotton is very demanding on the soil and a poor cover crop is well documented in general (e.g., Prentice, 1972) and for the specific case of southern Mali (Vanderpol and Traore, 1993; Girdis, 1993; Schrader *et al.*, 1998; Bingen, 1998). Bingen (1998) notes that, due to cotton induced land degradation, cotton production has begun to level off in some of the oldest areas of production, leading to a shift to the cotton frontier in the east of the country. Since the upturn in cotton prices around 1994, cotton production has also become increasingly extensive, that is, relying on increases in area farmed rather than on improved yields to augment production (Tefft *et al.*, 1998).

Globalization of Ideas and Paradigms of Environmental Change

In explaining environmental degradation, global paradigms often suggest that local people do not have the capacity to adapt to changing environmental conditions. Some development practitioners feel that while local knowledge may have been suitable to past situations, it has become increasingly less viable in a period of rapid change. The representatives of development organizations meeting at a major conference in Segou, Mali in 1989 generally agreed 't]hat existing production systems were not simply outdated, but that growing demographic pressure and environmental crisis have created the need for entirely new land management strategies' (Shaikh, 1989: 12). A Mali-based, expatriate administrator interviewed by the author in 1992 stated 'there is 20% less rain than in the 1960s but the villagers haven't adopted new agricultural practices'.

Local versus National Interpretations of Environmental Problems

Contrary to these assertions, the present research established that local people in Southern Mali were adapting to environmental change through a variety of ingenious strategies (Moseley, 1993). Chief among these was a switch from well-drained soils to water-retentive soils in response to decreased rainfall. Villagers are also cultivating a new variety of rice in an area that had rarely been cultivated before (demonstrating their ability to recognize and exploit new opportunities). Finally, the traditional land tenure system was flexible enough to accommodate dramatic shifts in land preferences (from well drained to water retentive soils). These cases suggest that local people possess the knowledge and flexibility to adapt to changing environmental conditions. Other authors have documented a similar adaptations (e.g., Koenig *et al.*, 1998).

Villagers' understanding of the environmental impacts of cotton production, may be compared to that of government extension agents, who serve as the foot soldiers of global capital in the villages. When extension agents were asked about the potential ecological repercussions of cotton cultivation, many felt that the cultivar did not present substantial problems. Some agents differed significantly from villagers in their assessment of the agroecology of the plant. One agent stated that cotton 'is like a tree that fertilizes the ground. It fights erosion in the same way that trees do.' When asked if any negative consequences were associated with the use of agrochemicals, another agricultural extension agent responded that 'herbicides do not have any negative consequences because they save farmers weeding time. Cotton can't work without it [herbicides].' A recurring theme among extension agents was that there is one 'correct' way to farm cotton and that way tends to involve the use of heavy capital inputs which place financial obligations on farmers that link them inextricably to global capital.

How the Malian government and the CMDT address environmental degradation is influenced by the fact that they depend on cotton as a significant source of revenue. Income from cotton is divided between the CMDT (40%), farmers (33%), the state (21%) and a stabilization fund[17] (6%) (Economic Intelligence Unit, 1998). The CMDT finances much of its operating expenses through the sale of cotton. The CMDT also has a contract with the state to provide general environmental management services in its zone of operation (Schrader *et al.*, 1998). This contract enables the CMDT to bias extension work and research in southern Mali towards cotton.

The state also depends on the export of cotton for a significant portion of it revenues, with 10.5% of government revenues deriving from cotton in 1998.[18] It is no surprise, therefore, that the state wishes to double cotton production over the next several years.[19]

Perhaps, due to the fact that the state depends on cotton as a significant revenue earner, it has few administrative checks and balances to temper the drive for increased cotton production. The Ministry of Environment (MoE) might logically provide a critical counterweight to cotton production goals set by the Ministry of Rural Development and Water. However, monitoring the environmental impacts of agriculture does not fall within the jurisdiction of the MoE (Moseley, 1999). Rather than having a broad oversight mandate on environmental issues, the purview of the MoE (reconfigured in 1999) is limited to urban sanitation and forestry.

Global Environmental Paradigms and National Policy

The IFIs and bilateral donors, such as USAID, are supporting a number of economic and environmental programs in Mali. The discourse on these programs makes few allusions to the links between cotton cultivation and environmental degradation, but frequently mentions poverty as a key obstacle to sustainable development. According to the World Bank (1997) 'Mali's agricultural potential is threatened by insufficient rainfall, poverty and competition between agriculture and animal husbandry.' Nowhere does the report mention cotton as a cause of soil degradation. Similarly, the IMF (1999) devotes several pages to agricultural reform, including significant sections on cotton, yet never relates cotton production to environmental problems. In a policy-planning document prepared for donors, the GoM focuses on increasing the efficiency of cotton production without mentioning its potential environmental impacts (GoM 1999). Mali's National Environmental Action Plan (adopted in 1998) also does not make any explicit connections between cotton cultivation and soil degradation.

In interviews with the government and donor community in 1999, a number of officials emphasized that poorer farmers were largely responsible for environmental degradation in southern Mali. A Bamako-based World Bank official observed that 'the poor are preoccupied with feeding the family today. They cannot think about the environment. They do not have the resources for [agricultural] intensification.' CMDT officials suggested, likewise, that general economic development and a wealthier farming community will lead to more sustainable agricultural production (as they believe wealthier farmers are more likely to invest in soil conservation and intensify production than poorer farmers). A high-ranking CMDT official explained that economic sustainability is required for agricultural sustainability.

Concerns within the central government and the CMDT regarding the environmental impacts of cotton cultivation are overridden by a desire to increase production to finance their budgets. The IFIs and bilateral donors have successfully peddled the notion that poverty leads to environmental destruction and that wealth gains induce natural resource conservation. The state has little short-term financial incentives to undertake research to test these assertions. As such and perhaps opportunistically, it has accepted and re-articulated the sustainable development paradigm of wealth induced environmental conservation. This influence of the sustainable development paradigm on Malian environmental discourse occurs at the same time that globalization forces are dominating the country's economic (liberalization) and political (democratization) agendas.

Conclusion

This chapter examined the evolving dynamic among cotton production; export production, environmental degradation and global development paradigms in Mali. The organization of commercial cotton production in Mali over the last 50 years is better characterized by continuity than change. Since independence, the private sector, as well as the French and Malian states has had a shared financial interest in cotton production in Mali. The volatility of the world cotton market probably would have dissuaded many farmers from growing the crop if it were not for policies that made much needed credit available to cotton farmers, dampened producer price fluctuations and guaranteed purchase of the farmers' crops. The IFIs have done little to change the fundamental relationship between private capital and the Malian government in the cotton sector.

If Mali is at all representative of other Third or Fourth World nations, then the nature of the world economy on the periphery is essentially the same as in the colonial era. This stasis is indicative of long-standing, dependent economic linkages between African countries and the former colonial powers rather than a new phase of collaboration between global capital and the state.

The Malian case supports the weak globalization argument that a global economy is not new, but a continuing and evolving phenomenon. However, the Malian case also raises interesting questions regarding the extent of the global economy. The world economy is truly global if one accepts the structuralist argument that nations on the periphery, while integrated into the world economy, are prone to have economies organized along different lines from those at the core (i.e., organized to produce raw materials for the core nations). In contrast, the spatial extent of the world economy is less expansive if globalization is defined as encompassing only those economies that are organized like those at the core.

There have been environmental costs associated with export oriented cotton production in southern Mali. Villagers are generally aware of these environmental costs, often much more so than government extension agents working in the field. The recent cotton boom in Mali has not led to more conservation as some sustainable development advocates would suggest. In fact, increasing cotton prices and pro-cotton policies have led to increasingly extensive agriculture, declining yields and high rates of forest conversion to agricultural land. Unless new approaches to cotton production are undertaken, the long-term viability of rural livelihoods in southern Mali will be irreversibly compromised.

Within the central government and the CMDT, there is some recognition that increasing cotton production carries environmental costs. This concern and recognition, however, is overridden by a desire to increase production to finance the CMDT and the state, both of which have opportunistically seized on the notion of poverty induced environmental degradation. This problematization, like democracy and market liberalization, has been marketed by the IFIs and bilateral donors, used to blame poor farmers for environmental degradation and to defend the interests of global capital (represented by the CMDT) with the tacit approval of the state.

In the introduction to the chapter, I discussed a set of connections between the world cotton market, the national level, local level production decisions and the environmental repercussions of these production decisions. I also described the interpretation of environmental problems by local farmers, national level decision makers and international environment and development organizations. The evidence in this case suggests that the level of interaction between decision-makers operating at different spatial scales is not of uniform strength. There is a strong link between the world cotton market and the organization of cotton production at the national level (by the CMDT and the GoM). Farmers respond strongly to cotton policies set at the national level (rather than responding directly to the world cotton market). The cotton production decisions of farmers strongly affect the natural resource base and farmers directly perceive the impacts of these decisions on the natural environment. Rather than directly interacting with farmers to discern the environmental impact of cotton farming, the state and international environment and development institutions generally construct their own perceptions of these problems, which are influenced by the prevailing sustainable development paradigm. There is a high level of interaction, facilitated by financial transfers, between the national government, global capital and the global environmental agenda, which allows the GoM and capital to continue to exploit the environment for short-term gain and blends the socio- ecological lenses of the GoM with that of the global environmental paradigm, perpetuating decades of global control over Malian cotton production.

Acknowledgements

The author is grateful to B. Ikubolajeh Logan, Kent Glenzer and Billie Lee Turner II for comments on earlier versions of this manuscript. Fieldwork carried out in August 1999 was paid for by a grant from the Cultural Ecology Specialty Group of the Association of American Geographers; and with support from the Sustainable Agriculture and Natural Resources Management Collaborative Research Support Program or SANREM CRSP (financed by the United States Agency for International Development, Contract # PCE-A-00-98-00019-00). Fieldwork conducted in 1992 was undertaken in conjunction with Julia Earl and in collaboration with the Government of Mali's Institut des Sciences Humaines. Major funding for 1992 fieldwork was provided by the Population-Environment Dynamics Project, University of Michigan.

Notes

1. The structural adjustment programs pushed by the World Bank encourage liberalization and a greater integration into the world economy (Roy, 1997).
2. This line of argument is similar to that made by world system theorists. Immanual Wallerstein suggested that a world wide system of capitalist production emerged in the 16th century (Wallerstein, 1974).
3. The dominant perspectives on ecological degradation s (Lambin and Ehrlich 1997; Behnke et al. 1993).
4. This represents the mainstream view of the relationship between poverty and environmental degradation.
5. The French government had a 60% interest in the CFDT.
6. The CMDT operates in the Sikasso Region while another Malian Governmental Agency,

the Office de la Haute VallÈe du Niger (OHVN) or The Office of the Upper Niger Valley, is responsible for all agricultural activities (including cotton) in the Koulikoro Region (where the Sanankoro-Djitoumou Commune is located). The CMDT manages 98% of Mali's cotton production while OHVN produces the remaining 2% and sells it to CMDT for processing and export. The United States Agency for International Development (USAID) provided substantial funding to the OHVN from 1978 until the mid-1990s (USAID, 1988; USAID, 1999). The OHVN has traditionally been involved in the supply of agricultural inputs as well as extension services for cotton production.

7. World cotton prices began to decline again in late 1998.
8. Agro-chemical companies marketing inputs in Mali include: Ciba-Geigy (French), AGAN (Israeli), SOCHIM CISA (Ivory Coast), SENCHIM (Senegal) and SIPAMA (Bamako based).
9. As discussed earlier, cotton profit margins in 1992 for poorer farmers were also lower than those for wealthier farmers.
10. However, this study did not include the cost of inputs and the residual effects of cotton fertilizers on cereal production (which typically occur when crops are rotated). It is noted that the use of commercial inputs for grain production is quite limited.
11. Actually, the price of cotton may vary from year to year, but in any given year a price floor is set before planting decisions are made.
12. This may be translated as 'the historical success of the cotton industry in comparison to other economic sectors in the countries of the CFA franc zone is partially due to government involvement in the development and monitoring of cotton policies'.
13. The cotton stabilization fund is used to subsidize CMDT operations and producer prices in years of low world prices. The fund is built up from cotton revenues in years of high world prices.
14. That is, the cotton company appears to radically change by becoming nationalized in the 1970s and privatized in the 1980s. This appearance of change allows the company to retain its political clout with government and donors. This change in appearance, however, is superficial and does not represent a fundamental shift in the partnership between the state and private capital.
15. That is, policies that have been put in place to support small scale cotton producers, such as a floor price and guaranteed purchase, would be eliminated under liberalization. In the absence of such guarantees, many small scale producers likely would cease to produce cotton given highly variable world cotton prices.
16. The oxen draw plow accompanied the introduction of long fiber cotton (hand held hoes were the major cultivation implements prior to this time) (Moseley, 1993).
17. This fund is used to subsidize CMDT operations and producer prices in years of low world prices
18. This percentage was derived from government financial information provided in the World Bank Country Brief for Mali (http://www.worldbank.org/afr/ml2.htm). Cotton revenues in 1998 were 250 million $US, with 21% or 52.5 million $US going to the government. Total government revenue in 1998 was 498.8 million $US (or 17.2% of GDP estimated to be 2.9 billion $US).
19. The target of doubling production was mentioned in an interview with Mali-based World Bank Natural Resources Management Officer in 1999).

References

Beckerman, W. (1992). 'Economic Growth and the Environment: Whose Growth? Whose Environment?'. *World Development* 20 (4), 481–496.

Behnke, R.H., Scoones, I. and C. Kerven (1993) *Range Ecology at Disequilibrium: New Models of Natural Variability and Pastoral Adaptation in African Savannas*. London: Overseas Development Institute.

Biladeau, D. (1992) Project Officer for DHV Project, United States Agency for International Development. Bamako, Mali. Interview with Julia Earl and William Moseley. Nov. 19.

Bingen, R.J. (1998) 'Cotton, Democracy and Development in Mali'. *The Journal Modern African Studies* 20 (4), 497–512.

Bracking, S. (1999) 'Structural Adjustment: Why it Wasn't Necessary and Why it Did Work'. *Review of African Political Economy* 26 (80): 207–226.

Brecher, J. and T. Costello (1994) *Global Village or Global Pillage: Economic Reconstruction from the Bottom Up*. Boston: South End Press.

Bryan, L. and D. Farrell (1996) *Market Unbound: Unleashing Global Capitalism*. NY: John Wiley.

Bryant, R.L. and Bailey, S. (1997) *Third World Political Ecology*. NY: Routledge.

Cheru, F. (1992) 'Structural Adjustment, Primary Resource Trade and Sustainable Development in Sub-Saharan Africa'. *World Development* 20 (4), 497–512.

CIA (1999) *CIA Factbook*. URL: http://www.odci.gov/CIA/publications/factbook/ml.html.

Cook, P. and C. Kirkpatrick (1997) 'Globalization, Regionalization and Third-World Development'. *Regional Studies* 31 (1), 55–66.

Davies, S. (1996). *Adaptable Livelihoods: Coping with Food Insecurity in the Malian Sahel*. NY: St Martin's Press.

Earl, J. and W.G. Moseley (1993) *Indigenous Knowledge and Non-Formal Education as the Core of Sustainable Community Development: The Case of Djitoumou, Mali*. Unpublished Mimeo.

Economist Intelligence Unit (1998) *Mali Country Report 1998–99*. London: Business International.

Eisa, H.M. (1994) *Cotton Production Prospects for the Decade to 2005. A Global Overview*. Washington, D.C.: The World Bank.

Fagan, R. (1995) 'The Economy, Culture and Environment: Perspectives on the Australian Food Industry'. *Australian Geographer* 26 (1), 1–10.

Fairhead, J. and M. Leach (1996) *Misreading the African Landscape: Society and Ecology in a Forest-Savanna Mosaic*. London: Cambridge University Press.

Famine Early Warning System (FEWS) (1997) *Living on the Edge. FEWS in Depth Report No. 2*. Washington, DC: United States Agency for International Development.

Frank, D.J. (1997) 'Science, Nature and the Globalization of the Environment, 1870–1990'. *Social Forces* 76 (2), 409–435.

Girdis, D.P. (1993) *The Role of Cotton in Agricultural Change, Land Degradation and Sustainability in Southern Mali*. Amsterdam: Royal Tropical Institute.

Glenzer, K. (1999) *La Secheresse: The Social and Institutional Construction of a Development Problem in the Malian (Soudanese) Sahel, c. 1900–1982*. Presentation at the Annual Meeting of the African Studies Association. Philadelphia, PA. November, 11–14.

Government of Mali (GoM) (1999) *Enhanced Structural Adjustment Facility Medium-Term Policy Framework Paper, 1999–2002*. Prepared with assistance from the International Monetary Fund and the World Bank. URL: http://www.imf.org/exernal/np/pfp/1999/mali/index.htm.

Greenberg, J.B. and T.K. Park (1994) 'Political Ecology'. *Journal of Political Ecology* 1, 1–12. (*http://dizzy.library.arizona.edu/ej/jpe/*)

Grant, R. and Agnew, J. (1996) 'Representing Africa: The Geography of Africa in World Trade, 1960–1992'. *Annals of the Association of American Geographers* 86 (4) 729–744.

Gupta, A. (1998) *Postcolonial Development: Agriculture in the Making of Modern India*. Durham: Duke University Press.

Hannerz, U. (1990). 'Cosmopolitans and Locals in World Culture'. *Theory, Culture and Society* 7(2,3) 237–252.

Harrison, P. (1987) *The Greening of Africa: Breaking Through in the Battle for Land and Food*. London: IIED.

Hirst, P. and G. Thompson (1996) *Globalization in Question*. Cambridge: Polity Press.
Imperato, P.J. and E.M. Imperato (1982) *Mali: A Handbook of Historical Statistics*. Boston: G.K. Hall & Co.
International Monetary Fund (IMF) (1999) *Mali: Selected Issues and Statistical Appendix*. Washington, D.C.: IMF African Department.
Johnston, R.J., P.J. Taylor and M. Watts (1995). 'Modernity, Identity and Machineries of Meaning'. In: R.J. Johnston, P.J. Taylor and M. Watts (eds). *Geographies of Global Change: Remapping the World in the Late Twentieth Century*. Cambridge, MA: Blackwell.
Klak, T. and G. Myers. (1997). 'The Discursive Tactics of Neoliberal Development in Small Third World Countries'. *Geoforum* 28 (2), 133–149.
Koenig, D., T. Diara and M. Sow (1998) *Innovation and Individuality in African Development: Changing Production Strategies in Rural Mali*. Ann Arbor: University of Michigan Press.
Kofman, E. and G. Youngs (1996) *Globalization: Theory and Practice*. London: Pinter.
Korton, D. (1995) *When Corporations Rule the World*. West Hartford, Conn: Kumarian Press.
Leisinger, K. and K. Schmitt (1995) *Survival in the Sahel: An Ecological and Developmental Challenge*. The Hague: International Service for National Agricultural Research (ISNAR).
Logan, B.I. (1999) *Environmental Security, Sustainable Development and Resource Management in Africa: Some Conceptual Considerations*. Paper presented at the Methodology Workshop, Southern African Political Economy Series Trust, Harare, Zimbabwe, July.
Loxley, J. and B. Seddon. (1994) 'Strangleholds on Africa'. *Journal of African Political Economy* 62, 485–492.
Marden, P. (1997) 'Geographies of Dissent: Globalization, Identity and the Nation'. *Political Geography* 16 (1), 37–64.
Marshall, B.K. (1999) 'Globalisation, Environmental Degradation and Ulrich Beck's Risk Society'. *Environmental Value* 8 (2), 253–275.
Miller, M. (1995) 'Where Globalization is Taking Us: Why We Need a New Woods, Bretton'. *Futures* 27 (2), 125–144.
Mortimore, M. (1989). *Adapting to Drought: Farmers, Famines and Desertification in West Africa*. NY: Cambridge University Press.
Moseley, W.G. (1993) *Indigenous Agroecological Knowledge Among the Bambara of Djitoumou, Mali: Foundation For A Sustainable Community*. Unpublished Master's Thesis, University of Michigan.
Moseley, W.G. (1999) *Assessment of Decision-Maker Priorities for Mali (West Africa): Findings from Field Visit #2*. Unpublished Mimeo. Athens, GA: SANREM CRSP.
Ohmae, K. (1995) *The End of the Nation State: The Rise of Regional Economies*. NY: Free Press.
Pearce, D. and G. Atkinson (1993) 'Capital Theory and the Measurement of Sustainable Development: An Indicator of Weak Sustainability'. *Ecological Economics* 8, 103–108.
Peet, R. and Watts, M. (1996). 'Liberation Ecology: Development, Sustainability and Environment in an Age of Market Triumphalism'. In R. Peet and M. Watts (eds). *Liberation Ecologies: Environment, Development, Social Movements*. NY: Routledge, 1–45.
Pieterse, J.N. (1995) 'Globalization as Hybridization'. In M. Featherstone, S. Lash, and R. Robertson (eds). *Global Modernities*. London: Sage, 1–12.
Prentice, A.N. (1972) *Cotton, With Special Reference to Africa*. London: Longman Group Limited.
Richards, P. (1985) *Indigenous Agricultural Revolution*. London: Huchinson.
Richards, W. (1991) 'My Experience: The More the Residue, The Less the Pollution of Surface Water'. *The EPA Journal*. November/December 1991, 43–46.
Roberts, R. (1995) 'The Coercion of Free Markets: Cotton, Peasants and the Colonial State in the French Soudan, 1924–32'. In A. Isaacman and R. Roberts (eds). *Cotton, Colonialism and Social History in Sub-Saharan Africa*. London: James Currey, Ltd.
Roberts, R.L. (1996) *Two Worlds of Cotton: Colonialism and the Regional Economy in the French Soudan, 1800–1946*. Stanford, CA: Stanford University Press.

Roy, S. (1997) 'Globalization, Structural Change and Poverty: Some Conceptual and Policy Issues'. *Economic and Political Weekly* 32 (33–34), 2117–2135.

Sandbrook, R. (1997) 'Economic Liberalization Versus Political Democratization: A Social Democratic Resolution?'. *Canadian Journal of African Studies* 31 (3), 482–515.

Sarre, P. (1995) 'Towards Global Environmental Values: Lessons from Western and Eastern Experience'. *Environmental Values* 4 (2), 115–127.

Schrader, T.H., B.H. Wennink, W.J. Veldkamp and T. Defoer (1998) 'Natural Resource Management in the Cotton Zone of Southern Mali: Merging Farmer Participation Research, Extension and Policy'. In S.R. Tabor and D.C. Faber (eds). *Closing the Loop: From Research on Natural Resources to Policy Change*. Maastricht: European Center for Development Policy Management, 142–155.

Serafini, Phil and Boubacar Sada Sy (1992) *Agribusiness and Public Sector Collaboration in Agricultural Technology Development and Use in Mali: A Study of the Mechanization of Cotton Production*. Submitted to USAID. Agricultural Marketing Improvement Strategies Project. Bethesda: Abt Associates Inc.

Shaikh, Asif (1989) *The Segou Roundtable on Local Level Natural Resource Management in the Sahel*. A report prepared for the Sahel Office, Bureau for Africa, United States Agency for International Development. Washington D.C.: E/DI.

Smart, B. (1993) *Postmodernity*. London: Routledge.

Smith, A. (1990) 'Towards a Global Culture?'. *Theory, Culture and Society* 7 (2,3), 171–192.

Stiles, D. and Brennan, R. (1986) 'The Food Crisis and Environmental Conservation in Africa'. *Food Policy* Nov., 298–310.

Strauss, A. and J. Corbin (1990) *Basics of Qualitative Research*. London: Sage.

Tefft, J., Staatz, J., Dione, J. and Kelly, V. (1998) Filiere Coton In *Securite Alimentaire et Flieres Agricoles en Afrique de l'Ouest: Enjeux et Perspectives Quatre Ans Apres la Devaluation*. Bamako: Institut du Sahel (CILSS).

Tenbruck, F. (1990) 'The Dream of a Secular Ecumene: The Meaning and Limits of the Politics of Development'. *Theory, Culture and Society* 7 (2,3), 193–206.

Todaro, M.P. (1985) *Economic Development in the Third World*. NY: Longman 3rd edition.

United Nations Conference on Environment and Development (UNCED) (1993) *Agenda 21: The Earth Summit Strategy to Save Our Planet*. Boulder, CO: EarthPress.

USAID (1988) *Mali – Development of the Haute Vallee*. Project Paper 688–0233.

USAID (1999) *USAID Mali Sustainable Economic Growth (SEG) Strategic Objective Team*. Unpublished description of strategy and programs. Bamako: USAID.

Vanderpool, F. and B. Traore (1993) 'Soil Nutrient Depletion by Agricultural Production in Southern Mali'. *Fertilizer Research* 36 (1), 79–90.

Wallerstein, I. (1974) *The Modern World System*. NY: Academic Press.

Warren, D.M. (1989) 'The Impact of Nineteenth Century Social Science in Establishing Negative Values and Attitudes towards Indigenous Knowledge Systems'. In D.M. Warren, L.J. Slikkerveer and S.O. Titilola (ed.) *Indigenous Knowledge Systems for Agriculture and International Development*. Studies in Technology and Social Change, No. 11. Ames: Iowa State University, Technology and Social Change Program, 171–183.

Warren, D.M. (1991) *Using Indigenous Knowledge in Agricultural Development. World Bank Discussion Paper No. 127*. Washington D.C.: The World Bank.

World Bank (1988) *Cotton Development Programs in Burkina Faso, CÙte d'Ivoire and Togo: A World Bank Operations Evaluation Study*. Washington D.C.: World Bank.

World Bank (1996) *Toward Environmentally Sustainable Development in Sub-Saharan Africa: A World Bank Agenda*. Washington D.C.: The World Bank.

World Bank (1997) *Partenariat Mali B Banque Mondiale 1997–98*. Bamako: Bureau de la Banque Mondiale au Mali.

World Commission on Environment and Development (WCED) (1987) *Our Common Future*. NY: OUP.

Chapter 14

Conclusion: From Globalization Towards Universalization in the Twenty-First Century

Alejandro Ochoa Arias and B. Ikubolajeh Logan

Summary

One important theme that runs through this book is the paradox that the same forces, which establish global political and economic interdependence, also create extreme poverty for large segments of the world's population. These dynamics work through the simultaneous disenfranchisement of the Third World state as arbiter between social classes and the ascendancy of neoliberal paradigms (primarily, market, democracy and sustainable development) as the main instruments of policy formulation at the global, regional and local levels. It may not be surprising, therefore, that globalization is perceived by many in the Third world as being suspiciously reminiscent of colonialism, neo-colonialism and hegemonic empire-building. Contrary to demurs of strong globalizationists, the Washington Consensus has not tackled poverty eradication with the same verve that it has approached market liberalization or democratization. Rather, neoliberal advocates respond to the negative impacts of globalization with claims that when applied properly, liberalization lifts all boats. This advocacy has lost some of its credibility, since several strategy changes in the past three decades (complete state removal in the 1980s; selective state participation in the 1990s; and civil society mobilization in the 2000s) have not prevented most Third World boats from becoming inextricably mired in poverty.

Is Globalization Immutable?

Debates over globalization have become characterized by an ideological fracture in which one side highlights its benefits and the other its negative impacts, especially on the world's destitute. Since both sides on the issue implicitly assume that globalization is immutable, the debates often ignore Third World responses to the unfolding global order. In fact, much of the discussion proceeds from assumptions that Third World states and peoples have no recourse but to surrender to the forces of neoliberal ascendancy, particularly the market and mechanisms of political control (for example, the United Nations system). According to this view, since market forces can operate in a 'stateless' global arena, globalization has become immutable.

The immutability of globalization is sometimes grounded in arguments that its intangible forms are as powerful, if not more so, than its physical and material manifestations. The world's financial markets are seen to be most representative of this power (as manifested a few years ago in the instability unleashed by currency speculation on emerging markets like Mexico, Brazil and Malaysia). Financial resources have become international commodities that seek and find shelter in the major markets of the global system, with or without state approval and support. Indeed, capital has become anonymous, faceless, virtual and consequently unconstrained by the state. Since financial markets lack a physical form that can be controlled by state regulations, their power is intricately linked to the 'hollow state' and strong globalization theses, both of which would suggest that 'the wealth of nations' has ceased to be state-owned. In the present global order, agricultural and mining economies can hardly compete with the high returns that investors can derive from financial markets. The accompanying loss of state revenues leaves it a mere caricature of its former self, a process that is further reinforced by conditionalities imposed on the state by the IFIs. Essentially, capital is becoming increasingly more powerful as the state is becoming increasingly weaker, in a zero-sum game in which the power of capital often comes at the expense of state authority.

Information is another intangible element of globalization that is said to have far reaching implications for the Third World. Technology has accelerated global integration by making it possible for information to be accessed simultaneously by people around the world. Rapid information exchange has become an economic activity and the ability to produce and diffuse information is important for authority in the global network. Since most Third World states and peoples are not privy to information commodity, they are unable to compete effectively in this very important market.

Other intangible forces said to demonstrate the omnipotence of globalization include ideas, culture, religion and language, to name a few. The claim that those who are connected to and by the internet represent a new global culture is a justifiable one. Undoubtedly, those in the Third World who have internet access tend to have world visions that are internationalized and often at odds with their compatriots.

Also, as noted in a number of chapters in this book, under globalization the state has lost much of its authority to capital, the IFIs and to bilateral and multilateral organizations, which shape global political, environmental and social policies. Democracy requires the state to adopt political transparency and decentralization, both of which are antithetical to paternalistic institutions; structural adjustment forces it to abdicate social welfare responsibilities; and civil society agitation forces it to adopt global environmental and social agendas that exacerbate poverty. It seems unlikely that the state can effectively counter these simultaneous forces and that the writing is on the wall for its role as ombudsman for the cultural and economic aspirations of the polity.

If the death knell is being sounded for state authority in the Third World, who or what must fill the institutional vacuum – the forces of globalization? The ability of both tangible and intangible global forces to shape political and economic outcomes in a variety of geographic settings would seem to indicate that this is the most obvious outcome. However, there is room for pause concerning the immutability of globalization, especially when viewed in terms of (i) Third World reactions and (ii) the universal legitimacy of the process in its economic, political and cultural forms.

Limits to Globalization or The Other Side of the Coin

As has been noted previously, neoliberalism in its various tangible and intangible forms, is a formidable force in the present global order. The AIM complexes referred to in chapter 10 control much of the world's financial, military, academic and political resources. Yet, even with such power on its side, globalization may not be immutable. For one thing, the Third World state is actively reconfiguring itself to adapt to the changing global order. Some of these responses are explored in this book: state-directed regional labor markets (as in southeast Asia), export processing zones (as in China), export oriented production (as in Mexico) and ideological change (as in South Africa).

Even more important than state strategies have been the responses of the general masses (civil society, if you will) to globalization. As the state tries to seek a solution to the global order, the polity has institutionalized its coping strategies, largely outside the realm of control of both the state and mainstream globalization (it may be important here to differentiate between mainstream globalization, those activities/processes typically recognized as constituting globalization; and non-mainstream globalization forces, equally important processes that are typically ignored because of their 'unsavory' or unacceptable attributes). Perhaps, the most noticeable mass societal response to globalization in the Third World is the robustness of the 'informal sector', as the main generator of economic output in many Third World countries (surpassing both the state and global capital). In chapter 11, Shaw discusses 'new regionalisms' by which informal sector has reorganized itself to meet the challenges of globalization. These reconfigurations include pseudo-legal activities like cross border trading by women, but also include illegal activities like poaching, drug-trafficking, labor-trafficking, global prostitution, the diamond-war nexus and child soldiers. All these activities constitute mechanisms by which the informal sector has addressed state withdrawal from resource allocation and the inability (or unwillingness) of capital to fill that vacuum. In essence, informality in the Third World and the rise of internationalized 'criminal activities' represent non-mainstream global organization. The Third World's poor, marginalized in and by mainstream are very active in this process.

What do these reconfigurations imply for arguments concerning the immutability of mainstream globalization? Are the coping strategies of Third World states and peoples (as discussed, for example, in chapters 1,7, 8, 11) equal to the task of poverty-alleviation? This is a difficult question to answer since the drama is still unfolding. What is unquestionable is that non-mainstream mobilization efforts to cope with global capital are also global in nature and will change the character and direction of mainstream globalization. The former may also prove to be more robust than the state in challenging the excesses of mainstream globalization, even if in undesirable ways (international terrorism comes to mind). However, since neither form of globalization is universal, neither can claim to be more legitimate than the other. The best that mainstream globalization can do is to claim that it has legality on its side.

Further Limits: Is Globalization Universal?

Prevailing notions that mainstream globalization is universal are questionable not only because they ignore the empirical 'underbelly' of the process described in the previous subsection, but also from a philosophical position. For a phenomenon to claim universality, it must be rooted in a global (universally acceptable) or globalizing (capable of being globally accepted) philosophy. These criteria are more readily satisfied, perhaps, by major world religions, whose principles allow them broad appeal in a wide range of geographic and cultural settings. The same cannot be said of the market, democracy, or sustainable development, the main cornerstones of globalization. To the contrary, the beneficiaries of globalization represent a small minority of the world's population while the majority remains in poverty. Even if one were tempted to view capitalism or democracy as dogma, their principles are far from universal, especially since they are unenduring and inconsistent. The rules of the game in mainstream globalization, whether in economics, politics or the environment, are changed continuously to maintain hegemony (this may be the case in non-mainstream activities also, but they are not being discussed here). The rules deliberately and inherently selective by class, race, region etc and have different explicit and implicit guidelines for different socio-economic categories. Under these circumstances, how, for example, can a poor farmer in India have the same view of capital as a New Delhi mogul; or how can an Asian sweat-shop worker or African miner view capital in the same light as the global enterprises which control their lives? Rather than being universal, globalization is alienating. In all its dimensions, it is designed to have clear winners and losers and the losers can hardly be expected to feel philosophical kinship with the winners.

Universalizing Globalization

If the argument is correct that globalization in its present form is not universal, then a further case can be made that its immutability (perhaps sustainability is a better word) can come only after its universality. What changes might be desirable to make globalization universal? One can argue that, for a start, the very definition of globalization must be subject to some modification. This is easier said than done, since any definitional change must be preceded by the following: a philosophical shift in the identification of globalizing parameters (for example, in economics, politics and society); and changes in dynamics within the material structures and institutions that control the process. This means, necessarily (but not sufficiently) a reconceptualization of what constitutes a global society. A reconceptualized global society should be based neither on principles of imperialism nor result from a struggle in which a dominant culture is viewed as THE valid global culture. To the contrary, a multiplicity of global cultures and their interactions should be its central attribute, not only in the interest of preserving cultures for their own sake, but also to promote universality. Western cultures must be willing to co-exist with others as equals; and the idea that progress must be equated with adoption of the traits of a dominant culture must be replaced with one that permits cross-cultural development.

The project for a new global society is predicated on two key tasks: a proper definition of common global goods; and the establishment of mechanisms to preserve such goods. Traditionally, the definition of common global goods is based on ideals surrounding human rights, individual autonomy and state sovereignty. These are all central tenets of globalization, yet they are not universal because they do not evolve as integral elements of political, social and cultural growth in the Third World.

Global Common Goods

An argument can be made that there are no universal rights, not even the right to life. Even if this is true, it does not preclude the fact that there are rights that are similarly recognized by different societies: the right to privacy, variously defined, is a case in point. Such (divergent) similarities could provide the basis for a more universal understanding of rights. The definitional task becomes simpler if one accepts that rights need not be universally defined; only universally accepted. For example, the right to basic needs cannot be universally defined simply because basic needs vary so much. However, if one accepts that basic needs, however defined, need to be accessible to all in society, the task becomes much easier to address. Similarly, human rights cannot be universally defined when societies are selective by race, gender, age and ethnicity on how to confer, take away, or prolong those rights. Again, if one accepts that there may be several definitions, none of which takes precedence over the other, the areas of convergence become the universal linkage. Thus, the definitional task for common global goods hinges on finding areas of cultural convergence, rather than on hegemony. This means that each society should be allowed room to articulate its own beliefs and traditions as co-equals. Co-equality would mean that the traits of each culture should stand the chance of adoption/adaptation by others. Freedom of cultural choice should be as privileged as freedom of political choice or market freedom.

Those who want to argue that freedom of cultural choice already exists in globalization need only examine the psychological and physical forms by which the printed and electronic media degrade Third World cultures while celebrating the supremacy of Western politics, economics, religions, fashion, cuisine, music, games, amusement, entertainment etc. The standard of universality applied by proponents of globalization is handicapped by severe cultural lenses, one of which is the notion that Third World societies are too primitive to provide meaningful cultural insights for the rest of the world. This notion is rooted primarily in Western assumptions that the value of a society to global development can be calibrated primarily in terms of its economic output and determined by positive comparisons with the historical development of Western Europe. Consequently, Third World development is conceived to be a process whose form and content is worthy of attention only as far as it replicates Western experiences. In this meta-narrative, the development process becomes synonymous with loss of Third World social and cultural identity (these attributes are seen to be actual barriers to development) and the goal of development becomes focused on molding Third World countries to become poor facsimiles of the West.

A related shortcoming of the notion of universality embedded in globalization is the idea that the Third World is incapable of articulating a social discourse about its own identity. Many Third World social practices, which are guided by a sense of community and interdependence, are essential for poverty-alleviation. Yet, these social constructs remain outside mainstream discourse, which persists in privileging economic indicators as barometers of socio-cultural change The dominant discourse, which organizes society around notions of individualism threatens the existence of social practices that are rooted in Third World community norms. For example, many Third World countries have now framed policy that place social security, health and pension schemes in the private sector. Culturally, this orientation departs from cultural norms of family-hood while, economically, it is not even logical in societies where large segments of populations are unemployed.

Final Thoughts

An important question at this juncture is why should the dominant culture deliberately engage in change that is likely to weaken its hegemony? The answer to this question is that multiculturalism is the only universal and sustainable social contract. Without it, even the dominant culture exposes itself to violent change, political instability and potential mass poverty.

A new global society is an imperative for those who are presently excluded from the benefits of mainstream globalization. Recent civil society action against the World Bank and WTO, for example, indicates that there are many who believe that the market cannot serve as a universalizing force that can effectively alleviate the plight of the world's poor and integrate them into a global society.

Poverty, however defined or measured, is a universal phenomenon. The commonality between different manifestations of poverty is exclusion from full participation in global common goods. This exclusion is a deliberate, orchestrated by the hegemonic powers and is not merely a side effect of hegemony. As argued in this book, poverty is an integral part of mainstream globalization and if non-mainstream globalization forces are to be controlled, poverty-alleviation, like poverty-creation, must become central to globalization discourse and policy design. Ironically, global communication networks make it possible for societies around the world to view and assess the geographic dimensions of poverty. The media continuously juxtaposes the extreme hardships of the many with the extreme affluence of the few, creating universal hungers and aspirations.

There are two obvious options to address this problem: continued hegemony and domination to rein in the desires of the poor; and a redefinition of global common goods towards universality and poverty-alleviation. The second option is likely to be more sustainable because universal poverty can only weaken the mainstream global order unless it is addressed by universal solutions.

Index